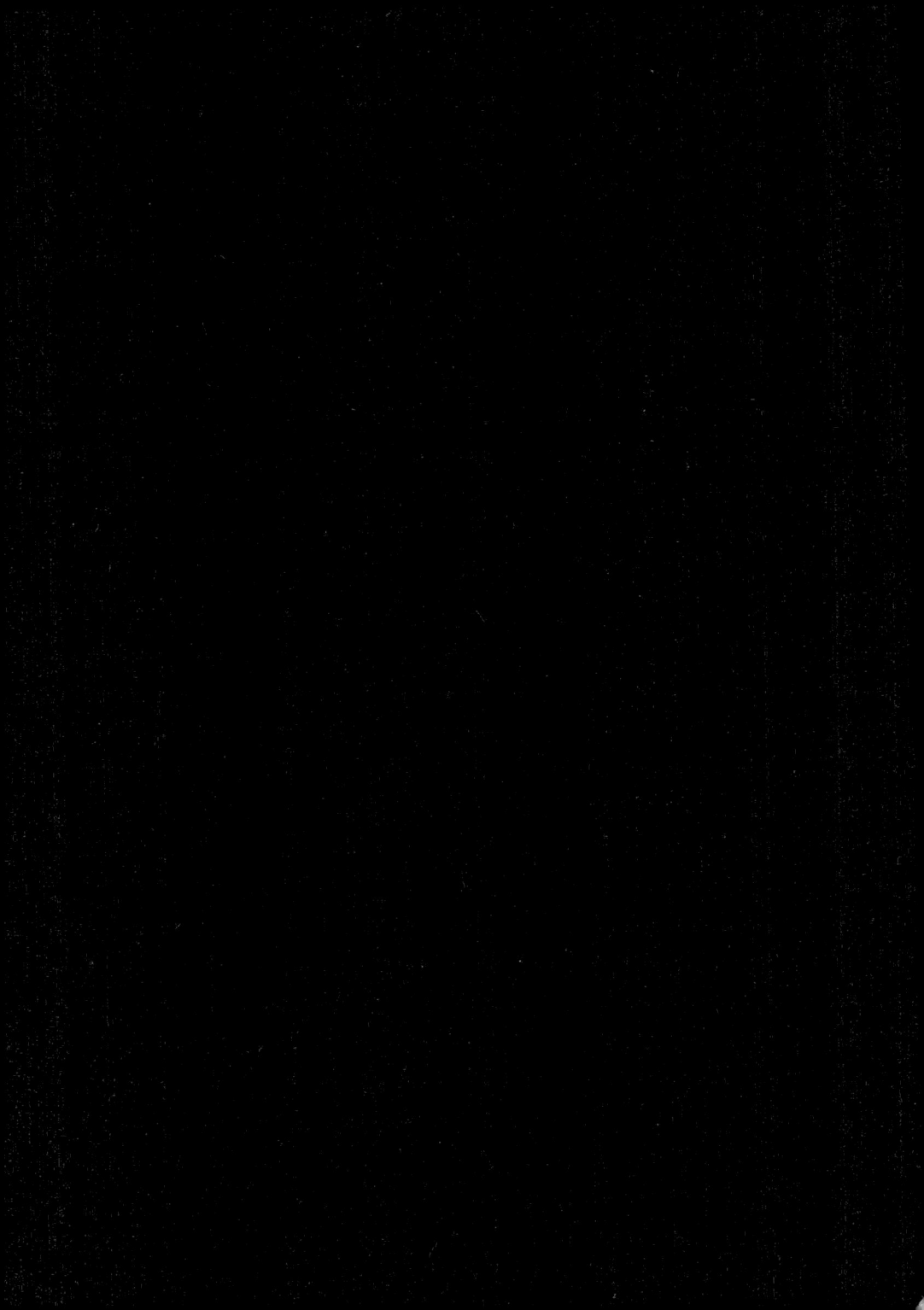

文
景

Horizon

社 科 新 知　文 艺 新 潮

徐梵澄 全集

孙波 主编

唯识菁华

徐梵澄 著

梁珏 译　　孙波 校

上海人民出版社

主编的话

徐梵澄（1909 年 10 月 26 日—2000 年 3 月 6 日），原名徐琥，字季海，湖南长沙人。幼塾就学于近代湘中巨子王闿运（湘绮）之再传弟子，其师杨度、杨钧辈，尝讲汉魏六朝古文。后进新式小学，开国领袖毛泽东为其地理老师。再后入教会所办之雅礼中学，接受全面现代教育，并得到了良好的英语训练。1926 年春，遵父命考入湘雅医学院。1927 年春，自作主张转入武汉中山大学历史系，开始发表文章，谋求自立。1928 年春，又考入上海复旦大学西洋文学系。同年 5 月，因聆听鲁迅讲演并作记录，遂与鲁迅通信，从此结下了深厚的师生情谊。1929 年 8 月至 1932 年 7 月，梵澄赴德留学修艺术史专业，分别就读于柏林大学和海德堡大学，其间为鲁迅搜求欧西版画，并自制作品寄与恩师，其作品为中国现代版画最早之创作，被业界誉为“第一人”者。回国以后，寄寓上海，为《申报·自由谈》撰写杂文和短篇小说，并受鲁迅之嘱，有规模地翻译尼采著作，包括《尼采自传》（良友公司 1935 年），《朝霞》（商务印书馆 1935 年），《苏鲁支语录》（含《人间的、太人间的》节译，生活书店 1936 年），《快乐的智识》（商务印书馆 1939 年）和《葛（歌）德自著之〈浮士德〉》（商务印书馆 1939 年）。又译出《佛教述略》（英译汉，上海佛教协会 1939 年）。

抗战爆发后，梵澄随国立艺专前往湘西，复又辗转昆明。1940 年底，艺专回迁至重庆，梵澄遂入中央图书馆，独自编纂《图书月刊》，并授课于中央大学。值 1945 年抗战胜利，梵澄加入中印文化交流计划，于年底飞赴印度加尔各答之桑地尼克丹的泰戈尔国际大学，任教于该校之中国学院，尝讲欧阳竟无唯识思想，并编辑《天竺字原》（佚失）。1950 年，梵澄赴名城贝纳尼斯（今名瓦拉纳西）重修梵文，其间译出印度文学经典《薄伽梵歌》和《行云使者》（迦里大萨）。1951 年春，梵澄又入南印度琫地舍里（今名本地治理）之室利·阿罗频多（Sri Aurobindo）学院，并受院母密那氏（Mira）之托任华文部主任。1950 年代，是梵澄于印度韦檀多学古今经典的译介期，古典有《奥义书》（梵译汉）五十种，今典有阿罗频多的《神圣人生论》，《薄伽梵歌论》，《瑜伽论》（学院版，六册，1957 年、1958 年、1959 年、1960 年），《社会进化论》（学院版 1960 年）和《伊莎书》，《由谁书》（学院版 1957 年），皆英译汉；以及院母的《母亲的话》（学院版，四册，1956 年、1958 年、1978 年），为法译汉。1960 年代，是梵澄于中国传统学术菁华的宣扬期，其以英文著译《小学菁华》（学院版 1976 年），《孔学古微》（学院版 1966 年），《周子通书》（学院版 1978 年）和《唯识菁华》与《肇论》。1970 年代，是梵澄将中、西、印三大古典文化思想之玄理整合的会通期，其标志乃为疏释室利·阿罗频多《赫拉克利特》之《玄理参同》（学院版 1973 年）。

1978 年底，梵澄回国。1979 年春，入中国社会科学院世界宗教研究所任研究员，直至 2000 年春殁世。此一末期，先生隐然有着确立中国精神哲学之努力的倾向，他的工作成果也不断被推向社会：1984年，《五十奥义书》（中国社会科学出版社）和《神圣人生论》（商务印书馆）出版；1987年，《肇论》（中国社会科学出版社）和《安慧〈三十唯识〉疏释》（梵译汉，中国佛教文化研究所）出版；1988年，《异学杂著》（浙江文艺出版社）和《老子臆解》（中华书局）出版；1990年，《唯识菁华》（新世界出版社）出版；1991年，《周天集》（英译汉，生活·读书·新知三联书店）出版；1994年，《陆王学述——一系精神哲学》（上海远东出版社）出版。先生故去以后，《薄伽梵歌论》于2003年面世（商务印书馆）；又由编者所辑《徐梵澄文集》十六卷于2006年推出（上海三联书店）。

纵观先生一生，注重非在某一学，如印学、西学或中学，尽管其治思于各家研讨极为深湛，要其着力所在仍为精神哲学，正如他自己所言："最是我所锲而不舍的，如数十年来所治之精神哲学。"这一端头是依鲁迅（"立人""改造国民性"）启始，这一线索是从希腊古哲赫拉克利特（永恒之"变是"）和德国近哲尼采（精神之回还），到印度古"见士"（由"无明"见"明"）和近代"圣哲"阿罗频多（自性高栖，有为人生，终与"至上者"合契），再回吾华儒家，并以中国文化为本位（变化气质，转化人生与社会），收摄、重治三家并塑模自家学说之雏形。于此可问：先生的尝试成功与否？或许"成功"不见！又有可说者，这是一"渊默而雷声"之事，影响或在久远的将来，它是浑融在中华民族未来希望之曙色中的，并渐行渐起，直趋"午昼"（阿罗频多语）。再问：到了"午昼"又如何呢？一个更高远的、更阔大的目标在上，即"超心思"之域，也可以称之为"精神道"。50年前，国内"文革”尚未消歇，只身寄寓南印度一海隅的梵澄就发出了其深情的期待，他说：“将来似可望‘精神道’之大发扬，二者（哲学与宗教）双超”（《玄理参同》学院版）。复问：“‘精神道’之大发扬”为何种境界？乃光明倾注天理流行矣！

先生著、译述，除佚失和未采者，文集之收录约合650余万字。据他本人的想法，全部文字可分为三个部分，他说：“编拙稿成集，细思只合分成三汇。属‘精神哲学’者一，则《薄伽梵歌·序》等皆收。属‘艺术’者一，则论书画者收之，当待大量补充。属‘文学’者一，则自诌之俚句，及所译文言诗，并诗说者属之，犹待大量补充。”（《梵澄先生》，上海书店出版社2009年）其中三汇之“艺术”者和“文学”者，极为粲然，可入乎美学畛域，编者无似，读者自鉴。此就“精神哲学”者略说，这一宗学问在我国古代属内学、玄学，也即形而上学，有伦有序而不违逻辑，立义黏柔而超乎知识，故“从此一学翻成西文，舍哲学一名词而外，亦寻不出恰当的称呼。”（《陆王学述》）

那么，当解“精神”二字，与寻常概念不同，他以人“型”（the Ideas）来打比方的：

> ……而人，在生命之外，还有思想，即思维心，还有情感，即情感心或情命体。基本还有凡此所附丽的身体。但在最内中深处，还有一核心，通常称之曰心灵或性灵。是这些，哲学上乃统称之曰“精神”。但这还是就人生而说，它虽似是抽象，然是一真实体，在形而

> 上学中，应当说精神是超乎宇宙为至上为不可思议又在宇宙内为最基本而可证会的一存在。研究这主题之学，方称精神哲学。这一核心，是万善万德具备的，譬如千丈大树，其发端初生，只是一极微细的种子，核心中之一基因（gene），果壳中之仁。孔子千言万语解说人道中之“仁”，原亦取义于此。（《陆王学述》）

这“精神”，在徐先生的语境中，也被称为“知觉性”“力”“气”，即一超乎现象的基本力，在黑格尔或叫作“自然”；亦被称为“心灵”“性灵”，即那“极微细的种子”，在柏拉图或叫作“灵魂”。前说好比大树之整个，后说有似其发芽破土的“种子”，二者是一事。又可表之：在本原性东西（宇宙之树）之内的一种自由（心灵或仁）。

先生所治之精神哲学，又分次第，初赫拉克利特和尼采，中诸《奥义书》和《薄伽梵歌》，后阿罗频多和儒家。初则赫氏与尼采之思想，不为“大全”，其精神只行进在半途，盖因赫氏不言“本体”，只说一永恒的“变是”，尼采否定“上帝”，只认一不歇的“心思”力。中则诸典，因受“空论”和“幻论”的消极影响，其真精神泯漠不彰垂二千余年。后则阿罗频多，欲挽沉滞，力振国运，重铸韦檀多哲学，并以《薄伽梵歌》为经，以诸《奥义书》为纬，教示其人民：以工作实践化除私我，以瑜伽精神奉献上帝。而阿氏之学，又与我国宋明儒家心学一路符契，梵澄说：“鄙人之所以提倡陆、王者，以其与室利·阿罗频多之学多有契合处。有瑜伽之益，无瑜伽之弊。正以印度瑜伽在今日已败坏之极，故室利·阿罗频多思有以新苏之，故创‘大全瑜伽’之说。观其主旨在于觉悟，变化气质，与陆、王不谋而合。姑谓为两道，此两道有文化背景之不同，皆与任何宗教异撰。亦与唯物论无所抵牾，可以并行不悖。”(《梵澄先生》)

又说先生之勤力，中年以后主要当在印度古典和阿罗频多诸书。其中翻译《薄伽梵歌》有句，“盖挥汗磨血几死而后得之者也”(佛协版“序”)；又有翻译《神圣人生论》曾云：“‘母亲’的精神力量是巨大的，我能够把室利·阿罗频多那样精深的《人生论》翻出来，没有精神力量支撑是不行的。”(《梵澄先生》)其自著之书，《老子臆解》也是颇费了不少心神，曾与友人说道：“这是‘狮子搏兔’的工作，是用过全身气力的，几十年来断断续续，不知费了多少功夫。”(《徐梵澄传》)对于这些文字的研读，仿佛有见一条基线，引向那本深而末茂的幽隧、高山而仰止的化境……于此可想，入蹊者定会兴味无尽，昭晰者必能疑窦释然，因为那是一注“神圣之泉”(阿罗频多)，“没有汲桶放下去不能汲满着黄金和珠宝上来”(尼采)！而先生的自著文字，皆是简洁、雅健、灵犀、深锐，其中传映着他优游涵泳、从容论道的儒者气象，使人读来每每如沐春风而怡然自适，如饮醇醪又不觉自醉。

然而，说到自己的工作，他尝言：“我的文字不多，主要思想都在序、跋里了。”“我的英语文字多于文言文字，文言文字多于白话文字。”惜乎在本次文集的编辑过程中仍未能如意尽收，可知其一生有多少劳作皆付之东流了，这又是人生无可奈何之事。好在“基线”昭然，于是可问：先生为什么要去印度并且一滞就是33年呢？回答：是为了实现鲁迅的理想，即挹取彼邦之大经大法。百余年前，鲁迅就已明示：“凡负令誉于史初，开文化之曙色，而今日转为影国者，无不如斯。使举国人所习闻，最适莫如天竺。天竺古有韦陀四种，瑰丽幽夐，称世界大文。其摩诃波罗多暨罗摩衍那二赋，亦至美妙。”（《摩罗诗力说》）故先生去国，译出经典是首要任务，因为“若使大时代降临，人莫我知，无憾也，而我不可以不知人，则广挹世界文教之菁英，集其大成，以陶淑当世而启迪后人，因有望于我中华之士矣”（《薄伽梵歌论》案语）。

诸《奥义书》乃韦檀多学之经典，韦檀多乃韦陀之终教，为刹帝利族所擅，其陈说巫术祭祀少，探讨宇宙人生多，被称为韦陀之“知识篇”，与婆罗门族所执之“礼仪篇”相对。大致公元前750年后，战事稍息，农耕始稳，刹帝利支配力扩大，王庭成为教学的中心，王者成为主宰者，一转婆罗门“祭祀万能”之外求，诉诸内中“心灵”之醒觉，迈出了寻求普遍性的步伐，憧憬最高者、最广者、最完善者，也即“真理”者——“大梵”“上帝”“逻各斯”“道”“太极”等等。德哲雅斯贝尔斯将其称为人类的“轴心期时代”。诸《奥义书》首推《伊莎书》与《由谁书》，是为其体系之两柱石。《伊莎书》主旨在：**揭示宇宙本然之大经大法，乃彰显大梵圆成之境。此是为入道者说法**。《由谁书》所表在：**由用达体，描述求道之过程，只止于“阿难陀”之境。此是为普通人说法**。前者可看作精神哲学，后者应当作精神现象学。尤其《伊莎书》，其密接韦陀之根本，反映古韦陀圣人之心理体系，即精神实用者也。徐先生指出：阿氏“疏释”之简约一卷，“而韦檀多学之菁华皆摄。有此一卷，即是书古今余家注疏皆可

不问。”（前记）

阿罗频多为印度近世韦檀多学之集大成者，其学说又可以称之为“大全瑜伽论”。1972年，阿氏百年诞辰，院母为其出版全集，煌煌然三十巨册。徐先生采译最重要者，乃其中四部，分属世界观者（《神圣人生论》）、人生观者（《薄伽梵歌论》）、修为观者（《瑜伽论》）和历史观者（《社会进化论》）。四者实“而一而四、而四而一”之论。设若以《薄伽梵歌论》为寻常本（俗谛义），后二者则皆为其系论；如果以《神圣人生论》为超上本（真谛义），余三者则又皆为其系论。《瑜伽论》补白“从成熟的低地（身体）出发”（康德），《社会进化论》注目集团、民族、国家的命运。四者或可一言以蔽之，曰：神圣人生本体论！于此足觇先生印学工作的重要性。我们说，他在这方面的贡献至少表现在二个方面：第一，于《薄伽梵歌》和《五十奥义书》之雅言风格的翻译与经典范式的注释——是基础性的；第二，于阿罗频多博大与精深之思想的介绍与显扬——是方向性的。阅读徐先生的文字，需要跳出寻常知觉性加以体会，或许我们能得出这样的结论：一方面，他造就了一种属于自己的思维风格和语言风格；另一方面，他指出了一个新的哲学工作的方向。

时光迅迈，陵谷替迁，《徐梵澄文集》出版已然17年了，先生示寂也23年了。这期间国家发生了多大的变化，何可计量？回想起上世纪90年代初，先生曾在街头看到一拨拨的农民工穿着西服，于是高兴得像小孩似的回来逢人便讲；又在90年代末，他尝与友人聊天，感慨地说道：“南水北调如果成功了，南方没有水灾，北方也不干旱，那中国就是天堂了。”

（《徐梵澄传》）如今，这梦想已经一步一步地变成现实。若果他在天有知呢，会对我们再说点儿什么？也许，他会勉励我们要把这一和平的局面再坚守“一世”（30年），或“两世”“三世”……“子曰：‘善人为邦百年，亦可以胜残去杀矣。’”“子曰：‘如有王者，必世而后仁。’”（《论语·子路篇》）他会希望我们将中国人和平发展的理想推及全世界。因为我们无论多么强大，其根柢都是以“文教”立国的理念，它保证了吾华族“宜尔子孙绳绳兮”之不竭的国运。今兹文集分期再版，正为长久，因为先生的目光始终是发到前方的。而前方正是我们的期许，也是现代文明世界所有人的期许，即“人类同一”的世界。虽然，这“期许”从未在人类社会实现过。然而，正如先生所言：

> 直至今日，这理想仍然只是理想，然而无论这一理想有多广大，却并非不可企及，仍属物理世界，终将实现于有限未来的某一刻，为一普遍真理的最终胜利。（《孔学古微》）

孙 波　写定于癸卯雨水日　2023年2月19日

目录

CONTENTS

唯识菁华

前言

历史上，希腊、印度与中国三个国家，都各自发展出了独有的各种哲学流派。这些哲学流派塑造了整个人类的命运。从某种意义上说，不论是现代的西方还是东方文明，都无法脱出由这些哲学所构建而成的基础。上世纪（编者按：指19世纪）自康德（Kant）开始的欧陆哲学（continental philosophy）被认为是德意志民族对古代雅典之荣光的怀旧与向往。这一荣光已不可重返，只余下了一道壮丽的彩虹，联结那些已逝而不可追的时代。若是将这些国家的历史分开来看，那么，各自的历史中皆有其空白；尽管有过去数代学者的研究，这些空白也难以填补。很多哲学流派与他们的重要著作已经佚失，很多大师也仅仅留下了名字，并无确切的年代与事迹可考。西方是这样，东方也是如此。在印度这一情况尤为突出：因为在印度，历史从未占据过十分重要的地位。一个民族因为对自身过去的无知而在前进的道路上没有任何心理负担或阻碍，这诚然是快乐的，但是，这种无知总会带来灾难性的后果。

历史的重要性在于它保存了人类在过去所能达致的最高成就的记录。过去的成败对于现在与将来的世代来说，都是宝贵的教训。已故的新儒家（New Confucianism）[1] 大师马一浮（1883—1967）认为，世界上只有两种知识体系：一是哲学，或者用他的话来说，形而上学；另一则是历史。[2] 现代社会的自然科学与社会科学体系无论如何细分或是专业化，皆可归于这两大类之中。大体来说，印度以哲学闻名，而中国则以历史著称。中国有“二十五史”，各朝各代也有无数其他的专门史；印度在韦陀时代之后（post-Vedic）则有六派哲学[3] 及各大宗教的不同学说。这在学界已广为人知。遗憾的是，历史留给我们的不总是珍贵或有用的信息，有时这些遗产甚至是有害的。哲学也是如此。在即将迈入 21 世纪之时，我们所见到的事物皆以前所未有的惊人速度前进着，我们也持有与过去全然不同的观点。因此，我们应当时时效仿两面神亚努斯（Janus）[4]，在向前看的同时，也要向后

1. 原文为 Neo-confucian，现在通行的用法是称新儒家为 New Confucianism，而称宋明理学为 Neo-Confucianism。——译者注（下文未作说明者，均为译者注）
2. 见马一浮的讲演集（1940 年代木版印刷）。——原注
3. 此六派为：数论（Sāṃkhya）、瑜伽（Yoga）、正理论（Nyāya）、胜论（Vaiśe-ṣika）、弥曼差（Mimāṃsā）、韦檀多（Vedānta）。
4. 亚努斯在古罗马神话中是具有前后两个面孔或前后左右四个面孔的门神，也是变化与时间之神。

看：只有这样，才能在最大程度上促进我们的进步。

现在，我们的文化中有一种特别的现象，这或许并非偶然。近年来，中文中“形而上学”（metaphysics）一词包含了许多的贬义；即使在人们的日常交流中，它也总是用来指称那些诡诈的、具有欺骗性的、难以确定的，或者是轻率而不够严肃的事物。这一词语的庸俗化似乎只是近三十年来发生的。年长的人或许还能记起，这一词语首次被译为中文时保留了它的原义，并且在《易经》中找到了完美对应：“形而上者谓之道”[5]。意思是，超出物理之“形”的（superphysical），就可称之为“道”或是真理。安德罗尼柯（Andronicus）[6]首先将亚里士多德（Aristotle）的哲学著作加以总结，并将它们列在物理学著作之后（译者按：meta-physics 中的 meta 在古希腊语中是表示“在其后”的前置介词），其中并无任何贬低之意。metaphysics 一词的所指与意涵不可能是今天的意思；它也与常常不受重视的中世纪经院哲学无关。我们今天所犯的这一错误或许是出于将形而上学与另一词“诡辩术”（sophistry）混淆了起来。无论如何，我们应该恢复它的原义，并与诡辩术区分开来。

一个词的误用或许并没有什么大影响。我在这里提到它，只是因为其可能造成的后果。这一误用暗示了一种非常现实主义的人生观，这种人生观谴责任何过于智性、微妙、抽象而不能为平凡人所理解的东西。因为在普通人的生活中并没有太多的抽象，更不用说思考了，这种人生观在大众中非常流行。这显然是源于唯物主义的兴盛。然而唯物主义，尤其是历史唯物主义，是高度智性的；它自身也是极为深刻的哲学思想。唯物主义并非是反对开化的；其人生观和世界观也是现实而理性的，因为它将所有事物都客观如实地对待，或者用俗话讲——实事求是。近来我们中的大多数知识分子也正是将一切事物用历史唯物主义的方法看待——将所有事物放在它所处的位置中观察，关注重大事件的历史与社会背景，并与经济基础、阶级关系等因素联系起来。如此看来，大众对“形而上学”这样一个旧词产生错误的理解，也是很自然的事。

在一个形而上学于文化中占据绝对主导地位的国家，这样的错误是极难发生的。印度是地球上唯一一个数千年以来为崇拜精神之真理而献祭并保持祭坛圣火不熄的国家。圣者们前赴后继，其中包括以其伟大精神征服了东方的佛陀乔达摩（Gautama）。佛陀的法统时有断续，但总是由另外的圣徒与智者再次承续下去；韦檀多哲学的传统也在今日的室利·阿罗频多（Śri Aurobindo）处达到了顶峰。于此不禁让人猜想，设若没有这些伟人，如此大规模的人类是否还会存在。在印度，这些人被叫作化身（Avatar），或是神在人间的化现。在无神论者看来，这可能不过是歌颂他们的一个名号；但他们的存在是必要的，他们所实现的伟大事业也不胜枚举，这就使得他们在普通人心中被神化了。

使人感到遗憾的是，印度现在的情况不容乐观；几乎所有的宗教对她

5. 《易经·系辞》。

6. 安德罗尼柯是古希腊逍遥学派（the Peripatetic school）哲学家，被认为是首位出版较为可信的亚里士多德著作集的人。

来讲都是弊大于利。但是要理解一个民族的真正价值，不能只局限在当下。正如一个人要想看到一幅景观的全貌就应当站在高处一样，我们也应当将我们的目光投向遥远的过去与更加遥远的未来。不论这一民族一时在世人的眼中是多么消沉，他们过去的荣光与对人类的贡献是不可否认的。对于伟大过去的觉醒，也就意味着对于一个伟大将来的期许。从自身灰烬中重生的凤凰，在接受了火的洗礼之后，会比之前更加美丽；这片次大陆的前景是光明的。

如果学术研究可以真正为人类服务的话，那么为迎来伟大的未来而追溯遥远的过去就应该是学者的责任；不然的话，他们的苦心研究就没有什么意义了。本书就是对一伟大宗教的过去追本溯源。依据批判哲学的方法，它探究了佛教诸重要的学说中一派之形成、短长，以及佛教整体衰落的原因。因为某些限制，这一研究不尽完整，但是主要的线索已经得以在此呈现。笔者在某些地方只是一笔带过，后来的研究者们尚有很多继续求索的空间。

1

中印文化之交流，在历史上十分繁荣。虽然中间有着很长的间断，但是，这种文化交流关系自公元纪年伊始已经持续了近千年。这些间断多由外部原因造成，两个民族之间从未有过根本上的对立。然而这种关系更多的是一种单向交流，因为只存在佛教自印度向中国的东渐。佛教首先间接由西域传入，后来又直接自陆路或海路传至中国。人们穿行在两国之间，经历了无数的艰难，只是为了一个目的——佛法。在形形色色的关于佛教传入中国的历史或传说记载中，最为可靠的应该是在公元前 2 年，大月支王使伊存为博士弟子景卢口述佛教经典一事，它标志着佛教在远东地区（the Far East）之开端。很多认为佛教传入年代更早的其他历史记载不应取信。[7]因为印度王侯（rājā）们数次请求将汉地的道家经典进行翻译，这些经典也被引介到南方与西方诸国，但似乎影响极为有限。著名的道家经典《老子》至少两次被译为梵文，但是如今已经佚失。

文化间的交流促进了两个民族的互相理解。汉地佛教徒们自称“释氏”（Śākyā），这一名号自古沿用至今。它不仅将佛教徒与家族分离开来，也使得他们与自己的民族产生了区别。如“旧时吾等之先兄伽叶（Kāśyapa）”等表达，在汉文佛教文献中随处可见。这些文献通常措辞典雅庄严，显示了与邻国之民的亲密关系。所有的佛教徒，不论印度或中国，在根本上都是出世的。他们的生活为一种出世间而不离于世间的苦行精神所引导，僧团内部有其自身的手足情谊。因此，这样的表达也就不难理解了。

中印之间的这种交流产生了许多正面影响。它引发了千数年来翻译佛经的活动；译经是与佛教文献学相关的一个专门题目，它过于广大，在这里不再深入。不论如何，这些翻译的成果正是这一宗教之灵魂所在。通常认为有四大译师：鸠摩罗什（Kumārajīva，344—413），玄奘（602—664），义净（635—713），以及不空（Amoghavajra，705—774）；其中鸠摩罗什来自西域，不空来自天竺，另两位为中国译师。译经工作由一群学僧与学者组成的团体进行，他们各司其职，形成了一个类似于今日之研讨班（seminar）的大型组织。这种集体合作十分高效，其组织形态值得进一步研究。

这群译者通常由一位将梵文原典进行口头翻译的译主主持。他的讲解被数名笔受记录下来。此外还有解释梵文口语的度语，检查梵文原义的证梵本或参译，负责润色文字的润文，以及负责全篇翻译的证义；这些人构成一个小组，在大译堂中集合。除开数名抄写与书记外，还有仅负责检查正字的校勘。每次集会皆由梵呗唱诵开场，并有监护大臣参加；监护大臣多是朝廷高官。所有参加集会的弟子皆为听众。对于译经团体成员的资格有严格考察。设若翻译工作进行得顺利有序，那么其成果通常是无可挑剔的。

这种集体合作即使在今天也是值得推崇的。然而，中国并不自居为这一翻译方法的发明者。最好的例子在古希腊。被称为“七十子译本”（Septuaginta）的古希腊文《旧约》（Old Testament）约在公元前270年被译出，它由72位学者合译而成。另一例子是英文的《詹姆士王圣经》（King James version of the Bible），这一译本集合了54位著名圣经学者之力，耗时超过四年（1607—1610）。只有在极少情况下，翻译宗教经典这样一项重大的任务可由一人独力完成；即便是马丁·路德（Martin Luther）在编定1522年《九月圣经》（September Bible）[8]的过程中，也有著名的助手梅兰希通（Melanchthon）相助。然而古代中国的译经活动并不限于一篇经典——单篇经典无论如何复杂浩瀚，总能在一定程度上被标准化。历史上自印度进入中国的佛教经典始终不绝如缕（或者更准确地说，奔流不息）。对浩如烟海的现存汉文佛教

7. 关于这一话题的讨论，读者应参考已故的汤用彤教授（1893—1964）之《中国佛教史》（译者按：此处应指《汉魏两晋南北朝佛教史》第一章“佛教入华诸传说”）。此书有英译本，详细探讨了佛教传入中国的方方面面。——原注

8. 因路德版《圣经》译本于1522年9月出版，因此亦称《九月圣经》。

经典进行最保守的估计，其部头也是《圣经》（包括《旧约》和《新约》）的六百倍。通读所有这些经典需要耗费毕生之力，也不值得推荐；不论古今，很少有大师曾通读过所有的经典。然而，这些经典作为一个整体，我们也应对之有些确切的概念。

2

汉文佛经整体上由三藏（Tripiṭaka）构成：经藏（Sūtra），律藏（Vinaya），论藏（Abhidharma）。依传统印度佛教的观点来看，“经”是一篇较短的文本或是一些教言的合集，如著名的《梵经》(Brahma-sūtra)；但汉文佛经也包括了由无数大小章节构成的长篇著作。一部佛经可能由多卷构成，如《大般若经》(*Mahāprajñāpāramitā-sūtra*）就有六百卷；也有较短的版本，如同属般若部的《心经》(*Hṛdaya-sūtra*）就只有一页，与一篇短奥义书（Upanishad）接近。这些都是极端的例子。总体上一部经有数卷，称为“品”；经通常被认为是佛陀亲授的教言。律藏也被认为是佛陀所授的，它包括行为准则与寺院清规。这些教言在佛陀涅槃（Nirvāṇa）之后，由弟子们在结集时背诵并记录下来。诸对法论（Abhidharma Śāstra）则是对那些同样是佛陀所授之教义的解释，由后世弟子写成。最新的三藏编目由曾任支那内学院研究部主任的吕澂（1896—1989）于1980年出版；这一编目清晰勾勒了三藏的全貌。[9] 笔者在此引用这一权威资料，并将其译为英文：

经藏（总688部，2790卷）	
宝积部	0001—0249
般若部	0250—0326
华严部	0327—0394
涅槃部	0395—0424
阿含部	0425—0688
律藏（总210部，879卷）	0689—0898
论藏（总196部，1094卷）	0899—1094
附疑伪外论	1095—1113

除开以上三藏，还有密藏，也应被纳入三藏之中，故此

密藏（总388部，639卷）	1114—1497
附疑伪目（7部，26卷）	1498—1504

这些只是译经，中国佛教徒对这一浩瀚文库的贡献亦十分巨大。在历史上，中国佛教逐步形成了六或七个主要宗派，这些宗派的经典包括论、注、疏、答问、历史、词典、目录及其他杂类著作共582种4172卷。这

种分类系统比日本《大正藏》(Taisho) 稍粗略些，但仍然足够全面且合理。仅仅是木刻雕版的历史、新版本的编纂与流布，已经是一门单独的学科了。关于这方面的研究，佛学大师欧阳渐（1871—1943）在半世纪前已有大成。[10]

上述的统计不过是让人一窥汉文（或者说在汉地的）佛教三藏之浩繁的卷帙。藏文的佛典翻译也是极好的参照。北京版《甘珠尔》(Bka' 'gyur[11])（其中包括经藏和律藏）有 1055 部，论藏则被收在《丹珠尔》(Bstan 'gyur) 中，共 3962 部。其他的蒙文或满文译本体量同样浩大，也同样重要，但此二者近来引用得相对较少。

当代的印度或中国学者不应忘记先辈们的宏伟成就。如果我们现在的视野仍局限于韦檀多哲学的某些流派的话，这些成就就是我们拓宽视野的理由。为研究这一如今在印度已几乎不复存在的宗教，人们的眼界也应放得更远。达斯古普塔（S. Dasgupta）的《印度哲学史》(*History of Indian Philosophy*)[12] 在探讨大乘佛教（Mahāyāna）教义时，仅使用了巴利文与梵文材料，他几乎不引用汉文资料，读者或许会对此感到遗憾。其他的欧洲佛教学者也多有同样的局限；在阅读他们的著作时，我们总会觉得其中缺少

9. 吕澂：《新编汉文大藏经目录》，济南：齐鲁书社，1980 年。

10. 欧阳渐：《欧阳大师遗集》，台北：新文丰出版公司，1976 年。——原注

11. 书中出现的藏文转写一律改为现在通行的怀利（Wylie）转写。下文不再作说明。

12. Surendranath Dasgupta, *A History of Indian Philosophy*, Cambridge: Cambridge University Press, 1922.

了什么。伟大的灵修大师室利·阿罗频多虽然被誉为“当代的柏拉图”，对古印度、古希腊与受希腊罗马影响的西方古典文明都有着深厚而广泛的了解；然而，他对古代中国却知之甚少。这是我们中国人之失，因为我们没有让自己的文化为人所知；不然，以世界文化的标准，中国文化，不论古代或现代，都值得人们研究了解。近三四十年来，随着梵文古写本的出土发现，以及印度传统梵文学者与中国学者合作进行的、对于汉文中留存下来却在印度佚失的经典的重构或重译工作的开展，我们可以期待这些由乔达摩佛陀所教授的佛法焕发出新的光彩。

3

一朵自远方移植而来的花蕾，即使能在他乡生长，也多会改变它的特性。从基因上来讲，这还是同一种花，但它生长的速度、叶子、开花结果的时间等等都可能改变。有时，这种改变会大到我们几乎无法认出是原来的物种的程度。月季或菊花的诸多品种就是例子。没有什么东西可以抵挡自然界中的演化与变迁。佛教也是如此，它在进入中国后的许多个世纪里发生了极大的变化。我们在面对这样一个形式多样、千变万化的主题时，为了研究目的而持合理的怀疑和保留态度总是没错的。

世界上的伟大宗教领袖总是被个人的超凡魅力（charisma）或者神秘感所环绕。一些西方学者甚至曾怀疑作为一个人的耶稣基督（Jesus Christ）是否存在过。至于乔达摩佛陀的历史真实性，则没有太多的怀疑。不论是南传还是北传的三乘，都认为以下事实是可信的：净饭王（Suddhodana）的王子萨婆额他悉陀（Sarvartha Siddha）[13]从他的宫殿里逃了出来，换上了苦行者的衣服，修习苦行，并在35岁证悟；此后他传法逾45年，并在80岁时（约公元前486年）于拘尸那罗城（Kusinara）入灭（Parinirvāṇa）。随后产生的佛本生传（jātaka）故事，应该被认为仅是优秀的传统文学作品。它们展示了丰富的想象力，对于人类学和语文学研究都有着很大的价值；但它们并不能被当作信史。

现在，我们或许可以说，耶稣存在与否并不重要，被钉在十字架上的那人是犹太人之王（Rex Judaerum）[14]或是其他人、他是被绳子还是钉子钉在十字架上，也并不重要；重要的是他的教法或福音：这并非诡辩。在这里，哲学——尤其是伦理学——比枯燥的历史更重要。但在佛教中，我们有两种并行的系统：小乘（Hīnayāna）或者说部派佛教与大乘（Mahāyāna）佛教。[15]此二乘类似基督教（Christianity）中的天主教（Catholicism）与新教（Protestantism），但大乘佛教与部派佛教之间并无争斗。而且，佛教从其开端就有北传和南传之分。上述所有佛经也都是经年累积而成的，没有一篇可以完全肯定是由佛陀本人所亲授。这种情况可与《薄伽梵歌》（*Bhagavad Gītā*）相比：我们知道它的作者是广博仙人（Vyāsa），然而《薄伽梵歌》中一定有非他所作的、被篡入的部分。我们现在所读到的文本很有可能不全是由黑天神（Lord Kṛṣṇa）在拘罗（Kurukṣetra）战场上所教授的，但在佛教中所有的佛经都被归为佛陀所授。佛经并非产生于同一时代，而是渐次出现的。

因此，我们应该假设所有的佛教文献都是由印度的智者们在发展佛陀教义的过程中创造出来的。但什么又是真正的、原初的佛教呢？这仍然是值得研究的问题。关于这一问题，我们可以勾勒出大致的框架，但其中仍有很多疑点。

就像对耶稣基督的崇拜先于对圣母玛丽亚（Virgin Maria）或其他圣徒的崇拜一样，对佛陀的崇拜也先于诸菩萨及之后的诸佛。如德国哲学家叔本华（A. Schopenhauer）所说，从一神崇拜转向多神崇拜或从简单转向多样是很自然的，因为普通人所崇拜的对象不可能永远局限于一个人或者一个偶像。因此，我们有理由相信大乘佛教是在内外因的共同作用下，基于原始佛教自发改变而成的。自佛教进入中国以来，所有佛教徒都认为大乘经典是佛陀真正原初的教法。许多佛学大师也是这么宣称的。但他们越维护这一点，越说明这仅仅是一个假设。虽然小乘经典也曾被译介，但在佛教进入中国之后，真正繁荣发展的只有大乘佛教。在基因上，大乘佛教仍然是佛教，但其外在形式与特色都是新出现的，汉地的社会风俗更使它逐渐远离了原来的形态。在这一问题上，历史唯物主义或许是正确的。因为法（Dharma）或者宗教总是监督并规范人们的生活，甚至就是生活的一方

13. 萨婆额他悉陀为佛作为悉达多（Siddhārtha）王子的另一名字。

14. 在《新约》中，耶稣被称为“来自拿撒勒的犹太人之王”（Jesus Nazarenus Rex Judaerum）。

15. Mahāyāna 的字面意思为“大车”，而 Hīnayāna 的字面意思则是“已被舍弃的车，劣等的车”。“小乘”佛教是大乘佛教对包括上座部佛教在内的部派佛教的贬称，是一个具争议的称号。如非另作说明，下文将 Hīnayāna 译为部派佛教。

面，而且因为不同国家的生活环境总是不同的，所以即使一个宗教的核心教义或许得以保留，它也必须适应新的环境而随机应变。此外，佛教进入中国时，面对的是儒家与道家这两个伟大的哲学或宗教系统。三教之间的斗争——尤其是在争取皇室支持方面——史籍多有所载，这也是所有宗教历史中都有的情形。无论如何，为了存续，佛教需要顺应并迎合形势，需要为生存而竞争；而为了自身的发展立足，它需要去除自身的某些方面，并与其他信仰甚至迷信系统结合起来：也就是说，佛教需要改变自己。因此，说在印度佛教之外另有一中国佛教，也是合理的。印度佛教中的大乘佛教在公元 10 世纪后就渐渐衰落，它与密教共存了近两百年之后，终于还是消失了；而中国佛教则存续至今。

在此，笔者想要简单地谈一谈部派佛教与大乘佛教的区别。二者都是佛教，但后者源于前者，并以龙树（Nāgārjuna）为祖师。龙树并没有创制出一套在此后被称为“大乘”的体系，而是对在他之前酝酿了百余年的思潮进行了系统化。龙树的年代无法确定：他最有可能生活在公元 3 世纪左右。在藏文译本中，他的著作有 118 种，其中 19 种为供唱诵的偈文（gāthā），51 种为对密教教义的注疏与阐释，48 种为对显教教义的注疏与阐释以及其他杂篇。这其中的 11 种有汉译本。瓦西里耶夫（W. P. Wassilijew）认为有两位名为龙树的大师，但这一观点仍须进一步论证。[16]

二乘之间区别显著。首先，二者的目的不同。部派佛教中修行者的目标在于证得阿罗汉（Arhat）果，永居于无生无死的涅槃境界中；而大乘佛教徒则以成佛为目标，这不仅意味着在进入涅槃之时将个人从一切苦难中解脱出来，而且要不顾自身去救助一切众生。其次，二者的教义也不同。部派佛教认为凡佛所言皆真实不虚，因此一切法都是真实义；而大乘则否定了包括“我”和一切法在内的世间万物的真实性，只有空性是真实不虚的。同属部派佛教一支的上座部（Āryasthāvīra）也讲空性，它认为法之空性与色（rūpa）之空性一样，但其解释并不十分全面。空性否定世间万物，意即一切皆为幻相（māyā）而并非真实：这就是法的自性。龙树的中道（Middle Path）就不立有或非有。再次，在修行上二乘也有不同。部派佛教推重禁欲与出家；大乘则并不向信众作此要求，其早期支持者也主要是在家众。最后，大乘更有三乘区分：下为声闻乘（Śrāvakayāna），中为独觉乘（Pratyekabuddhayāna），上为菩萨乘（Bodhisattvayāna）。佛教寺院中所供奉的很多造像都是菩萨（Bodhisattva），这在部派佛教中并不常见。

16. 佛教（以及印度教、耆那教）历史上有许多位名为Nāgārjuna的大师，除了中观派哲学的创始人龙树以外，还有密教注疏家龙树、成就者龙树、炼金士龙树等等。参见 David Gordon White, *The Alchemical Body: Siddha Traditions in Medieval India*, Chicago: University of Chicago Press, 2012, pp. 66–69。

4

在汉地，印度佛教的模式整体上发生了改变。律仪必须根据不同的居住条件进行修正。在新情况下，戒规（Śīla）也应作出很多调整。律藏在此后的发展过程中更进一步成为独立的一宗，以道宣（596—667）为祖师。在诸部派的律中，只有《四分律》或《法藏部律》（Dharmagupta）被广泛接纳并采用。《四分律》中有比丘戒 250 条，比丘尼戒 348 条。道宣作为一位注疏家也广为人知，其注疏的哲学基础最终还是建立在唯识理论上的。律宗与密教截然相反。通常普通人无法读到如《摩诃僧祇律》（*Rules of Mahāsaṃghikā*）等关于律法的书籍；它们通常被密藏在寺院之中。如今在精神医学研究中应用了很多这方面的材料。

除律宗之外，其他宗派也十分兴盛。这些宗派的区分是由对三藏的系统分类而产生的。天台宗（天台山是一座名山）以智顗（538—597）为其宗师，以《妙法莲华经》(*Saddharmapuṇḍarika-sūtra*) 为根本经典，教授止观禅修之法 (Śamatha-vipaśyanāni)。以法藏 (643—712) 为祖师的贤首宗[17]或华严宗仅以《大方广佛华严经》(*Buddhāvataṃsaka-mahāvaipulya-sūtra*) 为根本经典。以窥基 (632—682) 为祖师的慈恩宗主要宣讲唯识理论，"慈恩"是唐高宗为纪念生母而修建的寺院之名。净土宗 (Sukhāvatī / "Pure Land") 则始于慧远法师 (334—416)，并为昙鸾 (476—542) 所发扬光大；净土宗以《弥陀经》为经典，其信众主要供奉阿弥陀佛 (Amitābha Buddha)，他们时时念诵阿弥陀佛的名号，就像一些印度教徒念诵"唵"(Aum) 一样。除此之外，更有"禅那 (Dhyāna) 派"，又称禅宗。尽管禅宗尊菩提达摩 (Bodhidharma, ?—526) 为祖师，其教法与任何印度佛教部派都不同，它自成一派，其中更有南宗北宗之分。在这些宗派之下还另外生发出一些更小的宗派；它们多受到儒家或道家思想的影响，更多时候则两者兼有；在此就不做讨论了。或许有人会问：如果这些宗派都是佛教的话，哪一宗才是人们应当信奉的正统呢？

历史上，很多学者信奉某一宗佛教，写成、编纂并保存了无数三藏译文的注疏。与此同时，其他哲学流派的观点也进入了佛教；这些观点在某种意义上并非正统，但从未被排斥。尽管儒家很难被称为一种宗教，我们也常常见到将"三教"合称的趋势。道教可以说是一种宗教，但道家哲学思想也是独立于其宗教性方面之外的。儒学或者说宋明理学与现代意义上

17. "贤首"为法藏之封号。

的宗教类似之处极少。我们常常见到想要将三教合而为一的努力，尽管它们从未成功过。这可能是因为寻求真理者先是窥见或观想到一些或大或小的启示，之后才从这些信仰系统中找到并使用了用来描述这些启示的专有词汇。又因为人们能在这些系统中找到等同或对应之处，所以不同宗教的结合是可能的。同物质的真相一样，一定有某种精神之真相；其本质可以被认知，而外在表现形式则未必统一。马克思主义学者在此也会考虑到各朝各代的统治者总是倾向于各宗教的合流这一社会因素。一个宣称有着数百万信众的宗教是一种不可忽视的社会力量；统治者们不仅不会无视这种力量，更会渴望得到它的支持。从反面来看，宗教融合可以避免过多的纷争；从正面看，统治阶级则可以通过宗教力量的支持来巩固自身的政权。因此，他们总是赞赏并支持因循守旧或者兼容并蓄。这种虚构的融合更使得各个宗教的独特之处改变甚至消失，但总体来说，后果并不严重。

如果我们承认中国佛教不同于其印度源本（事实也确实如此），那么我们也应该注意到中国佛教自身的另一重鲜明特色。通常，一个人成为佛教徒时，需要一段见习期。这种现象在绝大多数宗教中都存在，如古希腊时期在秘仪（Mysteries）之前有一段用于洁净仪式的时间。一名佛教徒也需要在寺院中居住数年，才能成为一位受全戒的比丘或比丘尼。但是在中国，有的佛教徒不曾受过任何戒律仪轨，却对佛教做出了巨大的贡献。这些在家佛教徒被称为优婆塞（upāsaka）或者优婆夷（upāsikā）。他们通常是在家信众，多为大学者、社会名流或显赫官员。他们自发形成了一个社会团体或阶级，并做出了巨大的贡献。在某种意义上说，没有他们的支持，僧团就不可能昌盛，有时甚至难以生存下来。成为优婆塞或者优婆夷也需要一个简单的仪式，但很少有人真正执行。事实上，只要愿意，任何人都可以称自己为优婆塞或者优婆夷。著名的在家众包括杨文会（1837—1911）、欧阳渐，以及他们的同时代人如梅光羲（1880—？）、李正刚；他们也都是大儒。正是由于他们的努力，佛教得以在本世纪复兴并发展。或许我们可以夸张地说，在中国佛教之内更有一种在家众佛教。学界，尤其是西方学界，只重视在家众佛教；这种佛教也是本书所关心的。

5

从前面提到的文化交流角度来看，我们就能很容易看到在完整理解佛教教法过程中将要遇到的种种困难。一切都取决于翻译。一名学者不论对传统汉文文献有多深的造诣，如果不曾从一开始就正确地学习佛法的话，就不能理解佛教的文献；这就好像尽管词汇相同，但所有内容都以另一种语言来表达一样。学者通常会被音译词难倒。如 Nirvāṇa 一词（指一种超脱生死的状态）被译为“涅槃”，这仅仅是标记了发音。其他同样意义丰富的词还有例如般若（Prajñā）、菩提（Bodhi）、三摩地（Samādhi）、兜率天（Tuṣita）、瑜伽、阿含经（Āgama）等等。此外，在公元 7 世纪，即玄奘法师的时代之前，尤其是佛教刚进入中国之时，还没有任何标准化的翻译。每名译师都可以用自己的方言标记发音。因此，后代的注疏就不可或缺。这些音译也为现代学者进行古代语文学的研究，尤其是音变的研究，留下了丰富的材料。

在这一方面，玄奘所带来的标准化翻译提供了很大帮助。相比于旧的译文，他的翻译被称为“新译”。他规定了五类应当音译的术语：密教词汇如“陀罗尼”（Dhāraṇi）；多义词如“薄伽梵”（Bhagavān）；非汉地本土之物如“阎浮树”（jambu tree）；此前已经音译的词如“阿耨”（Anuttara）、“菩提”；以及使人生敬畏庄严之心、超脱凡语之词，如“佛”（Buddha）、“菩萨”等。

一名本土学者自然是不能理解佛教文本的，因为它是一门特别的学问，是在他眼界之外的一种知识体系。然而因为译文中的中文比传统文言文简单很多，对他来说这也终究不是难事。如果他熟悉旧译本的话，那就更容易了。在此，读者需要注意一点：玄奘推助新译，在保守派中引发了很多不满：习惯于旧译本的正统佛教徒们不能容忍他所做的改动。这不仅仅是语言的问题，而且是内容的问题。同一文献有很多不同的梵文原本，而从佛教史来看，在玄奘之前的数百年里，印度佛教在理论上也有很多进步。如关于空性的理论就是逐渐发展而来的。这些争端与反对最终使得唐高宗下敕，令玄奘“所欲翻经论，无者先翻，有者在后”。[18] 仅从语言角度来看，旧译本表述合宜，容易理解，便于阅读，也适合汉族的思维模式；因此在今天旧译也很受欢迎。然而玄奘所作的新译则更精确、齐整，也更接近原文；但这些新译文风独特，有时仅是通顺，谈不上文采斐然。所以

18.《大慈恩寺三藏法师传》卷九：“法师在京之日，先翻法智论三十卷，及大毘婆沙未了。至是有勅报法师曰。其所欲翻经论，无者先翻，有者在后。”

如今在研究中与梵文原本进行比较时，学者只使用并依据新译本。有意思的是，前文提到的梅光羲居士不懂巴利文、梵文，或藏文，却能够在“相宗（the Lakṣaṇa school）新旧译本”的比较中有精彩发现。他的论述虽短，却超出了同领域中很多的长篇大论。

此外，不同民族的思维模式基本上都是相同的，但其思想的表达方式则不同。足目仙人（Akṣapāda）的正理论与亚里士多德逻辑学中的三段论非常相似，而其推理过程则不可并立。通过比较研究，威提布萨那（Vidyabhusana）在他的《印度逻辑学史》（*A History of Indian Logic*）[19] 中认为，逻辑学比正理论要更易于应用。在印度的正理学中其实可以见到些微独裁主义的痕迹，而在希腊逻辑中则有一种民主的精神。圣教量（Āgamapramāṇa）是不可以被质疑的：上师的教言要求绝对的信仰与服从。而在逻辑推理中，先是提出一个假设，此假设如果被认可成立的话，就到此为止；如果需要的话，则引入论证；要是对方还不理解，则再给出一个正面或反面的范例。希腊式三段论在外在形式上更开明，也更使人信服。用历史唯物主义观点对此进行解释也能成立：在古雅典，尽管社会底层存在奴隶制，自由民们却发展并享受着一种自由精神，这在他们以归纳法与演绎法来进行论证的逻辑中也是可以见出的。而在古印度，种姓制度则存续了很长一段时间；在这种制度中，婆罗门居于金字塔之顶，并在精神领域如同独裁者一样对大众行使绝对权威。从实用角度讲，正理论在现代世界已经不被使用了，然而人们仍然需要了解古代佛教文献作者们对于它的应用。

梵语的语法结构也可能为学者造成困难。这一语言中充满了精确、微妙与优美之处，但它与汉语的区别之大也显而易见。另外，古印度人的数字思维也十分特别，如在《华严经》（*Avataṃsaka-sūtra*）中出现的数字之大，就超出了凡夫的想象力。[20] 或许有人认为这只是凭空想象而成，但它们仍无疑是数字。古印度哲学的表述方式中尤为特殊的一点还包括重复。在偈颂中的内容经常在散文中再重复一次。因为教法的内容可以通过重复多次被确认，这应该是有益的。在僧伽（Saṃgha）或僧团中，讲法与讨论前后通常会有唱诵。这种形式与今天在教堂仪式中布道前后唱颂赞美诗并无不同，不过佛教偈文是专为每次讲法所作的，其内容也与通常为散文形式的讲义相对应。然而即使在散文中，同样的意思也可能被再三重复，就像旋转的古埃及汲水车一样，这在佛教术语中又被称为“转法轮”。这一形式也被负责的译师保留下来了。在中国有一很老的笑话，说佛陀的教义就像水被来来回回从一个桶倒进另一个桶里一样，到最后还是同样的一桶水。对同样字词的单调重复，听起来使人感到压抑甚至昏昏欲睡，它或许并不那么鼓舞人心，甚至也并不算有意思；然而我们在阅读这些长篇大论时也应注意到，这些重复常常以螺旋的形式存在，观点虽然一样，次第却在逐步

19. Vidyabhusana, Satis Chandra and Irach J. S. Taraporewala, *A History of Indian Logic: Ancient, Medieval and Modern Schools*, Calcutta: Calcutta University, 1921.

20. 如实叉难陀译《大方广佛华严经》阿僧祇品第三十：“一百洛叉为一俱胝；俱胝俱胝为一阿庾多；阿庾多阿庾多为一那由他……不可量转不可量转为一不可说；不可说不可说为一不可说转；不可说转不可说转为一不可说不可说；此又不可说不可说为一不可说不可说转。”

提升。

以上就是阅读佛教文献可能会遇到的种种困难，我们应懂得如何立足解决。大量的佛教文献就像热带雨林一样；雨林中有数条被清理出来的大路，其中能找到许多珍稀的植物品种。如果以水作比方，那么它不仅是一桶水，而且是一条大河。现在或许已经没有人再立志成为精通三藏的大家了。作为在家弟子，如果一个人相信佛法并有信仰（这在任何宗教中都不可或缺），并追求心中的平静与个人的解脱（mokṣa），那么信奉其中一两个宗派就足够了。禅宗否定宗教中的一切，而净土宗则确信有传说中超越的净土存在。如果有人想要同时信奉这两种看上去互相矛盾的说法，那么他就会像俗话所说的，"有禅有净土，犹如戴角虎"。一个人去河中饮水是为了止渴，不必像因陀罗（Indra）一样将河中的水都喝完。[21] 净土宗仍有三经一论，而禅宗则不立文字，只有一些公案——即使这些公案也是可以弃之不用的。如果一个人想要通晓佛教，他可能需要先学习数个学派的教法，然后再参考前面所提到的那些博学的在家居士的论著。我们现在也有很多研究工作需要完成；因为许多传统都已被废弃了，我们尤其需要大力神（Hercules）之力来清理奥革阿斯（Augeas）的牛圈。[22]

21. 此处或指《梨俱韦陀》(1.32.1-2) 中因陀罗与弗栗多 (Vṛtra) 之战：蛇神弗栗多阻挡了雨水，导致人间发生旱灾。因陀罗与弗栗多交战，并以工匠神陀湿多 (Tvaṣṭṛ) 为他提供的雷电之杵杀死了弗栗多，使得雨水降下，水流汇集流向大海。
22. 希腊神话中大力神的十二项功绩之一就是在一天之内清理奥革阿斯的牲口圈。奥革阿斯是埃利斯 (Elis) 王，太阳神赫利俄斯 (Helios) 之子，拥有大批牲畜。传说他的牲口圈三十年从未打扫，极其污秽。因此“奥革阿斯的牛圈”常常用来比喻长期积累、不易解决的问题。

6

唯识学属于相宗，而已过世的佛教大师欧阳渐将其独立于一派。我们在此无须过多探讨他的论述，因为归根到底这只是分类的问题。前文所提到的慈恩宗尊窥基为祖师，窥基在 17 岁时（648 年）被玄奘收为弟子，并一直追随玄奘直到圆寂（682 年）。严格地说，作为唯识理论的首要倡导者，玄奘应被认为是唯识宗的创始人。然而作为当时最伟大的佛教领袖——玄奘在 19 年内译出了 75 部 1315 卷作品——仅称他为一宗之创始人远远不够。窥基作为他的弟子也著述颇丰，被称为“百部疏主”。这一称号源于那烂陀寺（Nālandā），用于指称一个人所精通的经论数量。然而窥基所作的 43 部注疏，于今仅存 31 种。他的杰作是对《成唯识论》（*Vijñāptimātratāsiddhi Śāstra*）的注疏《成唯识论述记》，这也是唯识宗得名的原因。

在《成唯识论》中，玄奘参考了以护法（Dharmapāla）为首的十位印度大论师，并以护法的观点为最终的权威依据。窥基请求玄奘将十位论师的观点糅合为一，玄奘同意了这一请求，并只将此学授予窥基。窥基为此苦心钻研。汉传佛教中著名的《成唯识论》及其注疏，就是这样写成的。

在玄奘之前，世亲（Vasubandhu）所作二十颂注疏《唯识二十颂》（*Viṃśatikā*）已有两个译本。其一由在北方的瞿昙般若流支（Gautama Prajñāruci，不是另一位印度译师菩提流支［Bodhiruci］）于534—538年译出，另一个由在南方的真谛（Paramārtha，499—569）译出。两位译师皆有他们的汉地弟子协助翻译。与《唯识二十颂》同时的安慧（Sthiramati）的《三十唯识释》（*Triṃśikavijñaptibhāṣyam*）则被纳入玄奘的注疏里。这两部注疏的梵文原本由西尔万·莱维（Sylvain Levi）在1922年发现于加德满都，并于1925年在巴黎编辑出版。[23] 因此，这两篇注疏在梵文原本与一部藏文译本之外，还有三个译本。通过比较三个译本，可以看出般若流支译本的原文可能与我们现在见到的原本略有不同，三个译本各使用了一套不同的术语进行翻译。[24] 三者的内容一致，很难说哪个译本最好；但玄奘的译本最晚，也最精确。严格说来，我们并没有一个“标准”的梵文写本原本。玄奘同时参考了数个梵文原本，其中自然有内容安排上的不同，后人篡入之处，此前的译师

23. Levi, Sylvain, and Vasubandhu, *Vijñāptimātratāsiddhi: Deux Traités de Vasubandhu : Viṃśatikā (la Vingtaine), Accompagnée d'une Explication en Prose et Triṃśikā (la Trentaine) avec le Commentaire de Sthiramati*, Paris: Honoré Champion, 1925.

24. 笔者在1948年对这三个译本进行了比较，结论可参考“《唯识二十论》钩沉”，载《世界宗教研究》，1982年第4期。——原注

们或正确或错误的修订，以及抄写者的错误，等等。正是玄奘将这些注疏的内容大体确定了下来，因此他的翻译也被认为是最可靠的。

唯识学是大乘佛教法相宗（the Dharma-Lakṣaṇa school）哲学的支柱。其发展过程是逐步由简至繁进化而来的，并在成为一个统一而独立的哲学体系的过程中不断地改进。唯识学的基本经典为著名的“六经十一论”。[25] 事实是，六经中的两部没有汉译，那么经只有四部；而论则只有九部——另外两部中的一部只有题目，而无本文，还有一部则已经佚失了。下面列举了这些经论的题目、译者以及译出的年代：

经：

（1）《大方广佛华严经》

两部译本：

（a）佛驮跋陀罗（Buddhabhadra） 60卷，418—421年

（b）实叉难陀（Śikṣānanda） 80卷，695—698年

（2）《解深密经》（*Sandhinirmocanavyūha-sūtra*）

两部译本：

（a）菩提流支 5卷，514年

（b）玄奘 5卷，647年

（另有求那跋陀罗［Guṇabhadra］和真谛译文各一卷，收录在（a）中。）

（3）《楞伽经》（*Laṅkāvatāra-sūtra*）

三部译本：

（a）求那跋陀罗　　4 卷，443 年

（b）菩提流支　　10 卷，513 年

（c）实叉难陀　　7 卷，700—704 年

（4）《大乘密严经》（*Mahāyānaghanavyūha-sūtra*）

两部译本：

（a）日照（Divākara）　　3 卷，676—688 年

（b）不空金刚　　3 卷，762—765 年

（5）《如来最胜功德庄严经》（*Tathāgata-abhyudgata-guṇa-alamkāra-sūtra*）

无汉译本。

（6）《大乘阿毗达摩经》（*Mahāyānābhidharma-sūtra*）

无汉译本，仅存引用。

论：

（1）《瑜伽师地论》（*Yogācārybhūmi Śāstra*）

弥勒（Maitreya）著。

25. 传统的“十一论”也可以包括世亲《三十唯识论》的译本，以及笔者曾译出的安慧《三十唯识释》。——原注

100 卷，玄奘译，646—648 年。

现存梵文写本。

（2）《显扬圣教论》（*Āryavācāprakaraṇa Śāstra*）

无著（Asaṅga）著。

20 卷，玄奘译，645—646 年。

（3）《大乘庄严经论》（*Mahāyānasūtrālaṅkāraṭika*）

弥勒著，世亲注疏。

13 卷，波颇密多罗（Prabhāmitra）译，630—633 年。

（4）《集量论》（*Pramāṇasamuccaya Śāstra*）

陈那（Diṅnāga）著。

4 卷，义净译，711 年。

（此译本已于唐代佚失，仅存《丹珠尔》藏译。已故的法尊法师有自藏文译出的节译本。[26]）

（5）《摄大乘论》（*Mahāyānasamparigraha Śāstra*）

无著著。

3 卷，玄奘译，648—649 年。

2 卷，佛陀扇多（Buddhaśanta）译，531 年。

3 卷，真谛译，563 年。

世亲注疏：

10 卷，玄奘译，648—649 年。

无性（Abhāva）注疏：

10卷，玄奘译，648—649年。

15卷，真谛译，563年。

10卷，达摩笈多（Dharmagupta）译，609年。

（6）《十地经论》（*Daśabhūmikasūtra Śāstra*）

世亲著。

12卷，菩提流支译。

（7）《分别瑜伽论》（*Vibhāgayoga Śāstra*）

弥勒著。

无汉译本。

（8）《观所缘缘论》（*Vidarśanā-alambanapratyaya Śāstra*）

陈那著。

1卷，玄奘译，657年。

1卷，真谛译。

（9）《辨中边论》（*Antamadhyaviveka Śāstra*）

弥勒著。

世亲注疏：

3卷，玄奘译，661年。

2卷，真谛译。

26. 陈那造，法尊译编：《集量论略解》，北京：中国社会科学出版社，1982年。

（10）《大乘阿毗达磨集论》（*Mahāyānābhidharmasamuccaya Śāstra*）

无著著。

7卷，玄奘译，652年。

师子菩提（Siṃhabodhi）注疏：

16卷，玄奘译，646年。

（11）《唯识二十颂》

（见前文相关讨论。）

7

玄奘在《成唯识论》中取其菁华而糅合为一的有十位大论师；除了窥基所作的一些含糊不清的记载（这些记载多为颂扬之词）之外，并无太多关于他们生平的具体信息。世亲被认为是唯识理论的始创者，但是他生活的年代并不确定。有两种记录：其一认为他活跃于佛入灭之后约 1100 年，另一则认为是约 900 年后。如果佛入灭的年代可以定于公元前 486 年的话，由 B. 巴塔查里亚（B. Bhattacharya）确定并被普遍接受的世亲的年代——公元 280—360 年——是很有可能的。世亲的传记由真谛译出（其中就有关于其生卒年的第二种说法），现仍存。亲胜（Bandhuśri，十位论师中的第四位）对世亲的《三十颂》则作了非常简要的注释，后世论师的详细注疏也是基于前者。世亲的另一位同时代人还有火辨（Citrabhāna，410—490，十位论师中的第七位），他也对这一理论做出了贡献。还有一位是德慧（Guṇamati，440—

520，十位论师中的第二位），他是安慧（475—555，十位论师中的第三位）的老师。安慧据称是真谛的老师。与安慧同时代的有净月（Śuddhacandra，年代未知，十位论师中的第六位）。然而在这些唯识派大师（Vijñānavādin）中最著名的是护法（十位论师中的首位），其生活年代为6世纪初。他是建志补罗城（Kāñcipura）一位大臣之子。护法曾任那烂陀寺寺主，29岁离开了那烂陀，居住在菩提迦耶（Bodhi Gayā）；他于32岁在摩诃菩提寺（Mahābodhi）去世。他是戒贤（Śīlabhadra）的老师，戒贤则是玄奘的老师。护法有三大弟子，胜友（Viśeṣamitra，十位论师中的第八位），胜子（Jinaputra，十位论师中的第九位），以及智月（Jñānacandra，十位论师中的最后一位）。与安慧和净月同时代的是难陀（Nanda，十位论师中的第五位），他是胜军（Jinasena）的师祖，胜军则是玄奘的另一位老师。胜军长期独居于那烂陀寺之外，并与戒贤齐名。在公元5世纪和6世纪这两百年间，唯识理论渐至完善，在玄奘编纂《成唯识论》时达到了顶峰。《成唯识论》作为一部奠基之作，时至今日仍然具有很大影响。

8

意识是宇宙中必不可缺的一种创造力；没有了意识，也就没有了存在：这是印度韦檀多（Vedāntin）派的观点。他们认为宇宙的实相即存在（真）—意识（智）—悦乐（乐）(Sachchidānanda)。[27]关于这一观念的正确理解，可以参考室利·阿罗频多的《神圣人生论》(*The Life Divine*)，这部著作也有法、德、中译本。[28]他对这一问题的探讨详尽无遗，其杰作不须易一字。[29]我们或许还须再加讨论的就是，在韦檀多派之外的其他学派之传统所持的观点。

27. Sacchidānanda 为三个梵文词复合而成：存在（sat）、意识（cit）和极乐（ānanda）。
28. 中译本见徐梵澄译，北京：商务印书馆，2011 年。
29. 室利·阿罗频多自称其为“杰作”(*magnum opus*)。——原注在开始对唯识理论的讨论之前，我们还须再离题一次。在我们的日常语言中，人人都知道“有意识”是什么意思。每名基督徒都熟知这一故事：耶稣在客西马尼（Gethsemane）花园发现自己的门徒睡着时曾两次提醒他们要保持清醒，因为有一件大事将要发生。[30]《圣经》中还有十处女迎接新郎的譬喻。[31] 在希腊神话中，我们可以看到古希腊人发明了各种形式的惩罚，如对于坦塔罗斯（Tantalus）、西绪福斯（Sisyphus）以及达那伊得斯姐妹们（Danaides）的折磨，或者是伊克西翁（Ixion）被绑的火轮，等等。[32] 然而即使是众神也对喝冥河（Styx）之水极为畏惧；喝了冥河的水，人就会陷入一年的无意识之愚蠢行为中，在此后的九年里也将失去所有的神力。古希腊人十分了解失去意识的意义。而在中国古代伦理学中，教育的主要目标之一，就是使学童们在言行举止上时时保持警觉[33]。在《礼记》中就能找到很多例子。或许每一重要信仰体系中都有类似的教诫。

理学与佛学互相对立，有一件逸事显示出儒家是怎样看待自己的对手的。有一次，一位友人问宋代理学大师程颐（1033—1107）谁是世上最忙的人，他的回答是“禅师！”——确实如此，因为禅宗需要破除一切，不立己说；因此，禅师们需要时刻留心自觉，心中一刻都不得停息。

所有真理的追寻者们欲想在修行之路上避免跌撞或者摔倒的话，这或许是他们需要意识到的一点。

以上是在日常理性中对意识的通俗解读。但如果我们要研究大乘佛教唯识理论的话，那么同时我们就得对认识论领域中的感官知觉有基本的了解。诸识是知觉性（智）的分支（或结果），如视觉可称眼识，听觉可称耳识，等等。这是一个由上文提到的十位论师逐步建构而成的、极为精微复杂的系统，也是相宗哲学的核心。

自很早以前开始，对五识的研究就吸引了许多哲学家；每一古印度哲学体系都不曾忽视五识，并有自己关于感官知觉的理论。爱德华·扎豪（Edward C. Sachau）所编的阿尔比鲁尼的《印度》（Alberuni's *India*）[34]中这样说：

30. 参见《新约·马可福音》14：32—41。
31. 参见《新约·马太福音》25：1—13。
32. 坦塔罗斯为宙斯（Zeus）之子，他在死后被逐出奥林波斯（Olympus），永远站在水中。他的眼前有唾手可得的果实，然而当他伸手去摘时，树枝就会升高；当他低头想要喝水时，水就会退去。西绪福斯是埃费拉（Ephyra）之王，他被惩罚的方式是将大石推上山顶；每当他接近山顶时，大石就会再次滚落，如此往复。达那伊得斯姐妹按照其父亲达那厄斯（Danaus）的命令，在新婚之夜谋杀了自己的丈夫；因此，她们被发配至冥府最底层，不停接水灌满那永不可能被灌满的无底之桶。伊克西翁因为对宙斯之妻子赫拉（Hera）起了欲念而受到惩罚，被永远绑在不停滚动的火轮上。
33. 著名的例子之一是大理学家邵雍在学《易》时，三年睡不沾枕，终于有所成而可以未卜先知。——原注（译者按：此处原文作“三十年”，根据邵雍之子邵伯温之《邵氏闻见录》卷十八，其父“三年不设榻，昼夜危坐以思”，故订正为三年。）
34. 阿尔比鲁尼（Al-Biruni，973—1048）为波斯学者，其研究横跨数学、天文学、物理学、医学、历史学、地理学等领域。作有《印度》（又名《对印度传统中合理与不合理之处的扬弃》），被认为是印度学的奠基人。

XV-XIX. 知觉有五，称为“根”(indriyāni)：耳之听觉，眼之视觉，鼻之嗅觉，舌之味觉，及皮肤之触觉。

XX. 再有意识，意识居于心中，并引领诸感官行使其功用，故又称“意”(manas)。[35]

在列举二十五谛[36]后，阿尔比鲁尼作出如下结论：

以上的各种被称为含识（tattva），一切所知局限于此。因此，破灭仙人（Parasara）之子广博仙人有言：“学习逻辑推论时，应学习此二十五谛之区别、定义与分类。此为定论，非口舌之言。再皈依任意宗教，则得解脱之果。”[37]

此为至今在印度仍然活跃的数论哲学的观点。一些大乘佛教徒在佛教衰落的时代也追随此派。耆那教（Jainism）关于感官知觉的哲学观点与数论相似，或者说基于数论派。耆那教认为对外界事物的知识来自从各感官得来的现量（pratyakṣa），但否认了意的存在。耆那教的大渡津者（Tirthaṅkara）[38]大雄（Mahāvīra）是佛陀的同时代者，他之前更有二十四祖师。不论是佛教或是耆那教，都很难自称五识之说的先行者。略晚于数论的《奥义书》以及《薄伽梵歌》也对根与五大（火、空、地、水、风）的关系进行了细致分析。因此，我们有理由假设在印度自古以来的不同哲学系统中，对于识的研究是一常见的主题；这些系统此后各有其不同的发展与创新。

唐代（618—907）由玄奘重新引入的唯识哲学有其自身的独特之处，我们现在来看中国的大乘佛教徒是如何理解这一哲学的。

35. Bīrūnī, Muḥammad ibn Aḥmad and Eduard Sachau, *Alberuni's India: An Account of the Religion, Philosophy, Literature, Geography, Chronology, Astronomy, Customs, Laws and Astrology of India about A.D. 1030*, Delhi: S. Chand, 1964, pp. 43–44.

36. 数论哲学将事物归类为二十五谛。此二十五谛为：（1）补卢沙或神我（puruṣa），原质或本性（prakṛti），觉或菩提（buddhitattva），我慢（ahaṃkāra），意（manas）；（2）眼（cakṣu）、耳（karṇa）、鼻（nasa）、舌（jihvā）、皮肤（tvac），以上五种为五知根；（3）口（vāc）、手（pāṇi）、足（pāda）、生殖器官（upastha）、排泄器官（pāyu），以上五种为五作根；（4）色（rūpa）、声（śabda）、香（gandha）、味（rasa）、触（sparśa），以上五种合称五根境；（5）地（kṣiti）、水（ap）、火（tejas）、风（vāyu）、空（ākāśa），以上五种合称五大。

37. Bīrūnī, Muḥammad ibn Aḥmad and Eduard Sachau, *Alberuni's India*, p. 44.

38. "渡津者"为耆那教术语，指已渡过生死之海而开悟的圣者。

9

我们在逐渐地深入唯识理论后，就会发现，对于现代思维而言，几乎它的每一步都有难以接受的教义或假设。现在可能只有出家的比丘、比丘尼和在家的信众会真的相信阿修罗（asura）、轮回、无色界（arūpadhātu）、十菩萨地等等。但如果我们选择迈出这一步并相信这些观念的话，就会发现在它们之上可以建构出一套自洽的教义。与之相反，我们如果坚持现实主义的观点并在每一步都挑战其真实性的话，则无法得出任何结论。设若我们从完全中立的高度出发来勘察这一理论的幽微之处，我们将会发现，尽管这些教义、假设或任何不合理的前提看似荒谬或者让人难以想象，但它们终究还是在人的思维模式之内，并且可能拓宽我们的知识领域甚至带来新的领悟。在大乘佛教中，实相一直被分为世俗谛（或俗谛）与圣义谛（或真谛），唯识理论所讨论的是前者。这一理论中有很多值得我们重视的理性与现实之处。对于一名西方学者来说，或许这一理论更应被理解为一门艺术；这样的话，欣赏这一理论中的每一元素如何极尽精准地构成一个整体则是让人惊叹的过程。这一系统中虽然有显然可见的修正之处，但整体上仍然可以引人入胜。

现在我们要问的是：唯识理论是由佛陀创制的吗？如果我们讨论的是现在的唯识理论的话，答案显然是否定的。佛陀教授的十二缘起（dvādaśāṅgaḥ pratītyasamutpāda）[39] 中第三因缘为“识”，第四为名色（nāma-rūpa），第五则为六处。这十二支因果链是早期佛教的关键教义，其权威性毋庸置疑，而其根深蒂固的历史背景也可为此提供佐证。在部派佛教及此后的大乘佛教中，“五蕴”（skandha）的学说成为用来对抗婆罗门教关于“我”（Ātman）的教义的壁垒，并使佛教也成为一种字面意义上的、与正统相对立的“新教”。五蕴大略可分为两组。第一组由四个元素组成：第一蕴为色，包括了身体、感官及对境；其次为受（vedanā），即感官之知觉；再次为想（saṃjñā），即观念知识；第四为行，即由感官知觉、感受、观念等和合而成的心理状态与作用；第五蕴为识（vijñāna）。在我们现代的思维模式中，第一蕴可以独立指物质世界；而作为心理活动的第五蕴则可包括余下三者。在寻找“我”或是自性的过程中，人们认识到这五蕴，并了解它们并非真有。不同学派对于“无我”有不同的理论，最终唯识论家将其发展

39. 十二缘起为：无明，行，识，名色，六处，触，受，爱，取，有，生，老死。

成一完备的系统。

需要注意的是，佛陀本人不曾想过要成为一位哲学家或是宗教领袖，而是致力于将人类从苦难中解脱出来。他发现了苦的起源是自无明（avidyā）开始直至老死（jarāmaraṇaṃ）、愁（śokaḥ）、悲（parideva）、苦（duḥkhaṃ）、忧恼（daurmanasyaṃ）的连锁反应。或许是因为这一问题不够紧迫，他极少探究存在或来世的意义。一个古老的譬喻是，当一个人被箭射中时，最紧要的是拔出箭头使伤口愈合，而不是去讨论射手是怎样的人、哪一种姓等等。[40] 与无明相对的是证悟，佛陀教授了如八正道（Āryāṣṭāṅgamārga）在内的达成证悟之道。[41] 识在八正道中一直是重要的一环，后来的论师也不曾对此加以增补。

因果之链又称为有轮（Bhāvacakra），它始于无明。祛除了无明之后，造作或者行（saṃskāra）也就不复存在了。saṃskāra 被理解为影响、行为或是建构等，在中文里则被译成“行”。再后，识、六处（ṣaḍāyatana，汉译又称“六入”）、触（sparśa）、受、爱（tṛṣṇā）、有（bhāva）、生（jāti）、老死都以其生起次序被根除。这是一种基于人类共同体验的深入分析。被后世大乘佛教徒所大量应用的第二、三、四、五种缘起还需要更多的解释。

40. 这一比喻出自《佛说箭喻经》。

41. 八正道是：正见（Samyagdṛṣṭiḥ），正思惟（Samyaksamkalpaḥ），正语（Samyag-vāk），正业（Samyakkarmāntaḥ），正命（Samyagājivaḥ），正精进（Samyavyāyā-maḥ），正念（Samyaksmṛtiḥ），及正定（Samyaksamādhiḥ）。——原注

10

接下来我们讨论在各部派佛教中与唯识学相关的一些早期理论。在佛陀入灭后的四百年中，佛陀的教法多次分裂为不同的部派。在印度北部就有不少于二十个部派。在此后的七百年中，部派的数量更多了。这些部派都属唯心主义，多持有早期佛教而非大乘佛教观点；然而最终大乘佛教正是从这些部派中发展出来。为了本书的讨论需要，在此引入如下观念。

大众部、一说部（Ekavyavahārikā）、说出世部（Lokottaravādin）、鸡胤部（Kaukkutikā）有共同承认的 47 个观点，我们从其中选取一些来讨论：

（1）（具有眼等五官的）肉身有或没有染污；

（2）在色界（rūpadhātu）与无色界皆有具六感之众生；

（3）五根（indriya）是物质器官，眼作为一种器官不能去“看”，耳不能去“听”，如此等等；

（4）智（dhī）为加行（prayoga），可以化除厄难，使人意乐；

（5）无无记法（avyākṛtadharma）；

（6）无为法（asaṃskṛta dharma）有九种：

a. 忘（Saṃpramoṣa）；

b. 不忘（Asaṃpramoṣa）；

c. 虚空（Ākāśa）；

d. 空无边处（Ākāśānantyāyatanaṃ）；

e. 识无边处（Vijñānānantyāyatanaṃ）；

f. 无所有处（Ākiñcananyatyāyatanaṃ）；

g. 非想非非想处（Naivasaṃjñānāsaṃjñānāyatanaṃ）；

h. 缘起支（Pratīyayasamutpada-aṅgāni）；

i. 圣道支（Āryamārga-aṅgāni）。

（7）随眠（anuśaya）[42]既非心法（citta），也非心所法（caitasikā）；随眠亦无所缘（ālambana）；

（8）一切随眠不同于缠（paryavasthānaṃ），前者与心不相应，后

42. 根据说一切有部（Sarvāstivādin）的观点，烦恼（Kleśa）指心理上的烦扰或痛苦；随眠是它的别名，指贪、恨等。根据大乘佛教的观点，随眠指潜伏于阿赖耶识（Ālaya-consciousness）的、苦与知识两重障碍之种子，这一种子时时增长众生之麻木。——原注

者则与心相应；

(9) 中有（Antarābhavaḥ，指人今生死后到来世生前的生命状态）不存在。

以上四部在一些次要的教义上持不同意见。以下仅举与我们讨论相关的几例：

(1) 业（karma）与异熟（vipāka，在意识中未定之内在变化）可以同时进行；

(2) 心田中种子即萌芽；

(3) 在色界感官所感知到的粗法之种子或许会发生变化；而心法及心所法则不然；

(4) 心遍于全身。

多闻部（Bāhuśrutīya）中各分派一致同意的观点有：

(1) 佛的五教法为出世间法（lokottaradharma），即

a. 无常（Anityā）

b. 苦；

c. 空（Śūnyatā）；

d. 无我（Anātmakam）；

e. 涅槃，即最终解脱；

（2）以上五种可以引领众生脱离轮回（samsāra）。此外的所有教法皆为世间法（laukikadharma）。

多闻部其他的观点都与大众部相同。

唯识宗的观点如下：

（1）十二入非真有；

（2）苦不是一蕴；

（3）没有不适时之死，一切皆是前世业果；

（4）在业因增长之时，异熟果也形成了。

唯识宗其他的观点都与大众部相同。

说一切有部其下所有分支皆认可的有六十二条基本观点，以下仅列举较重要的数条：

（1）一切有法都可被归入名或色之下；

（2）一切法皆可为四念住（catvāri smṛtyupasthānāni）摄受；

（3）一切随眠为心所法，与心相应，以所缘或境为果；

（4）一切随眠为缠所摄受，反之则不然；

（5）中有一定存在于欲界（kāmadhātu）与色界中；

（6）具有眼等五官的肉身有染污（kliṣṭha），不可能无染污；

（7）心法与心所法为真有；

（8）二者皆有所缘；

（9）没有任何法可以被自一世传递至下世，只有世间众生认为有轮回。

（上述观点皆摘自世友[43]的《异部宗轮论》；这一论著有四个译本：真谛译本，鸠摩罗什译本，玄奘译本，及藏译本 *Gshung-lugs-kyi bye-brag bkod-pa'i 'khor-lo*。南京支那内学院 1930 年版参考了这四种译本。[44]）

43. 此处原文为Vasubandhu，即世亲。然而《异部宗轮论》的作者是世友（Vasumitra），不是世亲。

44. 支那内学院辑：《藏要》，南京：支那内学院，1929年。此后有上海书店和台北新文丰出版公司的影印本。

11

目前为止我们简要介绍了自古以来不同的印度哲学系统对识的理解。佛陀自己在解救众生于苦难中的教法里也大量应用了这一理论。自部派佛教所持的各派观点发展创新而来的大乘佛教，则逐渐将其完善为一个以世亲为代表的独立理论系统。这一系统更由十大论师加以完善，在护法的时候达到顶峰，并最终由玄奘引介进入中国。很难讲后来的印度教圣者商羯罗（Shankarācarya）[45] 所宣讲的幻论在多大程度上是受到了唯识理论的影响；因为他所讲的“幻”与佛教讲的相之幻都认为世间事相即是幻相，影响一定是存在的。当然，商羯罗和世亲的理论存在很大的差异，后者甚至在某种意义上可以被认为是无神论者。尽管唯识理论复杂精深，却能在佛教体系中自圆其说而不自相矛盾；它并不像空性理论或者禅宗一样，需要通过许多悖论来揭示真相。唯识学更多依靠理性与可理解的语言，而非信仰与神秘主义。因此，它更多的是一种哲学而不是宗教。考虑到这一历史背景，我们就能更好地了解这一理论。

45. 商羯罗（788—820）是婆罗门教韦檀多派的集大成者。他认为“我”与最高的梵的同一就是解脱，即“梵我如一”。

12

理解唯识理论可以从五识开始。每一哲学系统中都讨论了五识。眼睛能视，耳朵能听；这似乎过于简单，不需任何说明。然而因为它们是整个理论体系必不可缺的基础部分，我们必须对其加以探讨，因为其相似之处，五识通常被放在一起讨论：

（1）五识皆需要依靠五根，即视、听、闻、尝、触之器官；

（2）五识皆与感知之对象相关；

（3）五识皆为现觉量（pratyakṣapramāṇam），现觉量需要满足如下条件：

a. 感知对象必须存在——不能像乌龟之毛一样，是不存在的东西；

b. 感知主体不应有幻觉或歪曲；

c. 感知仅限于现时，不包括过去或未来；

d. 感知对象确实显现，而非处于“种子”状态；

e. 感知对象之显现方式是明确可感知的；

f. 此时主观认知之表现尚未有任何分别心、指向性或猜测；

g. 感知与其对象紧密相连，并区别于主体。

（4）五识皆为间歇性运转，并不永远作用。

以上就是前五识的共通之处。对于一位现代思想家来说，对于现觉的解释或许过于肤浅，但它为此后深入唯识系统提供了路径，因此仍是必要的。以上关于五识的四个共同点也是了解后三识——第六、第七、第八识——必不可少的。

与五识相伴的必有第六识，即意识。如果意不在此，即使双眼大睁，也无法看到任何东西。我们日常经验中耳、鼻、舌、身也是如此。第六识是一种意识，它并非心中的复杂思维，然而只能称之为心。

这种现觉理论在客观上是经不起深入探讨的，因为它仅限于瞬时的范畴。在印度一个时间单位被称为一刹那（kṣaṇa），其长度为心中一念的1/900，或者是一弹指的1/60或1/65。一旦认识到此刻，此刻就已经过去了。然而凭借在这极短时间内的初步感知，识就可以接触到事物的自相（svalakṣaṇa）。这就是前五识与第八识最重要的功用。唯识理论认为世间一切事物的自相都是真如（tathātā）。真如超出了名言，不属于任何知识范畴。与自相相对的是共相（sāmānyalakṣaṇa），即一组或一类事物所共有的特性。一切名言皆可被用于描述共相，而知识也可以通过推论而得以掌握。

13

在唯识理论中，即使是认知这样一种简单的行为，也被分为了四个部分。与韦檀多理论中的所知者、所知物和知识相似，在此识的四分为：

（1）相分，即客观现象；

（2）见分（dṛṣṭi），即主观认知；

（3）自证分；

（4）证自证分。

相指一切事物的显现。它并不限于如眼所见的颜色、大小等，而是包括了听觉中的音调高低，嗅觉中的香臭味道，味觉中的酸甜苦辣，触觉中的粗糙精细，以及诸法（即事物或心的显现）。宇宙中万物皆为相。

见指可以将认识主体与心中所反映出来的客体相联系的功用。

因为每一种认知皆基于因缘而生，自证分以见为其自身功用，此为外缘。

自证分只与自身的功用相关；因此，自证分相对于其他三者被称为“自”。需要注意的是，此处的“自”（self）与印度教中的“我”（Self）是不一样的，尽管这一“自”也被包括在“我”中。自证是一个人自身不通过任何其他中介的直接感知，如用手指触碰某一物件。根据陈那的说法，心的自性与其功用同时发生；也就是说，当见分发生时，自证分对其功用进行验证。

第四分证自证分缘于第三分。第二分只缘于第一分；第三分则以第二、第四分为内外缘；而第四分则只缘于第三分。

当需要量度一块布的长度时，尺子是量度者，量度之后得出的长度是量度的结果。认知也是这样：见在与相的关系中是量度者，而二者关系的结果是自证。自证在与见的关系中是量度者，而证自证则是其结果。在第三分在与第四分的关系中，第四分是其结果；而第四分在与第三分的关系中，也以第三分为结果。因为第三分与第四分的功用相同，所以不必再单立第五分。

前二分很容易理解，因为它们是外在的；第一分就是对象世界。后二分是内在的，二者皆与现觉有关。对于见所产生的知识的比量在不同的识中也不同：前五识与第八识中的见为现觉，第七识中的见是虚妄知识，而第六识中的见则包括了现觉、推论与虚妄知识。相在此范畴之外，不属于这三量。

现在，如果我们考虑到唯识理论的历史，就可以更加清晰理解四分。前两分是由难陀基于将识分为十一种的《摄大乘论》建立的。在将这十一种归纳为八之后，难陀将相与见进行了区分，使得这一整体分类更为清晰。他认为见为自身，而相则是幻觉，并因见而产生并转化，并非真有。这与世亲的观点也相符合。因为难陀否认相之真有，他的理论在后世被称为“无相唯识”。

见依于相而起作用，其结果就是认知，或理解；陈那称之为自证分：这就是第三分。陈那作为正理派论师，其理论源自经量部（Sautrāntikā）。在四分的因缘关系中，他承认外物存在于人心之中，是感官所缘的对象，并能使感官生起主观执念。这种执必然与其作用的显现同时存在，也就是说，执在起作用时必然带有其对象的相。这种相的显现就像映于镜中的影像一样，它是被感知对象的一个形象，但却只存在于心中。因此，在考虑前二分时，相应该被认为是内在于心中的。因其作用而产生的知识只是表面的，或许更应称其为“理解”；这就是自证分。这一理论在后世被称为“有相唯识”或是“三分说”。

另一位唯识论师德慧的弟子安慧则依三分说而将陈那与难陀的理论合二为一。安慧认为前两分是虚妄分别，并非真有。只有自证分才是真有的。因此，在他的修订之后，三分又事实上成为一个整体。他的注疏仍存梵文本，玄奘在《成唯识论》中也采纳了他的主要观点。[46]

玄奘也学习了由法护所添加的第四分，但此法在印度不传。法护英年早逝。他认为见与相之间的所缘仍在心法之外。在主体与客体，或者说认知者与被认知物之间，还应存在一线内缘。在佛教术语中相是物质之特征或外表，它只能源于唯一真有之物，即真如。与感官相应的外境，被识化现的事物，以及任一主体的意义：这些都包括在相中。法护采纳了将相比拟于映射于镜中的形象这一说法。见与具体的事物或色法（rūpa-dharma）相关。识在将其自身化为相并与相产生联系时，这种联系就是见。这可被比作镜中的光线。在更高一层意义上，这种关系也是在理解并以理性进行的推论。然而，见虽然能够知晓客观之相，却并不能知晓自身，就像刀不能切割自身一样。识的存在即是内在认知者，而见则正是这一内在认知者与其自己构建的外在世界发生联系的功用。这就是自证分，就像镜子因反射光线而映照出各色影像一样。

证的过程就是去验证、确认，或体验。因为真如被立为唯一的实相，识的八支不离于真如，真如的存在亦可验证八识：这就是证自证分。证自证分可以真切不虚地理解第三分与第二分之间的所缘。它被比为镜子的背面（这里所说的镜子是古代金属制成的镜子）。

我们对感知的分析在此就告一段落。一“分”是一种整体行为的一部分。通常人可以将第四分理解为内在心理行为，但这并不是这一哲学体系所讲的内容。唯识宗认为，第四分是识的行为中被暂且承认为唯一实在的一部分。

46. 安慧的《三十颂注疏》有 H. Jacobi 的德文译本，然而此译本早已绝版（译者按：Jacobi, Hermann, *Triṃśikāvijñāpti des Vasubandhu mit Bhāṣya des Ācārya Sthiramati*, Stuttgart: W. Kohlhammer, 1932）。吕澂亦有节译本（译者按：《安慧三十唯识释略抄引言》，见《吕澂佛学论著选集》第一卷，济南：齐鲁书社，1991 年）。笔者于 1948 年完成了全译本，即将付梓（译者按：《安慧疏注释》，见《徐梵澄文集》卷七，上海：上海三联书店，2006 年）。——原注

14

现在我们来对感官进行逐步分析。任何一种感知都需要一个基础，这种基础在梵文中被称为 indriya，在中文中被译为各感知之“根”。根包括了如眼耳鼻在内的器官。然而根也有内外之别[47]：眼球与视觉神经为外在的器官，如果外在器官受损或被破坏，那么视觉就不复存在；然而视觉不独包括外在器官。非佛教徒或许会立刻想要将“生命”纳入考虑。生命存在于肉体之中时，诸感官只要不受损，就可以正常运行；当生命不复存在于肉体之中时，感官就不能正常地运行：就是这么简单。相宗则认为外在器官之外另有一种内根，被称为净色根或是胜义根（rūpaprasāda-indriyaṃ），它是五根之基。净色根可以被认为是感知的主体。只有当内根与外根同时与外物（viṣaya）产生接触，识才会生成。

如果确是这样的话，那么净色根究竟是什么就值得继续追问了。我们可以推论出净色根是通过外在器官而产生感知的，然而与外在器官不同的是，它不会受损或被破坏。根据唯识理论，认知者与所知物皆为识之化现，外在的不可知之物不能产生任何识，可知的认知主体则可以产生识。任何生成的识皆有生成与灭失之时；净色根却并非如此，它是独立自主的。特定的识有生有灭，净色根则恒常不变。它生起五根，并为五根之增上缘（adhipatipratyaya），或者说是最胜的助力之缘。五根必须依靠净色根来感知。

换句话来说，净色根就是识的内在之色。色即是相；在相宗中，色指一切有形之事物。实在的色相或者外在事物属于相中不可被真切感知的部分，而净色根则是相中可被真切感知的部分。因为它超出善恶之分别，净色根被称为“净”。这一“净色”也被认为是“无明”的外壳，对此我们将在后文中进行讨论。

净色根无须在肉体内建构任何一个真有的感知者，这一解读也与佛陀关于因果链的教义完全符合：

无明缘行；行缘识；识缘名色；名色缘六入；六入缘触；……

唯识学派的大师们基于佛陀的教法精心构建其理论，而并无违逆之

47. 密宗佛教的性力（Śakti）理论也采用了这一词语，但并不对内外根加以区分。它被认为是心的一种功用，并被用来解释一些瑜伽士们所成就的、独立于外在器官的神奇之举或者催眠过程中的一些现象。这些现象可称为超心理学，是一个尚待发展的学科。——原注

处。在世亲之后的两百年中，佛教贤哲们仍然能够使用理性哲学的力量，而非依赖于盲目的崇拜。这种盲目的崇拜与各种不同的信仰体系混同在一起，产生了无数的迷信。而在另一方面，过度的理性化与哲学化也导致了禅宗的兴起。禅宗整体上超出并脱离了语言和理论，在其最终发展阶段甚至无视佛陀本人的存在。但是唯识理论并不只对五识或六识的分析，我们的研究应当更加深入地探寻其所假设的第七或第八识，正是这二者将这一理论构建成为一个完整的体系。

15

A

大乘佛教之缘起论（pratītyasamutpāda）认为，宇宙万物皆由一系列相依的因缘和合而成。换言之，事物只在某些特定条件下或只在与某些特定因素相关联时出现。如视觉就是由九种因缘和合而成的：

（1）视觉预设了空间。在眼睛与物体之间需要存在一定的距离。如果物体离眼球太近，那么或者它无法被观察到，或者眼瞳会受到损伤。对于任何一位合格的眼科医生而言，这都是显而易见的。

（2）必须要有光。

（3）必须要有如前所说的感官之根。

（4）必须要有可见之对象。

（5）必须要有使心可见的作意（manaskāra）。

（6）必须要有第六识。

（7）必须要有第七识。

（8）必须要有第八识。

（9）必须要有种子。

如果时间也被纳入考虑的话，那么我们还需要加入例如等无间缘（samanantarapratyayaḥ），即在心中相续不止的相等之因缘。

接下来是听觉，以上所述九种因缘除了光之外都应起作用。我们在暗中或明处都能听见声音。

接下来是触觉，不包含这九种因缘中的前二者。余下七种仍然起作用。

B

众因缘生法，我说即是无。

这是龙树所作一句著名偈颂的前半句。[48]因缘是由起因与结果的原则所引导的行为。它仅指向这一事实而非其他；然而宇宙万物都被包含于其中。在这一佛教术语中，有一处强调值得注意："因缘"一词中是"因"（原因）与"缘"（次要条件），而不是"因"与"果"被并举。"因缘"这一复合词本应指起因（causation）而非因果关系（causality）。在梵文中 hetu 指原因；而 pratyaya 指的不是结果，而是次要的、相关的或同时起作用的因素，有时也被译为条件。因为因果关系更通常多被理解为一条前进的直线，这一

48.《中论》观四谛品第二十四。

对原因的强调使得佛教的因缘理论更倾向于循环的而非线性的。缘可作为基础或踏脚石，可被关联或接触，它分为四类：

第一，因缘（hetupratyaya）。如谷种为因，土壤、水、劳力等为在种植稻米中所需的缘或条件。六根为因，六尘为缘，六识为果。

第二，所缘缘（ālambanapratyaya），指相应或提供支持的条件。如一名病人因为身体虚弱，需要依靠拐杖行走一样，心法与感官可能也需要外在支撑。所缘缘正是心所依之处。

第三，增上缘（adhipatipratyata）。这是最主要的决定性因素，可与种植稻米的田地相比。因此，眼根为视觉的增上缘。

第四，等无间缘（samanantarapratyaya），即彼此相等、接续不断的相关条件。它即是基于不断心念相续的心法。心中升起的第一个念头被第二个念头所取代，就好像一个走在独木桥上的人向前一步以让位给后来者一样。心中或脑中的前一与后一念头或有增减，但它们的存在是相同或相等的。前者引发后者，后者紧接前者，其中没有任何间隔。除了阿罗汉或是一位即将证悟的圣者（这位圣者心中的最后一念将不再引发接续的心念）之外，任何一个人的心皆有此种相续性。

在明确了上述四缘之后，就可以很容易理解视觉如何由九种因缘和合而成，听觉如何由八种因缘和合而成，如此等等。然而仍有一点我们应该牢记：根据唯识理论，因与果都是假立且为相对的。为了解释作为此前某种情况之结果的当下情况，我们需要建构前因；考虑到当下的情况也会导致未来的后果，我们需要假设现因。二者皆为假立，只能说是相对成立。

15

C

我们现在来讨论第六识，即意识（manovijñānaṃ）；意识有时也被译为心念或心识。它是上述五识所依赖的分别之识。意识伴随前五识，以其境为境，但它也与诸法有着自己的联系。如第一识与外境接触的第一步是现觉，而在接下来的一刹那心中出现关于外物的颜色、长短、形状的观念，则是第六识在起作用。有时心中一线思维的产生也是因意识的作用而成为一个单独的想法。意识是由五种因缘和合而成的：

（1）根——此根是基于第七识，不由前五根产生；

（2）境；

（3）作意；

（4）根本依，此根本依位于第八识中；

（5）种子。

接下来是思维。第六、第七、第八识皆被称为“意”，然而三者间有着微妙的区别。第七识在形成想法与观点的过程中，一直思维活动。第六与第七识都被称为意识（manovijñāna），然而指第六识的 manovijñāna 是一个依主释复合词或限定（tatpuruṣa）复合词，而第七识则是一个持业释复合词或同格限定（karmadhāraya）复合词。[49] 对一位印度教学者来说，二者区别明显：前者即是我执或“我”，或者更适合的说法是“我识”。我识是前六识分别染污与清净所依之处（āśraya），它因三种因缘和合而生：

（1）其自身所生之种子；

（2）作意；

（3）根本依，即第八识。

或许在此值得一提的是，在东方，于现代意义上的思考，尤其是哲学思辨，并不占据重要地位；人们所追求与尊崇的是精神上的解脱。唯识理论也不强调思辨，因为它只将意识作为第六识。此后的禅宗更为“思考”敲响了丧钟。

D

前面所谈到的七识中并没有很多哲学或心理学方面的探讨；然而第八识则不然。在古代文献中，我们可以找到不少关于第八识的同义词。在我们现在的列表中，此为第八识；而在从内向外列举的诸识中，此为第一识；梵文中称为阿赖耶识（Ālayavijñāna）或阿陀那识（Ādānavijñāna）。阿赖耶（Ālaya）有储存之意，因此也称藏识或一切种子识。储存于藏识之中的是业力种子，由习气（vāsanā）"熏染"而成。阿陀那（Ādāna）可被理解为"执"

49. 依主释复合词或者限定复合词指梵文复合词中前节与后节有格限定关系，或者说前节之语限定后节之语的复合词，如"山泉"即"山中之泉"，"我执"即"对于'我'的执念"；持业释复合词或者同格限定复合词指前后节具有相同格的复合词，如"大树""高山"。

或"持"，因为《入楞伽经》中提到，阿陀那识执持一切种子，这些种子就像迅急的水流一样，不应被误解为"我"。[50] 此二者皆为音译。又因为第八识是一切知识所依之处，它又被称为"所知依"，即可知物之依所。因为它含有世间及出世间一切法种子，又被称为种子识。早期佛教称之为根识，因为它被认为是一切法之根，但这一名称略为含糊。

在合适的条件下，种子会生出果实。因果关系的规律在所有唯物或唯心哲学体系中都有探讨。在唯识理论中，因果关系因其朴素的特质而成为支柱。对于叔本华来说，两件事物互为因果是一种谬见。为了避免误解，此处笔者需要说明，在传统上解释不同因素何以构成识的例子中，用到的经典比喻是一捆芦苇互相扶持，才能支撑于地面。这一比喻通常被误会为芦苇之间互为因果，然而事实上却不是这样的。这种状态应该被解释为均等势力集聚在一起，其以互相扶持为因，以支撑于地为果。这种"果"的意思和与种子相关的果实相同，然而"果"更常用来指代由某些原因所产生的后果。起码在中文里是如此的。

在此我们需要区分两个词：如果果实与种子是同属的，果实就是等流果（Nisyandaphalam），意味着物种的延续。如果物种发生了变化，那么种子就可被称为异熟因（Vipākahetuh）。在精神活动领域，当一种行为的因有无数个，而其果与可能的直接原因毫不相关时，果常常成熟为另一物种或在另一时间成熟。因为这一切都发生在第八识中，因此第八识也被称为异熟识。异熟识从不同的因中结出生死善恶种种果。

第八识的另一名字叫阿摩罗识或者无垢识（Amalavijñāna），它是无漏法（anāsrava-dharma）的居所。无漏法离出一切染污与苦难，只存在于如来地（Tathāgata-bhūmi）的净土之中。一些古时的大师称之为第九识，这是多余的。

第八识的每一个名字都指代了它的一些特征。在汉语中最早的翻译为“不死识”“恒识”，或“无分别识”；这些都是不准确的。根据大乘佛教的说法，第八识在菩萨到达不动地（acalābhūmi）时或者当成就金刚身时就被忘失。玄奘在他的“新译”中已经弃用了这一译法。

第八识的因缘有四：

（1）根，此即第七识，意；

（2）境，指一切事物，一切世间；

（3）作意；

（4）种子，其自身的种子自无始时就已因现行（samudācāraḥ）而形成。

因为第八识是其他七识的基础，它本身就不需要其他基础。它与现代心理学中所说的“本能”可以部分对应：二者都是在出生前无数的前世中形成的。就像一朵芳香的花散发出香味一样，一个人的行为也会在他的意识底层留下痕迹，并通过“熏染”的过程形成所谓的“种子”。通过这一过程，行为产生了种子，而种子又再次使得行为出现。在唯识理论中，这一循环不断持续下去，直到涅槃境地或菩萨地中的最后一地。

50. 《大乘入楞伽经》卷二：“自心所见身器世间，皆是藏心之所显现，刹那相续变坏不停，如河流，如种子，如灯焰，如迅风，如浮云……”

阿赖耶识理论从起源上来说绝不是大乘佛教的发明；它是在佛陀入灭之后不久，由各不同部派所持的一个基本理念逐步发展而形成的。早期佛教通常只谈六识，化地部（Mahīśāsakā）所独有的秘密教法中另有一识，称为“随生死识”，他们认为此识是另一蕴。因为六识是有间的，因此需要假设另一精微且接续不断之识作为它们的基础。同属早期佛教的说一切有部认为必有命根（jīvitendriya），与一切生命的共通之处或者说众同分（nikāyasabhāga）才是真正的异熟。而大众部则仅称其为“根识”；分别说部（Vibhajyavādin）也认为必有此“分别识”。所有的这些假设都指向一个在相宗中被改良为“阿赖耶识”的概念。

16

在我们智人（homo sapiens）中，总有极少数完全欠缺智慧（sapientia）的人。这些人生来并无任何生理缺陷，也无任何外在畸形；除了极其愚蠢之外，他们并无什么不正常之处。在汉语里，这些人被认为是“缺少慧根”。在唯识理论中，他们被认为是在第八识中一定只有很少或者根本没有智慧的种子。第八识通常被喻为一片播撒种子的田地；在外部条件允许时，这些种子就长成为各种植物，并生发出更多的种子。

很显然，先哲们所认为的“种子”只是现代心理学中的一个因素。《瑜伽师地论》中提到种子有两种：第一种是遗传或者说先天的，自无始之时就存在于人身中；第二种是出生后获得的，或者说后天的。在现代教育中发展孩子潜能的原则被认为比“强制喂食”知识要好。然而如果潜能或（按唯识宗的说法）种子并不以潜藏状态存在，那么就没有什么东西可以提供发展。如果没有新形成的种子被加入藏识之中，那么一段时间或数代之后，储备就会被消耗殆尽，就像一个人的银行存取款记录一样。心中的印象或受到的影响逐步沉入阿赖耶识或意识最底层中；它们可能会在记忆中消失，然而当有特定条件出现时，它们也可能会浮现出来，这就是我们所说的回忆。但是究竟需要几代人，甚至几十亿年，才能使这些新取得的习气成为一种遗传的本能，使后天的成为先天的？——便无须回答了。

关于新种子形成的理论仍然值得我们注意。一个人的所说、所做、所想，无论好坏，都被称为现行。正如在纯芝麻油中浸入鲜花可以使油变得芳香一样，种子识也持有一切现行的印迹，就像花的香味一样。这些印迹被称为习气，也是种子（bīja）的异名。这一过程被比作将心“熏染”上或好或坏的习气，或者用佛教术语说，染污或纯净。这一熏染过程包含了持续不断的接触或碰撞，六识中所形成的名熏习（nāmavāsanā）、色熏习（rūpavāsanā）、烦恼熏习（kleśavāsanā）等皆与第七、第八识相合，并成为新形成的种子被储存在第八识中。

对我们来说，这里提到的种子新旧之分或许并不重要，而在佛教对有漏法（sāsrava dharma）与无漏法的区别中，这一分别很关键。此外我们也应考虑到古印度是有着严格种姓区分与压迫的社会。区分有漏法与无漏法的关键就在于，最低种姓或者被排斥于社会之外的人是否生来即在意识中具有正法种子；如果没有的话，正法的新种子能否形成也是一个问题。于是，最终归结为贱民能否加入僧伽的问题。

17

于此，我们也可以承认种子的存在，并来看唯识学是如何解释种子的。种子有如下几种特点：

（1）刹那灭。种子具有一种独特的效力，使得其生灭俱在一瞬间。这就是所谓的“化”。

（2）果俱有。种子和与之同时存在的行为并不冲突。理论上一个必然比另一个更重要，但此处不作考虑。

（3）恒随转。种子必为一类，恒常流转，直到其最后终结为止。

（4）性决定。种子的特性是已经决定的，所以它与善恶之因相应而产生果。

（5）待众缘。种子的产生需要其他各缘的作用。

（6）引自果。种子引发同类的果实。如果因不同，那么果也必然不同。

种子被储藏在第八识中；也可被认为是第八识独有的作用。中观派关于种子的理论听上去很像诡辩：种子不同亦不异于果。这一理论的论证过程是这样的：如果根识被认为是存在（being）的话，那么种子就是这一存在的作用或者说生成（becoming）；如果种子是因，那么其产物便是果。如果因与果是同样的，那么就不应该有任何的因果关系或是存在与生成的原则；如果因与果不同的话，就会出现不同的结果，像麦种生出豆子一样。否则，因果法在其起作用之前就应该消亡了，因为在此因果完全不同。

尽管因不同亦不异于果，它们却是两种相关的假设。如果这一假有的法不存在的话，那么也不应该有因果之法。这就是为龙树等所应用的中观派的古老准则，即“中道”。中道不倾向于任何一端，而是持中。中道在穷尽了各边的推理之后，在更高的意义上独立并超出了两端。

这就是种子最基本的特征。种子可以大致分为两类，心法（caita-dharma）及心与外物相应的色法（rūpa-dharma）；通常二者也被称为内法或外法。无性所作《摄大乘论疏》（*Mahāyānasamparigraha Kārikā*）中对二者不作区分，都归为“内法”一类。窥基与其他的汉地唯识家则兼采二者，认为上述种子的六个方面应该包括了心法和色法。这些观点尽管看上去简单，但我们深入探究时就会发现，关于种子的理论牵涉唯识宗与某些其他教派的争议。

第一，有为法（saṃskṛta-dharma）必有生灭，因此也必有变化。在每一变化中，都必然有形成种子的潜力。这一形成的过程同时也伴随着自身的消亡。这种特点因之就超出了正量部（Saṃmatīyā）所持由生至死四步为恒常的理论。而这一变化所导致的无常，也就自然地使得数论派所认可的自在主（Iśvara）与本性（Prakṛti）不再可能，并且进一步否定了最高的创世者。

第二，种子与果的并存也代表了它们的同时性。无性认为这一点指的是内种子。在现代观念中，我们可以将其理解为动机与行为同时存在。这一看法看似是否定了由上座部与经量部（现在思想家们也是这样认为的）所强调的因先于果的观点。但此处的动机，却是通过其行为而判断出并称之为行为的种子；因此二者是可以同时显现的。种子自身的种子必然在前，故因先于果。但是对于种子及另一种不同种子的果而言，其生成可以是同时的。尽管同时共存，然而它们必须在同一人的心续中和谐共处。如果种子可以同时生成同类的种子，那么生成种子的存在必然是无限的，而其生成的种子也是无限的。而当生成者与生成的对象并非同类时，即当新种子通过“熏习”而被生成时，尽管旧种子尚未生成果，它们的数量也不能是无限的。在那一瞬间不可能有两个果合而为一。

梵文词 samudācāra（sam+ud+ācāra）[51] 有时被译为“正用”或者是“目的”。于此它与种子相关，我们称之为“果”。需要注意的是，在此它是一种心法；种子作为一种极精微的心理动机，其果就是 samudācāra 或现行

51. ācāra 意为行为、习俗，或规则；sam- 和 ud- 为前缀，其意思分别为“聚集、结合”和“在上、在外”。

的作用。阿赖耶识或藏识与烦恼法（saṃkliśta-dharma）或有漏法是互为因果的，就像烛芯与火一样。火燃烧烛芯，就像果通过熏习生成新的种子；而烛芯所产生的火就像种子生成果。然而这一例子并不准确，因为火并不能产生一根新的烛芯。如果我们不用烛芯而是用产生的烟为喻的话，这一燃烧的比喻仍然是成立的。火焰燃烧产生了更多的烟，而烟又带来了更大的火焰：是这样一个循环。如今我们或许可以用电火花来作比喻：火花由电力产生，但是它又与电流不同。二者并存，同时出现且同时消失。如果电火花可以产生新电流的话，那么这个例子就完美了。

人心的本质是多变的，若非经训练将其平静下来，心中之事相总是不稳定的。人们通常觉得心绪的出现与消失几乎同时，有时就像火花或是闪电一样。从朴素唯物主义的观点来看，这可能就是即灭理论的起源。

第三，同类的种子必然互相接续，直至最后它们在更高的菩萨地被对治（pratikṣepah）或灭失。前七识因喜悦或痛苦等感觉会遭遇变化与中断，因而与种子法不相应。这一观点超出了经量部所说的六识皆可持种子的说法。第八识则是纯意识而非感官的。

第四，自性的决定性意味着，不论其善恶或中立，果是由因正向决定的。只有这样，种子才不是随意形成的，而是总持续地在熏习过程中与现行之因果相应。这一观点否定了说一切有部的说法。说一切有部认为作为因的法，不论善恶或中立，都是同类因（sabhāgahetuh），且互相之间可以相关。在唯识理论中，因与果的本性一定是相同的，善不能生恶，恶也不能生善，这就意味着互相矛盾的本性不会互相生成。善因必有善的种子。

18

依循这一解释，我们就可以探讨唯识理论中的另一观点。前文所述之因果关系似乎意味着种子只能生成同类或同等性质的果，即等流果。那我们又应该怎么解释异熟果呢？与前五识一样，第八识自身是中性的，脱离了善恶的区分。前五识在感知中不作任何分别；一件事物的善恶可以立刻被辨认出来，是因为第六识的作用。第六识通过分别生出了一种特定的种子。识本身是纯净或者中性的，它根据不同性质的心理因素而产生变化。阿赖耶识尽管自身中性，却含有各形各色的种子。善业与恶业分别带来快乐与痛苦，然而痛苦与快乐不应被认为是一种品性：它们本身是一种感觉的状态，非善亦非恶，而是中性的。在其品性方面它们属于另一种类别。异熟意味着在另一时间将事物转化为另一种类。

即使是印度教诸神也对因果的铁律感到畏惧，这一规律只能为神之恩典所宽宥。大乘佛教并非否认或忽视因果，而是认为通过觉悟超出善恶的真谛可以超脱因果。这一觉悟可以是顿时获得的证悟，也可以经由逐步修证得来。

第五，种子需要不同的所缘缘才能产生化，或者说生成现行。换言之，同类的种子如果没有所缘的话，就不能成为种子。这一理论与其他支持单一原初之因的理论相反，如韦檀多哲学中所说的造物主或生主（Prajāpati），或者胜论派所说的时间或空间（胜论派认为时间或空间不靠任何助力而在一瞬间创造了宇宙）。

最后，作为对这一论证的延伸，在生成果的过程中，果必须是与种子同类或相应的。这就进一步说明了如果因只有一种的话，那么果也不能是多样的；或者说如果果有许多种，那么因也必然有多种。这一特点也再次否认了单一原初之因的理论，并与说一切有部所认为的色与心可以互为因果相对。根据唯识理论，因为二者作用不同，不能互相紧随而无违碍，所以色不能是心之因，心也不能是色之因。种子的特性是深藏而精微的，而其生成之果的特性则显现于外。因此种子只有与果相应时，才能称之为种子；也就是说，种子必须与现行相随。

一切种子，如麦种、稻种等，在某种意义上都是假立之名；它们都是为识所化出的。我们所谈的因果只是包含识之种子的内在的心法；这些种子就像人体中的微生物一样，可以有无限多个——在这里，种子与时间相关。

19

如前所述，第八识也被称为种子识，因为它储存了从色法到心所法在内的各类种子。一切行为以及由这些行为导致的一切法都由此生起。种子有生起的能力，其本身却并非真有。因为它们是第八识的自性，相，或者说见分的对象，它们的存在也需要依靠第八识。种子并不持有第八识，而是被包含在第八识中。此识的特性就在于可以包含种子，而种子的特性则在于可以产生现行。第八识也被认为是一切法的自性，没有第八识，包括神佛在内的世间万物都将不存在。根据世亲的观点，除了我们对于宇宙的感知，宇宙本身并不真有。这也就是为什么现代译者将唯识学派称为“绝对唯心主义”。

第八识常常被比作平静无波的大海，其中的水也是纯净透明的。根、境、观念、一切种子就像是风。当风吹在海面上时就有了波浪；当外部因缘接触其表面时，第七识就开始运作，人就开始看见、听到等等。波浪或许有时被中断或暂归平静，然而海水并不因此遭受任何中断或终止。第八识永远持续运作着。

这听起来就像是我们的心，却又比心多了一些东西。根据唯识观点，这就与轮回相关。

20

我们已经进行了很多关于第八识及其内容的讨论，现在我们可以回到第七识“意”，来看它与第八识的关系。

正如商羯罗所论说的，没有人会说“没有我”。[52] 然而从古至今的每一个哲学系统都提倡否定、忘记或是抹去“我”（ego）。印度的伟大精神领袖室利·阿罗频多苦心证明了“我”是不存在的，他只肯定意识中心的存在。不论在部派佛教或是大乘佛教中，“我”都是被否定的；它是一种内在的幻相，一种与生俱来的（sahaja）执念。根据唯识理论，“我”没有任何实质，

52. 有意思的是，明代（14—17 世纪）的一位理学大师（译者按：王阳明，1472—1529）也持同样观点，尽管他并不知道商羯罗的存在。这应该是巧合，不然我们就需要假设思想可以自行在全世界传播，并在不同时期为不同的人所用。——原注

被详细解释为补特伽罗无我（pudgala-nairātmya）。玄奘写作《成唯识论》的主要目的就是解释补特伽罗无我和法无我（dharma-nairātmya）。

“我”只是一个习惯表达。在理解“我”时有不同的词汇，如行识、转识、表识、分别识、接续识等。行即是业，是由行为者做出的行动，在“我做的”“我干的”等表达中显而易见。转识（pravṛtti）指的是由识创造出来的对外境影像的意识；前六识都有这一功能，但第八识没有。表识指识对外物的反射或反映，但它与“镜识”不同。分别识指的是分别染污与纯净之识。接续识指的是业力在过去、现在、未来三时接续不断。这每一个词语都指向第七识的一个方面。

我们在此略过各派对于自我存在的否定。这些派别在印度教哲学中包括数论派、胜论派、尼乾子派（Nigranthaputrā）、乞者派（Parivrājakā），在早期佛教中包括经量派和正量部，在大乘佛教中则有中观派。概括地说，唯识理论认为“我”是一种从第六识中生起的假象。人不过是五蕴和合而生成之物，因为它由种种因缘而生起，所以其中并没有自性。人只是看上去存在，就像幻相一样。记忆、认知及其他心理功用可以用种子来解释：这些种子因熏习而新近形成或是在第八识中早已存在。

一个人或许与万物一样，都是一个幻相。然而问题在于第七识是如何将第八识认为“我”的。于此，我们又可以看到这一理论是如何逐步完善自身的。在唯识宗十大论师的不同理论中，四位对此有不同的看法。其中只有护法给出的答案最为究竟且最具有说服力。其他的论师们或许对此也有论述，但是我们还没找到相关的记载。根据难陀的说法，第七识于心有我执（ātmagrāhaḥ）；当其与心所法接触时就将其所有持为我所（ātmīyaṃ）。火辨认为第七识与识的见和相相联系。当它与见发生联系时，第七识将见持为“我”；而当它与相发生联系时，则将相持为“我所”。

联系的意思是与之生成正向接触并生成果。安慧在他为世亲所作的《三十唯识疏》中认为，第七识在现时的行为中与第八识相关，并且因此认第八识为“我”，它在与第八识的种子发生联系时将其认为“我所”。这在理论上推进了一步。在护法的分析中，第七识只与第八识的见关联，而不与其相、种子或是其他方面发生联系。见接触外境，其作用显然可见，因此会有“我”的出现。如果第七识与相关联的话，那么它就像前五识一样与外境发生了关系。第七识也不能与种子关联，因为种子（例如色种子 rūpa-bīja）在五取蕴（pañcopādāna-skandhā）中不属于识蕴，而属于另一蕴。第七识也与心所法无关，因为心所法不可以自主，也不可以为其他法所依。因此，第七识或者说“我”就只与第八识的见分相关。比较来说，护法的解释是最让人满意的。

我们也可顺带一问：那生命应该如何解释呢？原初佛教中的说一切有部认为，有一个称之为“命根”的原则，它既非色法，亦非心所法。命根在一段时间内支撑着肉体的生命力与意识。然而根据唯识宗的看法，命根也可以被种子所解释。因为过去的业力吸引，第八识中的种子生发了两种效应：首先是果或者行为，其次则是在识中暂时对果加以维持。这种对心与色的持护就可称之为生命。在这一假设中并不存在任何真有、独立的个体。这就是所谓的心不相应行法（viprayuktasaṃskāra-dharma）。

生命依赖于业的存在。设若要问既然没有“我”的话，那么是谁创造了业，又是谁收获了果呢？唯识理论的回答是心法与心所法；因为它们总是接续不断，为因缘所驱动而生成业与业果，并被第八识看作是一个假造的“我”。同时，业力也带来了生死轮回。

欲想达成我不是“我”，或者将“我”完全消融的认知，是绝不容易的：这意味着身份的消失。一个人过去的身份，不论是圣者还是盗徒，都已经不复存在了。如果他不为过去的业所羁绊，那么他或许可以心如止水般的与他人共存。这就是大多数宗教的魅力所在：从一个旧人中生长出一个新人，并以这新人的身份继续生活下去。相宗之法也不例外。但相宗的观念比其他各派更为激进，因为它不仅否定了“我”，也否定了法的存在。

21

我们还应对第六识再加解释。有时第六识被译为“意识”，有时被译为“心”，在现代汉语中，这一词指“意识形态”。第六识与前五识相伴并依于前五识，它将自己与五境相连并执持五境。第六识包括了知识生成过程中的现观、推论或者是谬误。当它与五识分开时，它就会在我们脑中成为独立的意识。第六识在冥想中是与现观相应的一种朦胧意识。在分散状态中，它就是我们醒觉时的精神状态。而当它与一切法相接触时，它就通过一切知识的三种比量而产生。它在睡梦中作为独立的意识而起作用；即使不在睡梦中，也有很多这样的意识混杂在一起。在这两种情形下，正确的知识是不能出现的。第六识的“德”（guṇa）或者其特质在于：它需要依靠前五识才能完整体验善、恶、中性之三性。然而，这种情况只限于普通人或者一个尚有烦恼（即有漏）之人的心理状态；而在无漏或者离于一切烦恼的状态中，则只有善性。

通常认为第六识为心主，第七和第八识则被忽视。第六识与其他七识不同，它总是处于运作之中；它是最强大的，也是行动最迅速的。因为第六识分别、决定并激发一切，我们身、语、意的所有行为都是由第六识引起的，一切不论好坏或者中性的业力皆由此发生。在善行或恶行之前必有意识；如果意识是好的，那么行为或语言就是好的。因此，可以说因为业本无自性，它就以第六识为自性。这就像说业即是意识，而意识即是心一样。

到目前为止，第六识所指的只是进行思维的意识。至于五受[53]，则没有统一意见。一些先哲认为第六识中只有乐、忧、舍，没有苦。另一些则认为与肉体感受相连的苦乐也能为第六识所认知。在极致的愉悦中没有欢乐之根；同样，在极致的痛苦之中也没有悲愁之根。或许人必须先要清楚分辨心中情感与身体的感觉，才能判断谁是谁非。

正如前文所述，第六识不依赖于诸多缘而生起。在某些情况下，第六识不起作用。例如，在无想定（asaṃjñāsamāpatti）与灭尽定（nirodhasamāpatti）状态中，一切思维都已经休止了，而修行者处在类似涅槃的完全寂静之中。这些状态只有通过一生的修行才能达成。当人陷入昏迷或因身体极度疲倦而进入深度睡眠时，第六识与前五识也不再运作了。而当第六识处于运作状态时，它则帮助前五识生起，是使前五识开始运作的关键。

53. 五受为：苦受（duḥkhavedanā）、乐受（sukhavedanā）、忧受（daumanasyavedanā）、喜受（saumanasyavedanā）、舍受（upekṣāvedanā）。

22

如果我们从外在的对象或者境的角度来看，或许能够更清晰地理解这一理论。宇宙中万物都是识的相或者说特征，识生成或者说“化”出了外境。事相或外境可被分为三类：

首先是性境。它们包括了前五识的一切相以及第八识，还有第六识的部分相。这些自然物由其相应的种子生成，并保有其自性。自性与真有在此是等同的。色是真有之色，心也是真有之心。因为万物皆由阿赖耶识转化为相，又因为阿赖耶识是由真如在特定条件下生成的，因此相原本也是无相的真如实在。尽管这一存在因为现时的迷惑而转为假有或者现法，然而它的自性仍是真有的。这一自性就是自相，它只能通过不分过去和未来的现观被感知；它自身并不与心法相应而被分为善、恶、中性等等。

唯识学中性境包括：

（1）有漏种子；

（2）肉体及诸感官；

（3）五感所能认知的物质世界；

（4）在禅定中出现的色（本书对此不作讨论）。

一切性境都是阿赖耶识或者根识所化现。

其次为独影境。

此处的“影”即是相。独影境独立生起，不需任何种子，也不依任何真有。它是随第六识而来的颠倒之见，例如龟毛兔角。极微（paramāṇu）原子之色相或者极远处之色相就属于这一类，它们在心中没有相应的种子。

再次则是带质境。这一类分两种：

（1）由心所生起的、与心所法相关的真有之物；

（2）由心所生起的、与色法相关的似有实无之物。

为心即刻所化的就是“质”，这就意味着心中的一切外境皆自第八识生出。这一生出的过程即为“化”。这是一个瞬间发生的过程，一切外在对象，或者说一切外在对象的影像就由此产生。这些影像是对外在对象的模拟，是相的外现。真有之物是不可知的，也不能产生自己的影像，它的影像只能从心或者第六识之见的作用中生成，故可以说它们皆生成于一端。

当第七识（意）与第八识或藏识中的见相缘时，第七识就带有了第八识之见的自相。第七识之相不由见而生，而是仅仅从二者之缘中生起；也就是说，其中一半是从主动的见的种子中生起的，另一半则是从被动的根识中生起的。缘与所缘的对象都在心中，在二者之间“我”的假象就出现了。“我”并没有自性，它不过是一个由心法之二端所生起的幻相，就像两盏灯互相照耀而产生的光一样。

但是在第二类独影境中还有非实在的假有对象，我们应该怎么样将它与真正的心法区别开来呢？非实在的假有对象并不依赖于与之相应的实在，它只是突然出现在第六识的见之中；而真有则从与之相应的实在而生起：这就是二者的区别。实在的假有对象看似真有。如果认知的对象是水中映出的月亮、镜中的影像，或是回忆中的过去，即使化现的过程需要依靠实物，这些对象及其影像仍非真有，并且都依靠第六识的相种子而成立。因此，不论是非真有或是真有的假有对象都依见而存在，并没有自身的种子。

这一认知过程看似复杂，但仍是一系统且合理的分析过程。我们在此只是略作论述，并没有涉及大量的细节。可能有人会问，既然色是可被感知的，有其自身的特质，那么它是如何得以被识所化而出现呢？

答案是：化并不指第八识可以生发物质。第八识之中储藏有色相种子，这些种子通过内熏习之因生成了色相，如眼耳鼻舌身等五官、色声香味触等五尘等。五识以转化之后的五官为增上缘，以五尘为所缘缘（此处缘指相关或同时起作用的条件）。如果五识不被第八识所化的话，那么它们自己就没有外境，这就如同说没有实在是一样的。在此否定的并不是实在，而是实在的真实性。只有识才是真实的。

23

如果识是宇宙中的最终存在的话，那么我们应该怎么解释生命和物质呢？唯识理论并未想要为物种或万物的起源提供解释。现代的一些灵修大师认为意识是分等级渐变的，不可以将世界简单地划分为精神和物质。在包括植物在内的一切有情之外，甚至连矿石也有潜在的意识，就像某些宝石的分子形态或者作为水结晶的雪花所展示的美丽对称态一样。一些神秘主义者还可以表演无中生有的神迹。我们在进行辩证哲学分析时，当然不需要引入如悬浮或无中生有等超自然的现象，唯识理论的导向也与神秘主义不同。中国佛教至少在整体上并未太过偏离其原始目标，即通过消除旧婆罗门世界中的各种迷信观念而达到证悟；这一目标也是反神迹的。唯识理论更偏向于知性主义和理性主义。为了解释物质，我们需要考虑明（vidyā）和无明。

世界中充满了无明。这种普遍的无明可以分为两类：一类是可进行认识的，另一类是不可进行认识的。八识与六类心所法属于前者，而如山河等事物以及一切物质元素都是由后者生起的；二者相合而形成了识的内根。这一内根，只要它还是物质的，就可进行认识并映射外物；五感即是这一内根的产物。内根是一，而其分别的感官则有不同。明在本质上是心理的；然而心或识的第一行为则是无明。在唯识理论中，明被认为是为无明所遮蔽的真如之心。因为明被遮蔽了很久，所以，此心产生了识之本质。见之本质反映出色，而色则发展成为肉体感官。尽管无明密密遮蔽了真如，但当它尚未形成四大（地、水、火、风）之色时，则称之为无明的外壳。宇宙中原初的精神本质是真有、精微、光明之心，但因为它被包裹在壳中，于是它起了分别，并成为无明所居之处；这也就产生了五蕴及一切有情。我们甚至可以说，如果不是无明之力，又是什么可以遮蔽此心呢？八识与心所法必须依靠某物而出现，而净色根则是它们的增上缘。

室利·阿罗频多认为在无明中亦有明，没有退化，也就没有进化。在这点上他的哲学观点与唯识理论很相似。

唯识理论认为根可以发展出感官并反映事物，但却不能以其自身与色相缘。只有自其发展而出的、具有分别能力的识，才能与色相缘。

前五识与第六识被认为是第八识的本质，或者说是第八识的精神之光通过这六个孔道而照耀出来。如果它通过的是眼睛，那么它就能辨认色相，故称之为眼识。如果它通过了耳朵，它就能分辨声音，故称之为耳识。另外的鼻、舌、身三识也可依此类推。到了第六识中，因其摄受一切法知识，所以被称为心或者意识。这也可以被比作一个有着六扇窗子的房间，其中关着一只猴子。如果一个人从任一扇窗子呼唤猴子，猴子就会从那扇窗作出应答，这就像认知一样。

我再谈一下被译为“作意”的Manaskāra。它是五遍行心所（pañca sarvatragaḥ）之首，每一段认知关系中的受、想、思（cetanā）皆依于作意。作意唤起心并将其引向外境。或许有人会问，它是在种子状态还是在现行状态引领心的呢？作意的自性是清明的，即使在种子状态中，它也能引领心及其他遍行开始运作。这就好像很多人在一间宿舍中入睡，其中有一人总是失眠；如果有小偷进入了这间宿舍，那么这个人就会唤起其他所有人。作意的种子在心入眠时将心唤起，并在其作用中将被唤醒的心也带起作用。一切感官的活动都需要作意的存在。

24

到目前为止，我们对八识进行了简要讨论，它们都与心法相关。“精神”（mind）在汉语中与“心”（heart）同义，但在不同的哲学系统中有着不同的解读。通常精神被认为是与基于大脑的思维相连，而心则与以心脏为中心的情感与感受相关。许多灵修大师都认为思维之所不在大脑，而在宇宙中的另一处。在佛教中，思维在原则上是需要被消除的；它在佛教中的地位不如在现代哲学中重要。根据唯识理论，心（mind）即是第八识。它在产生现行的过程中集合了一切种子；然而它在集合种子并加以熏习的过程中也包含了其他七识及其现行。心将自己与外物相缘，进行分别并加以考虑。总的来说，心的所行即是思考。分别、考虑与思考都是心的功能，并因此被纳入心法之中。然而心所法所指则是那些永远与心相应、依于心而存在的法。读者需要注意的是，相应指同时存在、互相依存的条件，这是一种平等的关系或事实。

心所法有无数种，一般列出51个，分为五类。[54]说一切有部认为心所法与心不同，经量部认为二者不异。唯识宗则认为因为心所法为心所生成，应将心放在首位，并称其为唯识，而唯识作为一种意识也一定包含了心所法。然而在终极意义上，心与心所法可以说是一，异，或者不一而不异，就像太阳与日光同时出现一样。

54. 见附录。——原注（编者按：见本书“附录一”。）

25

整个唯识理论的关键在于种子。种子分为两类：原本就存在于藏识中的和新形成的。新形成的种子是在长期的熏习之后形成的。熏习者与被熏习的对象是不同的：被熏习的对象是第八识，熏习者则是余下七识。关于这一点，两位先哲有着不同的意见。难陀认为一切种子皆是新形成的，而净月[55]则认为一切种子原本就存在于识中。他对于难陀的反驳就在于，最高等级的无漏种子与中性（即不善亦不恶）的种子不需要重新形成，如果它们不是本来就存在的话，那么是由什么生起的呢？如果要反驳净月的话，那么，我们可以说，若使只有这些非凡的种子存在，它们并非新生起之种子，而余下七识生起的结果又是什么呢？我们还可以进一步问，如果水的自性就是湿润的，它不需要沾湿外物以证明其自性，那么火也不应该燃烧，风也不能使物体移动了。最后，第三位论师护法得出的结论是，两类种子皆存在于藏识之中，这就解决了一个关键的问题。

此推论并没有被进一步演绎下去。很显然，这里的问题是本有之种子的起源，然而这一问题并没有得到回答，这也是可以理解的。

熏习的过程也需要进一步解释。第八识是被熏习的对象，因此是被动的。前七识是熏习者，因此是主动的。熏习的内容为善、恶，或是中性；就像极小的香味分子一样，它们被保留下来。然而为什么前七识不会被熏习呢？

熏习的产生需要四个条件。第一，熏习的对象必须是稳定的，或者说自始至终都保持了自性，因此它才能保有熏习之气息。其他七识从未稳定下来，因此它们不能接受任何熏习。第二，这一对象必须是中性或者无偏向的，这样它才能接受或者形成新的习气。就像麝香与檀香自身的味道过于强烈而不能被熏香一样，善与恶也不能被熏习。第三，被熏习的对象必须可以接受熏习。它需要是自由的，并且是可以接受操控的。因此才可以很容易地被熏习，不像石头。所有的心所法皆不能自主，并且过于固执；而一切有为法也是如此。第四，熏习者与被熏习的对象之间需要相应。二者需要同时同地存在，不离亦不即。这指的是一个人的前七识不能熏习另一人的第八识。这也与经量部所讲的心之前一刻熏习后一刻不同。一个人

55. 此处原文为月护（Chandragupta），月护并非唯识论师，应为净月（Śuddhacandra）。

或许能对另一人产生影响，然而将其保持下来则是被影响者才能做的事。

考虑到这四点，只有第八识才能被熏习。而作为熏习者的前七识也需要先满足一定条件才能开始熏习并产生新种子。首先，熏习者必须是不恒常的，有始有终，或者说有成有毁；如此才能形成新的习气。这就排除了恒常一致且不能作用的无为法。其次，熏习的对象必须有熏习之力。不论好坏中性，熏习的对象必须足够有力才能产生印象。这就排除了无力生成行为的第八识。再次，熏习的对象的行为必有起有落，这样才能促成习气的形成。因为成佛之果总是充满了至善，不增不减，因此它不能进行熏习。最后一点与此前提到的关于被熏习的对象的第四点相同，即二者必须总是相应。因此，熏习者与被熏习的对象同生同灭。

26

A

到目前为止我们所谈的唯识理论是一套在大乘佛教体系内的、精心安排且表述完善的哲学或心理学系统；然而它也是佛法，也有自身的目的。在最终分析中，此法既不是西方意义上的哲学，也不是西方意义上的宗教。它的目的在玄奘的名著《成唯识论》第一段中已经明确写出了：

> 今造此论，为于二空有迷谬者生正解故。生解为断二重障故，由我法执二障具生；若证二空，彼障随断。断障为得二胜果故。由断续生烦恼障，故证真解脱，由断碍解所知障，故得大菩提。[56]

56. 参见《成唯识论》卷一。

于此可见，这一理论的目的是实用性的。余下的长篇大论都是为了这一目的服务的。

根据世亲的说法，一切法归结起来共有一百种：九十四种有为法与六种无为法。他在列举的百法最后，提出了补特伽罗无我与法无我。在世亲的时代，此二者或许不言自明，无须加以解释，然而后世的唯识学者则对此有所注解。

唯识宗在词源分析上不亚于韦檀多学派，后来的密教也对此加以仿效。这种词源分析是为了宣扬本宗教法而形成的一种帮助记忆的工具，并不考虑真正意义上的语文学或者词源学的规律，只在对自身有利时才会将其采纳进来。例如“补特伽罗”（pudgala）一词是这样被拆分的：

补 *pu*：再三，常常；

特伽 *dga*：取，经历；

罗 *la*：有情世界，如天、人、动物等。

词义为“我”。

一切个体或有情（sattva）总是迷惑的，在有生之年总是要有所行为。一切行为无论大小，都被归结为业。因为过去的种种业，众生辗转于轮回诸道之中，然而他们不能自主，也没有自由意志。这就是补特伽罗无我。

有人可能会天真地问，补特伽罗或者“我”就是心吗？如果是的话，应该有八个补特伽罗。“我”就是心所法吗？如果是的话，应该有五十一种“我”。“我”就是物质原则吗？因为五内根不可见，五外根与外物相同，它们生灭不息，“我”应该立于何处呢？……如此这般，我们可以追问百法中的每一项是否为补特伽罗，然而真正的“我”却无处可寻。

法（dharma）被解释为源于词根 *dhṛ*，通常意为“持”。这是正确的词源分析。法无我指的是法不具有自性，或者说法不是自性。从世俗谛（saṃvṛtisatyaṃ）来看，百法皆根据其分别而立，而从胜义谛（paramārthasatyaṃ）来看，一切法皆如梦幻。因此，无即是有，有也即是无。一切皆如虚空，如幻中花，如水中月，如露如电。由此观之，世界是空的；与之相伴而生起的人间诸苦也是空的并被湮灭的。

大略分之，法只有如前所说的有为法与无为法两类。宇宙万物处在恒常的变化之中，因此宇宙也被认为是在不断变化中的。在记录这些变化的过程中，中国先哲所作的《易经》时至今日仍被人研究。佛教所观察的是同样的宇宙现象，却得出了不同的结论。一切存在都被认为是因缘和合的结果，这种和合意味着作用。一切心与外境的原则也都被包含在其中。这就是缘起论。此外还有与之相对的无为法，它最终归于真如。

世间万物皆为缘起，故一切法皆无自性。心能够感知到的只有法的外在形象或者说相。因此，万物看似真有，再将此理论推进一步，则可得出万物皆是心所化出的结论。

与色相关的是用以指称色的“名”。如果我们说某些东西“无名”，这仍然是一种命名方式。名离事物的本性就更远了。

第三[57]为分别法，即心中分别事物为善恶、宾主的功能。

57. 名法与相法为前两种有为法。

第四为正知识法，即关于前三者以及佛菩萨的知识，或关于无漏法的知识。漏即是拥有悲喜情绪的凡人心中所出现的折磨或可厌之事等。漏就是烦恼；它包括了痛苦，也包括了享受。一个人可以为享受所折磨而感觉快乐，因此快乐也是烦恼。

以上四种被归结为有为法。第五为无为法。此五法与三自性是相宗所要深入探讨并最终否定的主要对象。

26

B

在进一步深入之前，我们需要明确一点。唯识理论包括了相宗十位论师的教法，它与中观相对，又可称之为瑜伽行派。瑜伽行派与中观派针锋相对，在本书的最后我将谈到二者之间的争议。然而要理解这些争论，我们先要理解瑜伽行派与瑜伽之间的不同。

佛教语境中所用的“瑜伽”一词，与现在我们通常所说的印度瑜伽不同。在汉语中，瑜伽一词是音译。在佛教中，瑜伽并非波颠阇利（patañjali）的修行系统。因为佛教常被贬入无神论一类（佛教与无神论确实有可类比之处），这里的瑜伽指的并不是个人与神的同一。在此，瑜伽被理解为“相应”或“相依”，即一切法的自性互不相违，且与对象相应。它被应用于定、慧（mati）等修行方式中，教授修行者如何相应于修行。它也可以用在建构或解构关于世间及出世间法的正见或者如菩提等修行之果中。如果胜法彼此相应，那么也可称之为瑜伽。当一副正确的药物治愈疾病时，也可以称之为瑜伽。

瑜伽行不是我们今天所知的瑜伽练习。瑜伽行者不是瑜伽士，而是一位了知佛教各派学说以及禅定的大师。例如僧伽罗刹（Saṃgharakṣa）就是一位瑜伽士，但他不属于瑜伽行派。瑜伽行派的名著为弥勒（事实上是无著）所作之《瑜伽师地论》，此论由戒贤三次教授与玄奘，并因此传入中国。其原本为梵文，今存汉文译本。

作为独立修行体系的赫他瑜伽（Haṭha Yoga）或者罗遮瑜伽（Rāja Yoga）似乎并未传入中国。道教中有类似的修行方式，但是很难说谁影响了谁，也难以确定二者是否为平行独立地发展而互不知晓。后世大乘佛教衰落之后，佛教瑜伽行派也逐渐衰退了。瑜伽仍在密宗中保存了下来并繁荣发展，但这又是另一个故事了。

27

A

本书无法涵盖唯识理论中的所有细节，但是我们可以讨论一些主要观点。有人或许会就唯识宗对于外物根本上之真有性的否定提出怀疑。这一观点涉及物体所占的时间与空间的有限性，以及感知及其功用的无限性。经量部对唯识宗有四问，世亲在《唯识二十颂》（*Viṃśatikā-vijñaptimātratāsiddhiḥ*）中作出了回答。

（1）如果色识之升起不依赖于真有之外法（即真有之色），那么何以此识只于一处生起，而非处处生起？

（2）同样的，那么何以此识只于一时生起，而非时时生起？

（3）于一时一地可以有多人而非一人，何以物识不依一人之识而决定？如有眼疾者视物时见有本不存在的发丝或飞蝇，而其他诸人则无此问题。

（4）第四个问题包含三个与作用相关的问题：

a. 为什么如发丝等幻觉没有真正发丝之用；

b. 为什么梦中所进饮食没有真正饮食之用；

c. 为什么乾闼婆城（gandharvanagara）没有真正城邦之用。

上述四点都被世亲以梦为喻加以解释。在梦中，物体存在于一时一地，而非时时地地。具有同样业之人所见之物才相同；我们作为人见河为河，而恶鬼则未必见之为河。因此，所见之物取决于见之主。虚幻之物也是有“用”的，就像男性可能在梦中遗精一样。

不论在世亲生活的时代这些解释是多么有说服力，它们显然超出了现在人类推理的限度。说到底这是一个信仰或者是迷信的问题。对恶鬼以及地狱中其他方面的描写（如移动的铁山，烧红的铁地面，或者地狱的狱卒）展现了一幅怪异可怖的图景，它们或许可以为文学作品提供素材，但却太过幻想化，不能被纳入哲学讨论的范畴。即使如此，我们仍然可以从先哲的思维中提取其精粹。

B

唯识理论的观点还涉及一个神学问题：如果心外无真有之物（如肉眼及肉眼所观之物），那么为什么佛陀要教授眼处（cakṣurāyatanaṃ）、色处（rūpāyatanaṃ）等十二处呢？

答案是：此十二处为识所化，并非独立的实体。眼识因各种因缘和合从自身种子而生，因此而有相或者物体的影像。佛陀所讲的眼处与色处也是基于其自身的种子与生成，然而他并没有说在识之外尚存真有之物。佛陀教授中有（中有是一种人死后之内有）的目的，在于驳斥认为人死之后就完全不复存在的绝对虚无主义观点，与此相同，佛陀教授十二处的目的在于使人生起无我之证悟。但中有也不是外在的真有，它只不过是幻相而已。

C

这就产生了另一问题：如果补特伽罗无我与法无我密切相关，那么唯识理论也是法，它是否也是无我或者说空呢？

答案是否定的。为什么呢？因为唯识并非所执，就是这么简单。也就是说，如果作为识所化的见与相将任何法执为真有，那么它就是错误的。为了对治这种将假有执为真实之顽疾，需要以法之空性为药方。而超出言语的、认识到了识之自性的正见则不空。在遍分别（sarvakalpita）被认为是依他起（paratamtra）之对象并非真有而是空；而圆成实之对象是真有不空的。如果这一正知识也是空的话，那么世间实相也不复存在了。没有世间实相的话，也就没有出世间实相了。最后我们就会得出一个绝对虚无主义的结论；而佛陀认为这是一种不治之症。如龙树、世亲在内的绝大多数大乘论师也极力反对这一观点。

D

又有另一问题：如果在一切情况下色皆依识而存在，那么何以色的幻相，如物体的存有性，可以不生变化呢？

答案是：色及其存续，是受自无始之时起人心中名色熏习之影响的。色是净法与不净法所居之处。如果没有此形象的话，识也就不会将非真有之色虚妄执持为真有之对象了，而染污法以及无染污法也将不复存在了。

换言之，问题其实在于，如果我们不承认任何外在、真有之色，那么为什么会有色相出现呢？回答是：因为有虚幻的外像与假有的实在，我们必须承认色识与非色识的存在。如果没有化现出来的色相为因，那么也就不会产生出幻化之真有作为其果，因为因果是在心中相连续的。

E

还有一个问题：如果识之外境是通过现觉被认知的，那它们如何能被认为是非真有呢?

回答是：在现觉之时，外境不再被认为是外在的。只有在第六识起作用之时，才会将物体认为是外在的。然而这是错误的。通过现觉所生成的是自相分，即识所化之果，它可以被认为是真有的。但是任何被心所执持的、真有的外在之色必须被认为是非实在的。这是由遍分别的特性所决定的。

关于这一点各家有着不同的说法。经量部认为外境的存续刹那接续不断。唯识宗的反驳为：当意识在五识之后与外境接触时，在那一瞬间，前五识的现觉就消失了，因此就不再有现觉。说一切有部认为色的消亡也是刹那接续不断的。当意识产生作用时，前五识及其外境必然也会消失，又如何可能会有现觉呢?

大乘佛教关于这一点作出了微妙的修正，提出第六识伴随前五识同时出现，并且在此后生成自身的执持。

大乘佛教论师认为，如果不是这样的话，那么在听到声音之时，就不会对声音有所执。第六识的现觉也伴随前五识出现。在第一刹那，其所执生成了第二刹那，并接续生成了分别；因此外境被认为是外在的。以此观之，我们日常生活中所见之对象也并非实物。它们并非外在，却被认为是外在的。一切皆如梦境，一切事物皆不应被执持为外在真有之对象。

又有一问：如果我们在清醒状态中一切外在对象都如在梦境中一样不离于识，那么何以当我们从梦中醒来时，我们记得梦中所见之对象为心中幻相，在清醒之时却不能认识到所见之对象乃是意识所造呢?

回答是：人在梦中时，不知道他是在梦中。只有醒来之后，他才能忆起梦境。这与我们在清醒之时所见之事物是一样的。在达到真正的证悟之前，我们都不能意识到我们是在梦中。故佛陀视生死为长夜，我们也尚未意识到万物皆是由心所造。

F

在此又有一个难点，即佛教心理学所说的他心通（paracittajñānaṃ）或者说了知他人想法的能力。这也被认为是已经证明了的事实。既然一个人的意识可以与另一人的意识相通，那么，这难道与心执持外境有什么不同吗？

回答是：他人的意识为什么不可能成为人自身之识的外境呢？在这里不被承认的只是他人之意识可以与自心紧密相联。识的作用不像是以手持物，也不像是日月或是火光照耀在外物上，而是像镜子反射外界的影像。他心通不是将一个人的心与另一人的心紧密地联系在一起。识所知的只是由其所化的幻相的部分，他心通也是如此，共生之色也是如此。

又有一问：唯识理论认为心外无物，如果在本心之外的他人之心可以为我们所知，那么……？

回答是：唯识理论只承认本心吗？如果是的话，那么又如何区分高下、圣俗、心法与色法呢?

我们需要认识到，唯识宗认为所有人都有八识、六类心所法、对识主外境的分别、二十四心不相应行法、二空及由空性所揭示的究竟真如。因为一切自性、相应、分别与化皆不离于识，此宗被称为唯识。它否认了识之外任何真有的存在。

上述问答已经可以解释清楚关于这一理论的一切疑虑。然而对唯识理论最有力的攻击不来自外道或者早期佛教，而来自大乘佛教内部。

28

关于阿赖耶识我们已经讲了很多，然而仍有一个问题亟待解决：阿赖耶识是如何与轮回转世联系起来的？

除了顺世论派（Carvaka）之外，几乎所有的印度古代哲学都相信生死轮回与不同轮回道的存在。一个人可以在死后再次转生为人，或者转向更高或更低之道，如天或地狱。佛教认为有六道，最高的为天，最低的为饿鬼；人道居于第二位，仅次于天。[58]然而即使是诸天也受制于轮回，在业报耗尽之后，他们必须降至人道再修证佛果。只有通过人身才能成佛。如果一个人尚未证悟，那他就将辗转于六道轮回之中。人类想象力中最奇异又最荒谬之处在于人可以转生为动物：任何一个懂得达尔文进化论的人都会觉得这是不经之谈。这或许是关于变态过程的原始信仰的残留；对于远古先民而言，诸如毛毛虫变为蝴蝶等自然现象虽然可以眼见，却是很难理解的。然而即使是相对较进步的大乘佛教也将轮回视为当然。

阿赖耶识含藏一切善恶种子，使之不致散失；它护持色根及肉身，使之不致腐坏。因此，它就生成了一个人的业，并将其前世今生联系起来。它被认为是人此世死后至下一世前仍存留之物，这一状态被称为中有。如前所述，关于这一点不同部派之间有争议。中有是诸有情之果，是在胎中形成其行为的心理种子。

人死后，中有游离于世间寻求居所，就像旅客寻找旅店一样。这很像印度教所说的灵，或者西方所讲的灵魂。如果中有正好见到（因为过去的业，中有具有可见之力）一男一女正在交媾，它即刻就被其吸引，附着其上。如果中有为男性，则附着于母亲身上；如果为女性，则附着于父亲身上。因为它对这对夫妇的嫉妒，它将自身等同为对方所爱之人，并如铁被吸附于磁石之上一般进入母亲的子宫中。这就是在通常情况下的受孕过程以及胎儿形成的第一步。男女之间的精子和卵子可以结合，然而没有中有，就不能形成胎儿。人死之时，中有是最后离开肉身的；人出生之时，中有是最先进入肉身的。一个人的未来在很大程度上是由其前世所造的善业或恶业决定的，这些业被转化为业种子的形式储藏在阿赖耶识中。

这种转世理论听上去很科学。尽管在印度的哲学传统中转世观念是如此普及以及根深蒂固，但在中国它却遭到了强烈的反对。古代中国人孝敬父母，并且几乎将父母敬为神明；孝被认为是百善之先。中有对于父亲或

58 其余三道为阿修罗、畜生、地狱。

母亲的依恋被认为是极为使人反感、应被驳斥的邪说。这一理论在很大程度上影响了或者说阻碍了佛教的传播。印度和中国的社会与民族传统之间，确实存在很大不同。

29

我们还可以再谈谈唯识理论中皈依的问题。在人身中所形成的一种不表于外的原则称为无表色（avijñapti-rūpa），它是生起苦乐的潜藏业因。无表色本身并非实在，却由构成身体的四大所生成，因此根据说一切有部的教法，它仍然是色。

无表色值得我们注意，因为它与我们所说的修行或教育相关。新沙弥通过特定的仪轨受戒：他需要回答戒师的问题，做出向佛像顶礼以及向师父及同修再三致敬等动作，并背诵戒律。这些身语意之业在新受戒的沙弥身上形成了一张戒律的保护网。它并非外在，却有阻止此人再行恶业的能力。就像通过魔术或者催眠术一样，他被引领着遵循戒律，不犯罪行。这就是无表色。

经量部认为无表色没有任何精神活动，因此与心无关。它也并非实在，因此与色法也无关。它二者皆非，却是在人身中所形成的一种本质。

《阿毗达摩俱舍论》（*Abhidharmakośa*）则认为无表色以色之业为性，就像表色或了别识（vijñapti）或者含藏之业一样。因为它不展现自身而为人所知，故被称为无表色。

根据相宗的说法，无表色是因为阿赖耶识中精神活动之种子的作用，因此它仍是心法。无表色分善与恶。善无表色可以阻止人行恶业并引致喜乐；恶无表色则与之相反。在受戒之后，第六识起作用而在第八识中创造新的种子，这些心所法之种子可以阻止人违背戒律，因此又可称之为戒之“身”。

这似乎就是我们所说的新人格的塑造。和其他启蒙一样，这并非是一时一日可以形成的；新习气的形成不是一夕间的事。合格的师父必须在弟子的识中灌入一些新的观念；如果他有很大法力的话，那么他对于弟子的影响可以是永久的。在识中播入新种子是对这一行为最贴切的解读。

30

如前所述，世俗谛与胜义谛之间的区分是一直存在的。后者常常被解释为不可言说、超出思维的。然而神秘主义者与其他人也常常以胜义谛作为非逻辑推理的最终落脚处，或者说在辩论中为尴尬或失败解围的天外救星（*deus ex machina*）。在唯识理论中，佛教正理论的论证方式无处不在，这对于缺乏深刻宗教信仰的高级知识分子来说是极具吸引力的。在窥基的注疏中，世俗谛与胜义谛各有四种。

谛即真相。真相也有不同层阶。最为著名的是由佛陀所教的四圣谛——苦、集（Samudayaḥ）、灭（Nirodhaḥ）、道（Mārgaḥ）。此四谛一直是不容辩驳之胜义谛，因为它们揭示了世间万法的真相。而在哲学讨论中，为了思维的清晰，我们需要对世俗谛与胜义谛加以区分。窥基（事实上是窥基的老师玄奘）将“世俗”（saṃvṛti）分解为“世”，即覆障、可毁坏，与“俗”，即显现、随世流；[59]“世俗谛”被认为是世间之真相或者是俗人之真相。此处世俗谛为“A”——

A

（1）有名无实谛或世间世俗谛。一切名相都是人任意假设的。自假设的观点观之，它们为真有，就像一个瓶被称为瓶，一个盆被称为盆：它们都是实物。非真有的抽象物也有名字。此二类皆为世俗谛。

（2）随事差别谛或道理世俗谛。依一种事物而安立此种事物之法，如蕴、界等。

（3）方便安立谛或证得世俗谛。被广泛承认、体验并证明之事实，如苦、集等。

59. 窥基《成唯识论述记》卷一：“世俗谛者，世谓覆障可毁坏义，俗谓显现随世流义。”

(4) 假名非安立谛或胜义世俗谛。这指的是作为世间实性的二空理论。其真实性只是被内在体验，而不能言说于外。它仍依假有之名而立。[60]

胜义谛亦分为四种。此处为“B”——

B

（1）体用显现谛或世间胜义谛。就像蕴及界一样，胜义谛有超凡之真性，因此为胜义，并因不同事相而得名。此胜义谛是显现的。

（2）因果差别谛或道理胜义谛。此指苦、集等。在认知、祛除无明、修行与证悟中，因果皆有显现并起重要作用，甚至超出了普通的理性。故此谛被称为胜义。

60. 窥基《成唯识论述记》卷一："真俗二谛各有四重。俗谛四者：一假名无实谛，谓瓶、盆等。但有假名而无实体，从能诠说故名为谛。或体实无亦名为谛。二随事差别谛，谓蕴、界等。随彼彼事立蕴等法。三证得安立谛，谓苦、集等。由证得理而安立故。四假名非安立谛，谓二空理。依假空门说为真性，由彼真性内证智境。不可言说名二空如。但假设故，此前三种法可拟宜，其第四谛假名施设。"

（3）依门显实谛或证得胜义谛。指的是通过超出世俗观念而悟得之二空理论。依赖空性而显现真性，此即胜义。

（4）废诠谈旨谛或胜义胜义谛。指的是唯一之真如，它超出言语，是胜义的；也因其超出一切世俗谛而是胜义的。[61]

唯识理论认为世间世俗谛（A.1）无真性，依虚名而立（但即使是虚名也不能被一笔勾销）。胜义胜义谛（B.4）不依名相而立，因此不是世俗的；它是胜义且真有的。余下各项（A.2, A.3, A.4；B.1, B.2, B.3）既是世俗的也是胜义的。我们在此只能得出一切都是相对而言的结论。真正的胜义谛不可能单独被称为胜义的；它有待于世俗之谛与之相对，才能成为胜义谛。而世俗谛也要依靠胜义谛才能被认可。因此二者是相对的。

这种分类一直被佛教学者高度认可，却并不见于其他古代哲学系统。

61. 窥基《成唯识论述记》卷一："胜义四者。一体用显现谛，谓蕴、界等。有实体性，过初世俗，故名胜义。随事差别说名蕴等，故名显现。二因果差别谛，谓苦、集等。知、断、证、修因果差别，过俗道理，故名胜义。三依门显实谛，谓二空理。过俗证得，故名胜义。依空能证以显于实，故名依门。四废诠谈旨谛，谓一实如。体妙离言已名胜义。过俗胜义复名胜义。俗谛中初都无实体假名安立，无可胜过，故不名为真，但名为俗。第四胜义不可施设。"

31

前述的种种又关系到另一重要问题：八识具有相同的自性吗？回答既是肯定的，也是否定的。我们不能说八识具有相同的自性，因为：

（1）八识产生作用所依缘及其果是不同的，而且——

（2）熏习者与被熏习物（即第七识与第八识）不可以是同一个。

然而八识的自性也不能说相异，因为所有八识就像海中的波浪一样，而波浪与水是不异的。如果八识的自性不同的话，那么它们就不能为因缘所和合，而是会像幻相一样没有常性。

因为在胜义谛中，一切名相思维都不复存在，这些区分都是基于世俗谛而非胜义谛的。这就是前文的 A. 2 与 B. 4 的对比；其中主观与客观的分界也被消除了。

万物中只有识是存在的，包括“我”和法在内的一切都是幻相，因为二者皆无真性，二者都是空。然而也并没有绝对的空；空不等于虚无，幻相仍然存在。这就又回到了世俗谛与胜义谛的共存关系上来，也就是说，二谛不能脱离彼此而单独存在。这也是居于有与无之间的唯识宗之中道。

32

在此还须进一步说明名相之非实在性。

自相与共相，或者说特殊性与普遍性之间的区别是一直存在的。相指形象或外观，也指性质或特质。名与言语构成了语分别（vāgvikalpa）。除了心中所形成的影像之外，并无其他可被执为真有的外境；虚妄知识与命名本身不是外境。至于心所执持的法及其相，它们是在言语之外的，其形成及因缘不能为虚妄知识所理解；因此它们为真有。名相可以通过超出言语及分别知识的现觉被认识；虚妄知识及命名则围绕共相而存在。如火有热性，水有流动性，实物有实在性，这都是它们的自相；自相可被证明并认识，然而却不能以言语来表达。第六识在前五识作用后生起，言语根据第六识的知识而产生，与事物之共相相关。

依据这一观点，如果语言同任一物体的自相相关，那么在说出“火”

一词时，嘴就会被烧伤。或者在提到“张三”时，我们就能知晓关于张三此人的一切。张三的自相是由不同法或四大和合而成的。在称他为张三时，我们所知的只是此人，而非构成此人的一切原素。因此，言语被认为是围绕共相而运作，而共相却完全不能被言语所了得。

这在整体上是一个二分或排除的过程。我们谈论一物体的颜色时，所谈论的是其外观，排除了如大小、重量等其他因素；这就是普遍中的特殊。而当我们提到一个颜色如红色，这就是一个普遍的特征，如红花、红果、红油漆等则是特殊的例子。普遍性即是共性，而特殊性则是自性。如果一物体由无数个原子构成，那么每一个原子都是其自性，而此物体则是共性。如此二分之后，自性是不可名说的，而可名说的共性则有限。一切虚妄知识、施设、名言都只能是共性，而不能再进一步了。

或许有人会问，既然水与火的自性同样不可知，为什么提到火时，人想到的不是水呢？其实并非如此，所有命名的区分，都是自古以来通过人类的习惯或风俗而形成的，与我们现在所谈的名相分别不是同一问题。比如见到红色物体并认出这是红色的认知过程，是通过比量（anumānaṃ）而产生的知识。眼识与颜色通过现觉相缘，但眼识并不能将这一颜色理解为红色；只有当意识或第六识与颜色之共相相缘，然却不附于任意颜色之上时，意识才将其理解为红色。这一红色物体不等于“红”这一名称，或者是关于何为红色的知识。我们是在排除了如蓝色、绿色等其他颜色之后，才得出了红色的结论。当然这是另一问题了。

除了名相与虚妄知识之外，自相的成立不需要依赖任何人为因素。知识的非真实性在于，它只是类似于自相而不能真正成为自相。知识不能与任何东西相缘，即使可以，它也不能知晓自性。在辨认出某一颜色为红色时，我们所见到的并不是红色的自性；即使我们可以见到其自性，我们也不会将其理解为自性。名相与虚妄知识只能成就模拟之物，却并不依于自性；然而，我们只能说它们依于自相。

名相与虚妄知识还必须依靠声音而存在；这就是语言的起源。语言不能到达之处，它们也不复存在。声音为听觉器官所感受，本身并没有任何意义。心与词汇或语句相缘，故而产生了意义以及由之而生的理解。指示物与所指对象并不是自相。此外，因为共相并非真有，所以它也不是一种独立存在的对象。语言作为假有法并不依于任何真有之物，它只是靠模拟真有之物而运行。比喻是附加于本体上的外物；共相也是叠加在自相上的外物。共有的特征中包含了许多独立的特质，因此共性也是附加于自性上的外物。在此，语言或声音也是靠叠加之比喻而运作，因此，不能说非真有之物一定要靠真有之物才能成立。（这也就回答了前文 27D 中提出的问题。）

根据唯识理论，宇宙万物皆为识所化，“我”与“法”皆为假立之比喻。二者皆只是名相，并非真有。在前文（15B）所引的龙树之偈文中，下半句为：

亦为是假名，亦是中道义。

33

识之三性，是大乘佛教尤其是唯识学中经常讨论的一个认识论观点。从唯心主义的角度来看，这三性即是世间之性。它们指向自性，自性也被理解为相，与人类存在之自相相等同。此三性为：

（1）遍计所执性（parikalpita），即对于执持外在对象时无处不在的分别与揣测之性。“执”在此意为感知，并隐含了执着之意。

（2）依他起性，即在生起之时需要依靠外在对象之性。

（3）圆成实性（pariniṣpanna），即周遍圆满成就之性。

对于第一性遍计所执性有着不同的理解。安慧认为心可以执持外在对象；前五识与第八识执持的只有法，第七识执持“我”，而第六识则同时执持法与“我”。护法则认为遍计所执性有二主，即执持法的第六识与执持“我”的第七识。通过执持法与“我”，便产生了对于万物的分别与揣测。

前五识与第八识如果不伴以慧的话，就不能产生此种执持。而与能够附着于法之上并熏习出善恶种子或习气的意相比，它们的力量则太微弱。只要心还未证悟，那么一切虚妄分别与揣测，就会因自无始之时成形的虚谬之习气而生起。而自证则被分为见与相，即执持者与被执持的对象；二者只是看似实在，却非确实真有。这就是遍计所执性，它具有无数种形态。

第二性依他起性指的是被执持之对象。“他”在这里指的是因果关系。安慧与护法两位论师关于此性亦有两种不同的观点，并在他们后来的弟子中分为两支。

第一支认为，心及心所法为假有所熏习，故看似分为见与相二者，然而根本上只有一者，即自证。在正理中二者看似实在，却非确实真有。此即“遍计所执”。

见与相之所依包括了因缘和合而成的有情及其识。因为这一特性是由虚妄分别的种子在因果关系中形成的，故而称之为“依他起性”。

我们何以得出这一结论呢？它们是圣说（āryavāda）或者由先贤教授而知。虚妄分别是需要依他而起的，而执持者与被执持之对象在总体上都是分别心。

第二支则认为，因为心、心所法及受熏习之后二者所产生的变化都是由因缘和合而生的，所以它们都是依他起的。在心与心所法的基础上，以四句法来推测有无、同异、一或多、相伴或相离的恒常性，这就是遍计所执性。四句法为：

（1）有；

（2）无；

（3）亦有亦无；

（4）非有非无。

这也是由圣说而知的。圣者所教授的知识比量、二分法等都属于依他起性。相宗所教五法中的前四法也是依他起的。[62]

第二支还认为，如果在依他起性中只有自证分而没有相分的话，那么在佛的无漏状态中被转化的此二分也必然是遍计所执性的。如果上述可以成立的话，那么证悟就不能自其中生成，因为真有不能与遍计所执性发生联系；如果上述不能成立的话，那么有漏的精神状态中则既有自证分亦有相分。如果这两分是遍计所执性的话，那么因为遍计所执性自身并非真有，所以二分也就像龟毛兔角一样，并非真有，且不在因果之中。因其并非真有，故而就像说不育妇女之子一样，对二分的执持也不会产生任何种子，因此而生的接续之识也必然空于此二分。一切习气都被包含在相分中，如果相分非真有的话，又如何由此产生因果呢？再有，一切因果所生皆不离于识，如果由因果所生之相分与见分并非依他起，那么因为并没有其他因的缘故，所以二分所依之有情必也非依他起。因此，我们可有此推论：

依因缘而生之二分为依他起性；

因为它们同自证分一样自因缘种子而生；

如果只有自证分的话，那么它又如何与种子相缘并引致证自证分呢？

62. 前四法为：心法、心所法、色法、心不相应行法；见本书附录一。

正确与错误的知识比量又如何可以独立与心相缘呢？如果我们承认见分的话，就没有这些困难了。

因此，一切心与心所法以及在有漏或无漏状态中的相与见，根据正理都是依他起性的，由各种因缘而生起。

第三性圆成实性，即是由二空理论所揭示的圆满成立之一切法的真相。

第三性是真有而非假立的，其中没有任何颠倒。在这里之颠倒指的是由外道及早期佛教部派所持的空、恒有等见。虽然其名称是一致的，然而对它们的理解却不同，因此，在唯识宗的观点中，它们是颠倒的。第三性无处不在，遍及一切，恒常真有，这就意味着它是超出的。

第三性就是真如。

在第三性的特质中排除了如自相等不能遍及一切之物，也不包括如无常、空、无我等在内的共相，因为共相虽然可能遍及一切，却不能自在。自在及作为其体现形式的真如一直被认为是一致的。

在依他起性的特征中有染污与无染污的区分。一切因果所生法都是分别的，因此被称为染污法。无染污的依他起之对象并无颠倒，自身清净，更是完全显现，遍及一切。与所有无漏法一样，它离于任何染污；因此无染污的依他起之对象被归入圆成实性中，它也被认为是圆满成就的。此圆成实之真有虽然在依他起中，却永无遍计所执性，无任何执取与揣测。它的自性如二空法所显示的一样，也是真如。

34

前文所说的圆成实性依于依他起性，或者说是依他起性的一部分，应该被理解为二者不离亦不异。如果二者可以合而为一的话，那么真如也会有灭时，或者依他起性则无始时。正是因为在依他起性之特性中有真如，所以二者才能不离。因为一者居于另一者之上，不能分离；然而二者却并不同一。

值得注意的细节是，tathātā 在汉语中被译为“真如”。“真如”指的是空性，而不是空自身。空为“如”所揭示，或者是“如”的原因。真如有别于有无之显现。因为它是空，它必然不同于有之显现；然而它却与空之显现并无二致。真如是超出有无二者的。

同样地，圆成实性与依他起性的特质也不一亦不异。如果二者全然不同的话，那么真如就不能是二者的共性；如果二者完全一致的话，那么真如就会和依他起性一般无常，二者也将有染污与无染污的分别，先天的根识与后天的知识之间也不会再有区别了。

这种不一亦不异的状态或许可以用无常来解释。如果无常之性完全不同于我们的日常行为，那么我们的行为就应是恒常的；其不同之处就像蓝色不同于黄色或者其他任何颜色一样。如果二者完全相同，那么无常就不能是共性，就像一切颜色的共性不能是单一颜色一样。共性与特性是不同的。

这就说明了圆成实性与依他起性不一亦不异。在正理中，法与法性也应如此理解。依他起性即法，圆成实性即法性。

它们与遍计所执性的关系也是如此。世亲认为心性和周遍分别与揣测之性是相同的。依他起性是物体被执持或相缘之性，因此能够引起周遍分别与揣测，故而也可称之为遍计所执性。然而另一位相宗论师无性则认为，等同意味着不能被分别开来；圆成实性与依他起性并存，却不存在于遍计所执性中。一个真有之对象与另一真有之对象不能被认为是相同或者相异的，然而对于非真有之对象来说，又有什么可以被等同或区分呢？此外，真有与非真有不能为一；依他起性是染污的，而圆成实性是无染污的，这就是二者的区别。故此普遍三性既非一致，也非彼此相异。根据另一种解释，依他起性是对我、色等法起分别之处，因此也可称之为遍计所执性。这与世亲的观点稍有不同，但结论却是一致的。

在论疏中对此三性有详尽的讨论，最终还是落在了相关性上；也就是说，离开其中一者，另一者将无法存在，反之亦然。如前文所说，没有世俗谛的话，也就没有胜义谛了。

最后，三性也与证悟有关。一个人如果没有悟出遍计所执性为空，就不能完全理解依他起性；或者说，应该通过对空性的领悟来理解圆成实性。换言之，只有通过无分别的根识才能体悟真如或者说明了圆成实性。人在了知世间万物依他生起之后，就可将一切视为幻相、梦境、镜中影像、光影、回声、水中月等等——一切心所化之对象都是看似存在，或者在假有意义上存在，却并非真有。自身或他人之“我”，真有或假有之法，同一或相异，相伴或相离，都因此被俗人错误地执持为真有。它们就像天花一样，并非真有，自性为空；一切都是虚妄的分别与揣测。最终三性就引致了证悟。

35

紧随三性之后是三无自性。这看似荒谬——如果没有自性的话，又有什么东西可以被区分或分类呢？此处的否定只是相对的。即使在胜论派哲学中，“无”也被分为四种：未生之无（prāgabhāva），已灭之无（pradhvaṃsābhāva），互为之无（itaretarābhāva 或 anyonyābhāva，如“如果有 A 则无 B”），以及绝对之无（atyantābhāva）。四者皆与“有”相对而成立。唯识理论的三无自性也是为说明三自性而构建的。

佛陀为一切众生说法而不论其智慧的高低；佛法是为了凡人而说。其中的否定也是相对的。首先，因为众生固有执持，佛陀教授了相无自性，它与遍计所执性相应。其次，与依他起性相应的是生无自性；世间万物皆由各种因缘而生起，因此其生无自性。再次，与圆成实性相应的即胜义无自性；因为遍计所执性的完全消失，即是最胜之法亦无自性。三无自性被比作遍及于一切实在之物中的空间或虚空，因物体的消失而得以揭示。第二无自性即使并非最胜义，也因为是空于第一性而可称之为无自性。无自性指的不是胜义非真有，而是胜义即空。

胜义分四种：世间胜义、道理胜义、证得胜义，以及胜义胜义。最后一种胜义即是唯一的真有，是唯识之菁华或者说真如。

这就是最超凡之真谛，然而如果对此产生误解，那么它只能带来最坏的果报。

36

我们需要时刻提醒自己，佛法尽管包含了各种理论，却并不是现代意义上的哲学。从瑜伽的角度来看，它是通过智性而到达涅槃的智慧瑜伽(Jñāna Yoga)。大乘佛教中也有对于菩萨尤其是观音的崇拜，则被贬称为敬爱瑜伽（Bhaktiyoga），关于此并无太多的讨论。菩萨地自下至上共有十地，在论中有详细论说，本书就无须引入了。修行五门是自入门到证悟之途的路标，在此也不多说。虽然，将天生就倾向于大乘佛教的人归为一类，是对印度种姓制度的严重挑战，但在现代世界中并无太大的价值。然而，我们不应忽视唯识理论中几点极精要之处。

首先是关于冥想的讨论。冥想有三种：

（1）居于舒适净法之中而不放逸；

（2）修证种种神通；

（3）为利益众生而成就。

上述三者都需要经过多年修行成就三摩地之后方可施行。修行者在其积极努力之外还必须要有极强的愿力；为行此道，他还需要有正确的精神与心理力量，尤其是取得成就之智慧。

真如是另一要点。它被分为十种：

（1）遍行真如。真如遍及一切、无所不在，为二空所揭示。

（2）最胜真如。真如于一切法为最胜，因此称之为最胜真如。

（3）胜流真如。“流”指教法之流传。

（4）无摄受真如。真如不为“我”或法所摄受。

（5）无别真如。真如中无生死涅槃之区别。

（6）无染净真如。真如之性为根本清净，而非染污之后再加以洁净。

（7）法无别真如。关于真如之教法或在各派之中有所不同，然而在根本上是没有区别的。

（8）不增减真如。如果祛除了任何染污或者添附了任何圆满清净之物，真如不增亦不减。

（9）智自在所依真如。证得了真如，就可以无碍了得一切法之智自在。

（10）业自在等所依真如。证得了真如，就可以成就一切神通。

真如为一，却又因其不同特质被分为十。这种十分法或许代表了一种典型的印度思维方式，它受到自韦陀时代的献祭仪式等影响，对细节极度看重。其精致入微之处实在不同凡响。

37

通过对于人认识过程的分析，可以将识分为八支。因为识完全基于缘起，在这一理论中并无特别深奥费解之处。我们可以假设宇宙之中有一基本准则，如在《梨俱韦陀》(Ṛg-Veda) 第一颂中所提到的火。如果一切因缘具备的话，点燃一根火柴就可以产生火——就是这么简单。然而唯识理论的特别目的在于祛除覆被于人对于法“我”之执着上的双重遮蔽。在云的遮蔽消散之后，太阳的光辉就会出现；在祛除了遮蔽之后，大智慧就可以完全展现出它的光芒了。成佛之路应该是直接而顺遂的。智慧不同于识，然而智慧完全依赖于识。在无漏状态中，一个人的识是微弱的，而智慧则是强大的；在有漏状态中则与之相反。为了证悟，我们自然需要将识整体转化为智慧。智慧是一种知识，但它却没有遮蔽的作用，可称之为大觉(Mahābodhi)，有四分。

凡人分很多种，其中的主要区分在于，出生时阿赖耶识中是否有无漏种子，也就是说，是否有成为佛或阿罗汉的先天可能。因为种姓制度在古印度的流行，故而这一点被讨论了无数次。这一制度根深蒂固，似乎可以抵挡任何激进或温和的攻击。印度民族的英雄罗摩（Rama）不得不砍下在苦行（tapasya）中的首陀罗（śūdra）圣者的头颅，因为他见到这位低种姓者做出了只有婆罗门才能做出的行为时感到了耻辱。[63] 在这方面，佛教不分种姓而允许所有人都加入僧伽，是更为进步的。这也意味着人的本性由善法的种子决定，所有人都可以成佛。然而善种子也成为佛教教义中一个常常遭受攻击的薄弱环节。

因为大觉的种子存在于人的阿赖耶识中，我们应当悉心培育使之成长。只要种子还被深重的无明所遮覆，它们就不能顺利地成长。我们可以凭胜义之力剖开这一遮蔽；如果无明的遮蔽分崩离析了，大觉就会出现，生长，并恒久地兴盛下去。

大觉分四种；这种分类只是一个比喻，此四分并不是分类，而只是因为其相应的精神状态而被区分对待。第一种为“大圆镜智”（ādarśajñānaṃ）。智慧就像镜子，它没有“我”，没有执持者与被执持物，也没有主宾之分。

63. 在《罗摩衍那》（*Rāmayāna*）中，首陀罗修行者商部伽（Śambūka）违反了首陀罗种姓不能修习苦行的规定而进行修行，导致一个婆罗门之子死去。作为国王的罗摩砍下了商部伽的头颅之后，婆罗门之子也复活了。Vālmīki, and Hari P. Shastri, *The Ramayana of Valmiki*, London: Shanti Sadan, 1952–59, vol. 3: 580–585.

镜智的内在本性与外在表现都是清净而离于一切染污的。因为其含有一切完备的善种子，因此可称之为“圆”。因为它可以不受时间和空间的限制，反映心中生成的种种外物影像，所以它被喻为反射万物的圆镜。它是第八识自有漏化为无漏之果。

第二种为平等性智（samatājñānaṃ）。此智认为一切法、自他、一切有情都是平等的，并以大悲观之。此即菩萨根据不同地（bhūmi）所显现之智慧。它立于无住处涅槃（Apratiṣṭhitanirvāṇaṃ）或者说为智慧慈悲所共同揭示的真如中。平等性智乃为将第七识化为无漏所成就者。

第三种为妙观察智（pratyavekṣaṇājñānaṃ）。智在观察中与一切法之自相和共相成就因缘。妙观察智了知一切陀罗尼之德，并显现人之各色行为，降下法雨，使人心中欢喜。此乃为将第六识化为无漏所成就者。

第四种为成所作智（kṛtyānuṣṭhanajñānaṃ）。为利益一切众生，菩萨根据其原初之大愿产生种种化身并成就种种事业。此大愿即愿世间一切众生皆能证悟，地狱不空，誓不成佛。此乃为将前五识各个化为无漏所成就者。

有大觉者即是菩萨。对于凡夫来说，将识之八支化为四智或许不可想象。即使它真的发生了，也并非显而易见。就像一根电线中充满了电流，从外表上看不出什么，但其内在却有着很大的分别。虽然识仍然存在，然而其功用或显现却全然改变了。识完全变成了智慧。此时，人已不再是凡人或是超人的状态了，而是已升入佛或菩萨的境界。人之成佛并非不可想象。

38

在唯识理论中，四智与佛境界中的三身紧密相关。首先是法身（Dharmakāya）。在这里“身”应该被理解为一种集合物或者说蕴。大牟尼（Mahāmuni）因成就静默殊胜法，也可称之为法身，但这只是一个颂词。在这里法身指的是一切如来的真实清净法身，是一种完美的抽象状态，没有任何外在的形式，其中含藏着无限恒有之德，却不能被言语思维所理解。作为殊胜诸法的集合，如来在取得第一大圆镜智时就成就了法身，也可称之为自性身（Svabhāvakāya）。

其次是报身（Saṃbhogakāya）。所报之对象是由如来所享有的法之悦乐，此悦乐也为他所化现的净土中之十地菩萨所享受。此身为智慧之集合，由第二智平等性智所显现。

最后为化身（Nirmāṇakāya）。化身意为如来因所集聚之功德而化现为不同世界中之有情众生。化身可在任意一处出现，为利益他人而教授佛法。这是由第三妙观察智及第四成所作智所成就。

上面我们简要介绍了识与四智及三身的关系。在古印度，三分是一常常被讨论的话题。基督教中也有三位一体；或许法身在此可被比为圣灵（the Holy Ghost）。在佛教语境中，三身是一种理想状态；寺庙中常有三尊塑像，代表需要顶礼的三身。从文化史的角度来看，将一分为三又将三合为一，或许是在复杂的三身理论成型之前已有的一种社会习俗。大乘佛教常常提到三身，但就本书的目的而言，我们却不必多言。客观地来说，除了传说的佛陀之外，是否真有任何人成就过三身是值得怀疑的。然而佛教徒谈论时间惯常以数亿年计，或许在甚久的将来会有人真能达成此一境地。与之相比，我们地球从成形到如今的时间还是太短了。

39

在前文中，十位论师逐渐修正并构建起了唯识理论的坚实基础。此理论在护法的解读中臻于完善，成了一个组织严密而无可辩驳的理论系统。在护法之后，再无关于唯识的著名论师，然而它却被玄奘传至中国并发扬光大。

这一严密完善的理论系统，即使遭到了其他各宗教以及部派佛教系统的各种攻击，仍屹立不摇。其中最有力的攻击来自大乘佛教内部，即以龙树为首的中观学派。“中道”最早为佛陀所教授；然而佛陀所教的是居于苦行与放逸之间的中道：对肉体的折磨不能解救灵魂，它和无常一样，只能带来肉体的毁灭。龙树所讲的中观则完全是在如有无、生灭、因果同一、始生与死灭两端之间的哲学探讨。

关于龙树有很多研究及译著。著名的苏联学者 W. P. 瓦西里耶夫在十月革命之前就进行了关于龙树的研究。然而龙树根据佛所说法的内容对教法进行的分期或者说他对佛教历史的重构，仍然未引起足够的关注。这一重构在理论上具有足够的说服力，为所有中国佛教学者所认可并接受。佛法被分为四期：首先是四阿含经所讲的有法（sat）；其次是诸般若经（the *Prajñāpāramitā sūtras*）所教授的空性；再次为一切大乘佛经所讲之有与无（asat）；最后是中观理论中对有与无二者之否定。这使得龙树的教法居于最高地位，在二端之平面上将自身理论垂直拔高并超出二端，在此基础上就没有再进一步发展的可能了。

瑜伽行派与中观派之间的争论在那烂陀寺持续了很久。有几位中观派著名论师值得一提。第一位是清辨（Bhavaviveka），他和佛护（Buddhapāla）都是僧伽罗刹的弟子。关于僧伽罗刹的生平我们所知甚少，但他作为一位中观派论师广为人知。在这些历史上的论辩中，佛护使用的方法与我们今天所说的否定法相类。他的论辩仅指出对手的错误而不立己说。然而清辨则不同，他的批判也是建设性的。他以正理论准则来正面表达自己的观点，包含了肯定与否定两方面。他对瑜伽行派关于相的理论的批判主要包括如下三方面：

首先，关于三自性，清辨对依他起性与其他两性究竟是相同还是相异提出了质疑。整体上，法可以被分为两类，染污法与清净法。瑜伽行派认为遍计所执性是染污法，圆成实性则不可染污，是圆满清净法；因为依他起性居于其间，两者皆非，故而并未被提起。清辨认为依他起性与遍计所执性必然是一致的，因为二者皆与圆成实性不同，且皆为染污法。因此，再别立依他起性作为与另外两者相依之性，是重复的且没有必要的。

其次，清辨质疑三性是成立于世俗谛或是胜义谛中。根据瑜伽行派的观点，胜义谛是最胜智慧所行，而最胜智慧所行是一定成立的；三性即是此智慧中之超凡真谛。然而清辨的观点则与之相反，他认为三性只是世俗谛而不存在于胜义谛中。

这一论争自然也就延伸到了如何理解二谛上。一般认为世俗谛是与世间凡人相关，而胜义谛则包含了先天的无分别根本智与后天所证得之最胜智。在此清辨对这一理论也作了修正：他认为只有无分别根本智才是胜义谛的，而后天之智不能算是胜义的，只能与胜义相随。

清辨不曾在那烂陀寺求学，我们可以推测他的观点与数论派和胜论派关系密切。因为他基本上承认心外之物为真有以及物质由原子组成。这些观点都是与唯识学派相悖的。

40

在清辨之后，另一位对瑜伽行派提出批评的学者，是佛护的第三代弟子，名为月称（Candrakīrti）。月称与清辨一样是中观派，但是他甚至对清辨也提出了批评，并和他的祖师佛护一样用否定法进行论证。

龙树所教授的缘起论指的是对四种生（自生、他生、共生，以及无因生）的否定。佛护对这一学说的解读为：如果事物可以自生，那么谈“生”就没有意义，因为所生之物已然在此，不然生的过程就是无穷无尽的。清辨反对这种推理，而月称则支持佛护的看法甚至否定了正理论本身。月称认为，因为中观学说的根本观点是宇宙万物皆无自性，所以正理论也不例外。如果清辨要在正理论中进行三段论证，那么他就必须先肯定自己的理由或例子是有自性的；因此，以三段论解释自性空是自相矛盾的。故为了不造成思维的混乱，即使是正理论也不应当使用。

月称接下来对三性理论中的第一性，遍计所执性，提出了批评。瑜伽行派认为遍计所执性是有自性的，而月称认为，遍计所执性因缘起而生，其自性为空。所以有生的话，就一定没有自性。他也认为瑜伽行派所持之空性理论不够彻底。根据瑜伽行派的观点，如果依他起性之上没有遍计所执性的话，那么它就是空的。〔一个经典比喻是，走夜路的人看见远处的一根绳子而误以为蛇，走近之后才意识到这不是蛇，只是一根绳子；〕[64] 在这一比喻中，消除了的蛇影被理解为空，然而绳子仍是真实存在的。但是月称认为这一比喻所谈的不是自性空，而是他性空。可以成立的空应该是自性空。

月称也对唯识理论提出了批评。唯识理论在以阿赖耶识为根的八识的基础之上特别强调业的作用，人过去所作业的种子被储存在阿赖耶识中，当其成熟时则产生了果报。然而月称认为这只是一种精妙的假设而非事实。业本身并不接续存在。外在的行为或许会消失，但是内在之力则不会，其自性一直处于潜藏的状态中；而在此只有潜藏与显现的区别。在业力消失、业报耗尽之前，它会一直存在，无须为了业及业报的储存设立藏识。我们一旦否定了第八识，其他七识也就被否定了。

另外，瑜伽行派还强调自证分以解释人的记忆。在记忆中人能想起听到或见到之事；而在听到或者见到之时，人能向自己解释所听或见到的为何物，这就是自证。因为有了自证，人才会有自我意识。月称则反对这一

64. 此处为使意思清楚而补充。

观点；他认为同一事物不可能同时既为主体，又为客体，因此，“我”是不能自证的。刀可以切割，手可以触碰；然而刀却不能切割其自身，手心也不能触碰手背。

最后，月称还讨论了心外无物的观点。唯识学派以睡梦为例：人在睡梦中所见的只是心中所造之物，他在醒觉时所见到的事物也是一样的。因此，睡梦与清醒状态只是程度上的区别而已。修行者在大悟之前都不能意识到自己的生命如同长梦。月称也批判了这一观点；他认为在绝对意义上，心与外境是相等的。如果在梦境中物体非真有的话，那么梦中之心也非真有；因此在梦中也必然有实在之物。

这就是月称对唯识理论的主要批评。唯识学派对此并无反驳。或许有人会认为唯识理论终究也并非坚不可摧。后来月称的观点被以相反的顺序进行论证：因为自性为空，一切法皆由因缘生起。这就将中观论点放在了首要地位。

在那烂陀寺，瑜伽行派与中观派之间的论争持续了很多年。玄奘到达那烂陀寺之后，深入了解了各边的观点并有了调和二宗的想法。因此玄奘作《会宗论》三千颂，并得到了戒贤的肯定。此论在一定程度上平息了各派（包括部派佛教在内）之间的激烈争论，然而这一妥协状态是暂时的，自然也是不稳定的。很可惜《会宗论》已佚失，而这些争论也还在继续。一份藏文历史资料中提到，此后在那烂陀寺月称与著名的唯识论师月官（Candragomin）之间有一场长期的公开辩论，这场辩论持续了七年。[65] 一方认为中道指的是无自性，另一方认为中道即是唯识。辩论的观众中有学者，也有村民和牧人；在最后，即使是普通人也了解了这两种教义的一些方面。这场辩论并没有达成最终的一致，然而大致结论为龙树的教法就像药一样，在治愈疾病方面有效，但其中也有毒性；而弥勒所教则是一切有情之仙馔。因此可以说月官在一定程度上取胜了。月官或对唯识理论有一些修订，然而我们并不清楚这场辩论是如何发生的。时间之轮与正法之轮皆滚滚向前，到了 10 世纪末期，随着密教的兴起，二宗都归于了沉寂。[66]

65. 藏族佛教史家布顿（Buston，1290—1364）与多罗那他（Tāranātha，1575—1634）均对月官的生平有所记载。关于藏文史料中月官与月称之间辩论记载的英文翻译及研究，参见 Mark Tatz, "The Life of Candragomin in Tibetan Historical Tradition," *The Tibet Journal*, vol. 7, no. 3 (Autumn 1982), pp.3–22, esp.13–15。

66. 关于密教或密宗佛教最早的文本证据可以追溯至公元 7 世纪，到了 10 世纪末期密教已经发展兴盛，具有一套完备的修习体系。参见 David B. Gray and Ryan Richard Overbey, eds., *Tantric Traditions in Transmission and Translation*, New York: Oxford University Press, 2016, pp.1–5。

41

在略过玄奘《瑜伽师地论》中很多对我们而言不是那么重要的内容之后，还有最后一个话题——涅槃。涅槃不仅在瑜伽行派或者相宗中，甚至在整个佛教中也被认为是生命的最高目标。涅槃有四种：

（1）本来自性清净涅槃。此即圣人内在证得之涅槃；其自性完备清静，不为名言所染污，也不能被指称。它离于一切法、一切分别，如虚空般透明，不生不灭。它与一切法不一亦不异。所有人皆有此含藏无量精微功德的本来自性清净涅槃。它就是自性清净而不离于染污法相之真性或真如。这与佛所教授的一切众生自无始起就居于涅槃之中是相符的。

（2）有余依涅槃。此即离于一切遮蔽烦恼之后证得的真如。虽然遮蔽已经被永久抹去了，但它仍然依于余下的极微之苦，即尚未死灭的人之肉身。这说明了人在证得涅槃之后仍然可以生存。

（3）无余依涅槃。此即离出包括肉身在内的一切遮蔽烦恼之后证得的真如。它跨越了轮回之海，将不会再有来世。

（4）无住处涅槃。此即使得人离出一切知识（甚至包括成为圣者之知识）的真如。证悟者为慈悲与智慧所协助，既不居于生死也不居于涅槃之中，恒常以利益一切众生为事业。其事业在恒常中静默施行，故而也可称之为涅槃。

第一种涅槃潜藏于所有人之中，第二与第三种涅槃可为二乘修行者证得，菩萨道修行者可以证得第二和第四种涅槃，但只有佛才能成就全部四种涅槃。

佛和如来为何还有余依呢？余依只是佛如来所显现之法，事实上并非真有。

因为涅槃是自古以来佛教各派所公认的最高目标，笔者在此处也想加上一些自己的评论。

从文化和历史的角度来看，在印度广泛存在的、由涅槃与轮回相结合而成的这种悲观人生态度，在古代中国是没有的。这些观念伴随着佛教被引入中国。在早期阶段，“涅槃”被误译为“无为”。“无为”是道家哲学中的核心概念，其事实上意为“自然而然”。后来这一错误得到了改正，Nirvāṇa 被音译为“涅槃”。佛教进入中国大约发生在公元前后。我们不能说此前各朝代的中国人比印度人多快乐，然而彼时如涅槃这样悲观的概念还未出现。在古希腊神话中，我们则可以找到一些与涅槃即使并非完全相同，至少也与之类似的观念。西勒努斯（Silenus）在回答弥达斯王（King

Midas）时说："可怜的性命只有一日之人！变迁与苦恼之子！为什么你要强求我告诉你对你来说最好从未听说的东西呢？对你来说最好的东西是遥不可及的——它不曾存在，不将存在，也终究归于虚无！对你来说次好之事，则是早一日死去。"[67]

这就是另一种文化中对涅槃的表达。在希腊神话中有阿波罗（Apollo）奖赏两位为他修建壮丽神庙的建筑师——特洛弗纽斯（Trophonius）和阿伽墨得斯（Agamedes）的故事；[68] 也有两名孝顺的兄弟代替牛亲自为母亲拉车的故事，他们的母亲对神祈祷，神对两兄弟的奖赏是满足他们马上离开人间的愿望。[69] 因为他们想要速速地摆脱俗世，我们可以推测他们将不再会降生人世。这也就是印度所说的涅槃。

涅槃的关键在于是否有轮回。在中国并没有这样的信仰，而在印度—雅利安民族中则很常见。著名的数学家毕达哥拉斯（Pythagoras）就深信轮回。从他所生活的时代（他于公元前 497 年逝世）甚至更早，直到公元 553 年君士坦丁堡（Constantinople）举行的第五次基督教大公会议（Catholic Convention）将轮回定为邪说，轮回信仰持续了足足一千年的时间。如果它不是影响巨大并且产生了不良的后果，那么这一信仰或许就不会被谴责了。即使是在今天，东方的很多民族仍然有此迷信。一位佛教大德去世后，人们常常委婉地在挽词中称他"入了涅槃"。

如果涅槃被认为是人类的最高目标，那么进化就失去了意义。根据智慧的西勒努斯的建议，生命终归是使人厌恶且可悲的，越早脱离它当然就越好。然而结束生命并不是解决方案。如果人们相信业的话，自杀或者安乐死虽然可以终结此生，但却不能终结业：死亡并不是出路。然而涅槃不总是绝望的：大乘佛教认为涅槃最终是以对事物真相的证悟，或者说是以对万物中共有之真如的认识为基础。修行者需要与众生一起朝着这一目标不断地精进。因此这是一项高上而恒常的追求。这一事业超出了生死，立乎于人世苦难之外。用一种辩证的方法来说，世界的真相是大空，而大空也就是涅槃。故而此世界和涅槃可以被认为是一种真相。只要世界还在运作，对涅槃的追求也就不能停止。普贤（Samantabhadra）菩萨发愿说，地狱不空誓不成佛而入涅槃，这就是所有大乘佛教徒的伟大决心。因此，我们不应当得出尽快结束生命的结论。

67. 西勒努斯在被俘后被带到弥达斯王面前，弥达斯在狩猎之后问西勒努斯，人最想要的是什么。一开始西勒努斯不愿回答，保持沉默，在弥达斯再三强求之后，他才很不情愿地说出了如上一番话。参见 Plutarch, *Plutarch's Morals: Translated from the Greek by Several Hands,* Boston: Little, Brown & Co., 1883, vol.1, pp.326–327。中译或可参考普鲁塔克：《道德论丛》，席代岳译，长春：吉林出版集团有限责任公司，2015。
68. 相传特洛弗纽斯和阿伽墨得斯为阿波罗在特尔斐（Delphi）修建了神庙。神庙完工后，神谕告诉他们可以在六天时间里尽情为所欲为，到了第七天，他们最大的愿望将被满足。二人照做了；第七天，人们发现他们死去了。
69. 克琉比斯（Kleobis）和比同（Biton）两兄弟是赫拉的祭司库狄普（Cydippe）的儿子。库狄普在前往赫拉神庙参加节日的途中，牛车不堪重负，两兄弟就拉着车走完了全程。库狄普向赫拉祈祷，希望赫拉能赐予两兄弟最好的礼物。于是赫拉满足了她的愿望，让两兄弟在睡梦中死去了。参见 Herodotus, A. D. Godley and Loeb Classical Library, *Herodotus,* Cambridge, Massachusetts: Harvard University Press, 1981, pp.35, 37。

42

在这样一部枯燥的长篇论述最后，如果再作总结的话就太多余了（何况笔者已经重复了太多）。然而笔者或许可以再于整体上评论一二。

对唯识理论的最终分析说明，它仍然是一种简单的、有局限的心理分析与泛印度信仰体系的结合。将宇宙分为六界或六道并非佛教的创举；基督教中也承认有天堂和地狱。在人道之下是阿修罗道。在韦陀时代，阿修罗（asura，字面意为“无光者”）一词并不含贬义，但它逐渐变为了指称一种类似于鬼怪的存在。地狱道之外还有饿鬼道；饿鬼道自成为一个世界，没有人能够给出关于这些饿鬼的确切描述，他们在六道系统中也并不重要。唯识理论中关于业的理论值得称道，然而业在印度教中也存在。业是一种联系因果的机制，很难称之为宗教信仰，其中不论善恶，并没有任何神秘主义或者神力的原素。相对而言，大乘佛教中的相宗仍然是诸派中最为进步的。正是因为其理性，所以，相宗对中国学者来说最具吸引力并持续了千年之久。

当今世界上的很多国家都处于变革时期，许多重大而突然的社会变化正在发生。在当代社会中，一名无神论者当然可以将古代的信仰视为迷信，一名自认正统者也会将其他宗教视为异端。但我们不应该轻易在整体上否认或谴责某一宗教，而是应当细心检视我们所继承的过去：如果有用的话，则取之为我所用；如果没有用的话，也应该细心地将其保存下来，它或许会对后人有用处，而这些用处是现在所不能预知的。这在经济上很容易理解：若我们要将长城夷为平地（这在今天是无用且可悲之事），所耗之功不会比修建长城更少，那为什么不将其保存为历史遗产或是对过去文明的纪念呢？在近年的修复与重建时期，人们意识到了保存传统文化的重要性，也对历史遗产采取了正面态度。

中国社会在历史上对宗教是宽容的。宪法中也明确规定公民享有宗教信仰自由，这是科学社会主义在真正的民主精神指导下的先进政策。

常常有人误会在唯物主义为主导的国家，所有唯心主义的观点必然会被废弃。这种误会使人感到遗憾。作为我国最高指导原则的马克思主义深刻而广博，它在根本上绝非故步自封而容不下任何拓展；马克思主义也从未要求全然废弃传统。因为错误信息与误解所造成的惑乱是我们这一时代的顽疾。中国曾在短时期内为这一顽疾所苦扼，然而很快就痊愈了。如今社会条件在逐步自行改善：绝大多数的佛教寺庙都被重建或者修复，道观与孔庙也是如此。佛教的三藏保存完善，并且出现了一份新的增订版；道藏也是如此。没有任何国家能够承受失去其文化遗产宝藏的损失。这些宝藏不仅仅是物质的，也是精神的；其中一个微不足道的证据就是这一唯识理论。唯识宗被认为是绝对唯心主义或客观唯心主义的代表之一，对它的研究仍在进行，并在此展现给了英文读者。

本书只是一篇阐释之作，并无任何新知。它就像沙中淘金一样，需要耗费很多无用的时间与精力，其结果也不能说完全使人满意。这种研究的一项原则，就是要知道如何除去在历史上层累起来的无用之糟粕，而揭示其原初之菁华。只有这样，我们才能公正看待或者说正确评价古代印度与中国的思想。

或许每一个有翻译经验的人都知道，要在英语中为另一语言（在此是梵文）的词汇找到其完美对应是很困难的。只有依靠古代的汉文注疏，我们才能大致理解梵文原文的确切含义。然而英语并非笔者的母语，故而这一结果也远非完美。如果有什么错误的话，皆为笔者的过失，因为他是作为一名学者独立工作的。博闻的读者诸君若有任何意见或建议，笔者也将无上欢迎。

On the Theory of Pure Consciousness

INTRODUCTION

From a historical point of view, ancient Greece, ancient India, and ancient China were the three lands that brought forth various schools of philosophy, original and genuine and independent, which shaped the destiny of humanity. In a sense both oriental and occidental civilization in modern times would be unthinkable without the philosophies that underlie them. In the last century the development of continental philosophy since Kant was figuratively described as the nostalgia and longing of the German race for the ancient glory of Athens, to which there was no way of return except by way of a magnificent rainbow that resembled a bridge overarching the bygone ages which, however, could not be trodden. Taking the separate histories of these lands into consideration, we find many lacunae existing in each, and in spite of the research work done over many centuries, there is little likelihood that they will be filled in. Many schools of philosophy together with their important works have been irretrievably lost, leaving only uncertain dates, vague accounts, and the empty names of their masters. Such is the case in the West, and such is also the case in the East. It is especially so in India, because in India history has never occupied an important place. Happy indeed is the race innocent of its past and therefore devoid of any psychological burden or hindrance on its path of progress, but that innocence has always proved to be disastrous or calamitous.

History is certainly important, because records of human achievement at their high peaks are preserved therein. The study of successes and failures offers salutary lessons which can be of immense value to the present and future generations. According to the late Chinese Neo-Confucian master Ma Yifu, only two main lines of knowledge exist in this world: one is philosophy, or metaphysics in his terminology, and the other is history.[1] No matter how ramified and specialized all the natural and social sciences in our modern world may be, they all fall into these two categories. Generally speaking, India is famous for the former, while China is renowned for the latter. We have in China our twenty-five official histories and numerous specific histories from all periods, and India has her six main schools of post-Vedic philosophy and various doctrines of miscellaneous religious sects. But unfortunately not everything left to us in history is valuable or useful, and sometimes the persistence of things carried down in history can even be harmful. Such is also the case with philosophy. As we prepare to step into the twenty-first century, we see things proceeding forward with marvellous and unprecedented speed and putting forth an outlook

1. See Ma Yifu's book *Lectures* (woodblock-printing in 1940s).

totally different from the scope of the past. It behooves us always to take the position of Janus looking forwards and backwards at the same time. Only that can greatly facilitate our progress.

Nowadays a very peculiar but perhaps not incidental phenomenon has appeared in the area of culture. In recent years the term "metaphysics" in Chinese has taken on such a bad connotation even in daily parlance among ordinary people that it is always used to denote something dishonest, deceptive, shilly-shally and flippant. The vulgarisation of this word seems to have taken place over the past three decades. Members of the older generation may well recall that its original meaning was kept when the word was first translated into Chinese, using this statement, which contains its exact equivalent, from the *Book of Changes* (*I-Ching*): "What is above form — i.e. superphysical — is called 'Tao' (or Truth)." When Andronicus first compiled the philosophical works of Aristotle and placed them *behind* ("meta-") the writings on *physics*, he had nothing deprecatory in mind. The denotation and connotation of "metaphysics" was not what it is now. The word also has nothing to do with scholasticism of the Middle Ages, which is often not highly appreciated. The mistake might have been due to certain confusion with the word "sophistry". In any case the original sense must be restored and a distinction made between the earlier and later meanings.

The wrong use of a single word may not be of any great consequence. It is mentioned here merely because of what it implies, which is issued from a very realistic view of life, denouncing things too highly intellectual, too subtle or abstract, beyond the grasp of average mentality. Such a view is prevalent among the masses because common people live without much abstraction or even without thinking. This seems to have resulted from the thriving of materialism. But materialism, especially historical materialism, affords the scope for the far-reaching activity of the intellect, is itself a profound philosophy and, so far as commonly understood, it is never obscurantist. We may say its view of life and its view of the world are both realistic and rational, since it treats everything objectively as it is, or, to be colloquial, it prefers to call a spade a spade. To see everything in its proper place, to appreciate the true value of any great phenomenon against its temporal and social background, with reference to its economic basis, class pertinency, and other factors, thus seeing all in the light of historical materialism, is precisely the course lately taken by most of the intellectuals among us. Under such circumstances it is natural that the masses should err in understanding an ancient term.

In a land where metaphysics preponderates in culture, such a mistake would scarcely happen. India is the only land on earth that has made its sacrifices and kept the altar fire burning throughout millennia in the worship of spiritual truths. Great saints followed one another in succession, among whom Gautama Buddha the Enlightened One made a great spiritual conquest in the East. The tradition was broken every now and then, but always connected again by other saints and sages, such as the great masters of Vedānta philosophy, culminating in Śri Aurobindo in modern times. Sometimes one wonders whether the existence or survival of such a vast mass of humanity would be possible without these great men. They were called Avatars in India, or incarnations of gods in human form. To atheists this may be merely a eulogistic appellation. But their necessity and their contributions, which were too great, beyond praise, brought about their deification in the psychology of common people.

In view of the present state of affairs it is highly regrettable to say that India is not in good condition owing to its internal strife, and all religions seem to have done her more harm than good. But in appreciating the true value of a people, one should not limit his scope only to the present. One should extend his vision to its long past and to a longer future, just as when one wishes to have a complete view of a certain landscape, he should station himself at a very high place. However low a people may have sunk temporarily in the eyes of the world, their past glories and contributions to humanity cannot be denied. An awakening to the great past means the promise of a great future. The new phoenix that appears from the ashes of its former self after purification by fire may be even more beautiful than before. Therein lies the great hope of the Indian subcontinent.

If scholarship does mean to do something of real service for humanity, then the task of scholars should be to go deep into the past in preparation for a great future. Otherwise there would be not much significance in all their laborious efforts in research. What follows is the exploration into the past of a great religion, an exposition of only one of its prominent doctrines with regard to its formation, its strength and weakness, and the causes of the decline of the religion as a whole, all viewed in the light of critical philosophy. The study cannot be complete owing to certain limitations, but the main lines are presented hereby. At certain places this study gives only brief indications, and ample room has been left for further research.

1

There were periods in history in which cultural exchanges between China and India flourished. This relationship lasted for a thousand years since the Christian era, interrupted by long intervals. Those vacant stretches were due to external causes, and there was never any essential antagonism between these two peoples. But it was, so to say, one-way traffic, because there was only the flow of Buddhism from India to China eastwards. This religion came first indirectly through Central Asia called in China the Western Regions, and later directly through other routes by land or by sea. Passing through endless hardships, people travelled to and from both lands merely for the sake of one thing — Buddhist Dharma. Among the diverse historical and sometimes legendary records, the story of the translation of a Buddhist classic dictated by an ambassador of the Great Yui Chi tribe, named I Tzen, to a Chinese scholar named Chin Lu in the second year B.C., marking the inception of Buddhism in the Far East, is most reliable. Many other historical accounts about earlier dates may be discarded.[2] Chinese Taoism was also introduced to southern and western lands upon requests by their kings or rājās for the translation of its texts on several occasions, but these made little impression. The famous Taoist work, *Lao Tze*, was rendered into Sanskrit on at least two occasions, but no trace of it can be found today.

This cultural relationship did much to promote mutual understanding between the two peoples. Chinese Buddhists actually called themselves Śakyās, an appellation that has existed from ancient times till today, thereby separating themselves not only from the patriarchal society but also from their own nationality. Expressions as "our forebrother Kāśyapa in olden days..." etc. are all too often found in Chinese Buddhist writing. These were usually couched in a dignified tone and particular style showing respect for and familiarity with their friends in neighboring India. This is understandable because all Buddhists, Indian or Chinese, were fundamentally otherworldly, as they lived in a spirit of asceticism believed to be outside secularity though never outside society, and cultivated a separate brotherhood of their own.

2. For this the reader is expected to refer to the *History of Chinese Buddhism* written by the late professor Tang Yongtong (1893—1964) which has been translated into English. There everything concerning this subject is treated in detail.

The relationship had fruitful results, one of which was the thousand year translation of Buddhist scriptures. This is a special subject connected with Buddhist bibliography, which is too big to be treated here. It is safe to say that the work of translation is the life of this religion. Generally we speak of the four great masters of translation, namely Kumārajīva (344–413), Xuan Zang (602–664), Yi Jing (635–713) and Amoghavajra (705–774) — one Westerner, two Chinese, and one Indian. The work was carried out by a team of learned monks and scholars each with his special duty, forming a huge organization somewhat like a modern seminar. This sort of team work was highly efficient, it is worthwhile to look into its organization.

The assembly was presided over by a Master who orally translated the Sanskrit text. His words were noted down by several Recorders. There were then the Interpreters of speech, the Verifiers of original Sanskrit texts, the Examiners of meaning in Sanskrit, the Writers or Wordsmiths, and the Revisers of the whole translation, all of whom formed into small groups and gathered together in a big hall, apart from a number of scribes and clerks. There were even Editors whose sole responsibility was to ensure the correct writing of Chinese words. Every meeting was formally opened by the Chanters and attended by a Guardian who was usually a great minister of the royal court. All the disciples attended the meeting as listeners. Strict qualifications were demanded of the members of the team, and as the work proceeded in a regular and orderly manner, its results were usually flawless and good.

This sort of collective work seems worthy of recommendation even today. Yet China does not claim the invention of such a method. The best example can be found in ancient Greece. The Greek version of the Old Testament, made about 270 B.C. and known as the Septuaginta, is the result of the collective effort of seventy-two scholars. Another example is the King James version of the Bible in English, which engaged the intellectual labour of fifty-four eminent Biblical scholars for four years or more (1607–1610). Rarely can such a gigantic task as the translation of a sacred book be undertaken single-handedly by one person. Even Luther had his famous assistant Melanchthon to help in shaping the *September Bible*, 1522. But the translation of Sanskrit texts into Chinese was not limited to a single book which, however complex and voluminous, could be brought to a certain standardization. A continuous stream or rather a torrent of sacred scriptures from India kept pouring into China over the centuries. A very modest estimate of the voluminosity of the Buddhist scriptures now extant in Chinese is about six hundred times the length of the Bible, both the Old and New Testaments included. It is a life's work to read over all these works, and this is not advisable. Even among the great past and contemporary masters, few have accomplished this feat. Yet we must have certain definite conceptions of the literature as a whole.

2

As is well known the bulk of Chinese Buddhist scriptures comprises three "baskets" or "stores" (*Tripiṭaka*), and these are Sūtra, Vinaya and Abhidharma. In the traditional Indian view, a sūtra is a short text or a collection of aphorisms, such as the famous Brahma-sūtra, but the Chinese Buddhist Sūtras can also be large works containing many chapters with numerous sections. A sūtra may run into many volumes, like the *Mahāprajñāpāramita-sūtra* which has six hundred volumes. There are short ones like the *Hṛdaya-sūtra* belonging to the same school but perfect in itself covering only one page like a small Upanishad. These are the extremes. Generally sūtras consist of several volumes, called fascicles, and are believed to be preachings of the Buddha in his own words. The vinayas are the rules of conduct and monastic regulations, believed to be the words of Buddha committed to memory by his disciples and repeated aloud after his *Nirvāṇa*. The Abhidharma *Śāstras* are the treatises explaining the doctrines, supposedly also preached by Buddha, but written by followers in later ages. A most recent catalogue of the *Tripiṭaka* by Lu Chen (1896–1989), Director of the Institute of Research on Inner Knowledge, published in 1980, gives a clear idea of the whole. The present writer takes the liberty to draw upon this authoritative source and to put it into English as follows:

Sūtras: (total 688 works in 2,790 fasc.)	
Ratnakūṭa Section	0001–0249
Prajña Section	0250–0326
Avataṃsaka Section	0327–0394
Nirvāṇa Section	0395–0424
Āgama Section	0425–0688
Vinaya: (total 210 works in 879 fasc.)	0689–0898
Abhidharma: (total 196 works in 1,094 fasc.)	0899–1094
Dubious works	1095–1113

Apart from these three collections there are the Tantric works which must be also included in the *Tripiṭaka*, thus

Tantrics: (total 388 works in 639 fasc.)	1114–1497
Dubious works (total 7 works in 26 fasc.)	1498–1504

These are only the Chinese translations. But the contribution from the Chinese side to this great storehouse is considerable. It includes treatises, commentaries, sub-commentaries, dialogues, histories, lexicons, catalogues and other miscellaneous works of the six or seven principal sects that were gradually formed through the ages amounting to 582 works in 4,172 fascicles. This catalogue is less sophisticated than that of the Japanese Taisho edition, but equally comprehensive and reasonable. The history of the carving of wooden printing blocks and the making of new editions and their distribution in itself forms a separate subject of research. A masterful study of subject was done by the great master Ouyang Jian[3] (1871–1944) a half century ago.

The above figures give only a faint glimpse of the voluminosity of the *Tripiṭaka* as it exists in Chinese. The Buddhist translations in Tibetan offer excellent supplementary material. The Kanjur collection (Beijing edition) embraces the first two piṭakas in 1,055 works, and the third piṭaka is included in the Tanjur collection, comprising 3,962 works. Other translations in Mongolian and Manchurian languages are equally bulky and important, but they are comparatively less referred to nowadays.

It seems to be meaningful here to remind scholars of the present generation, Indian or Chinese, of those monumental achievements of their forerunners ages ago. If the current view is still limited to certain schools of Vedānta philosophy, these achievements give us reason to expect that view to be extended and enlarged. By exploring this religion that has grown almost obsolete in India, the scope of current thinking can be greatly magnified. In reading the *History of Indian Philosophy* by the late world-famous professor S. Dasgupta one can oftentimes not keep from feeling a slight regret that he was limited to Pali and Sanskrit materials for his discussion of Mahāyāna doctrines; Pali and Sanskrit texts have almost none of the necessary references to Chinese sources. Other European writers on Buddhism have generally been under the same limitation, and in reading their works we always have the same feeling that something is lacking. Even the great spiritual master Śri Aurobindo, said by some to be a Plato of the modem age, who had profound and comprehensive knowledge about ancient India, ancient Greece and the Graeco-Roman world in general, knew little about ancient China. The fault lies with us Chinese because we have not made ourselves known. Otherwise in our traditions there is a wealth of knowledge worth knowing, judged by world cultural standards, ancient or modem. Yet during the past three or four decades Indian pundits in collaboration with Chinese scholars have done much work in the restoration, or rather re-translation, of lost texts that were preserved in Chinese, and along with the discoveries of ancient Sanskrit manuscripts, we can expect to see some new light from this Dharma, the teachings of Gautama Buddha.

3. *Ouyang Dashi Yiji, A Collection of Posthumous Works of Ouyang the Master*, Xinwenfeng Press, Taibei, 1976.

3

A flower transplanted to new soil far from its native place is likely to change many of its characteristics if it grows at all. Genetically it is the same flower, but its rate of growth, its foliage, its flowering time and its fruits may change, and sometimes it may change so much that the original species is barely recognizable, like the Chinese rose and chrysanthemum. Nothing can withstand the forces of evolution and transformation in Nature. Likewise, Buddhism, as it was introduced to China over so many centuries, underwent considerable change. In the handling of such a multiform and protean subject, a certain reasonable skepticism and reservation in the attitude of research is always advisable.

Great religious leaders of the world have always a certain charisma or mythic aura surrounding them. Certain Western scholars have even doubted the existence of Jesus Christ the person. About the historicity of Gautama Buddha there is not much doubt. The prince of Suddhodana named Sarvartha Siddha fled from his palace at the age of twenty-nine and donned the garment of an ascetic, practised austerity, attained enlightenment at the age of thirty-five, preached his own convictions for more than forty-five years and entered *Parinirvāṇa* at about eighty in Kusinara (circa 486 B.C.) — these things are generally agreed upon among the three Vehicles in both the northern and southern traditions, and are believable. But soon we encounter the *jātakas* or stories of the Buddha's birth. *Jātakas* must be taken as they are — fine pieces of classical literature rich in imagination and important for anthropological and philological studies, but not to be taken as authentic history.

Now, we may argue in this way without falling into sophistry, saying that it matters not much even if Jesus the person existed at all, or the one crucified was the supposed Rex Judaerum or someone else, or the crucifixion was done with ropes or nails. What matters to us is his teachings or gospels. Here philosophy, especially ethics, outweighs the dry and barren history. But in Buddhism we find two distinct systems side by side: Hīnayāna the Lesser Vehicle and Mahāyāna the Greater Vehicle, somewhat like Catholicism and Protestantism in Christianity but without any bellicosity between them. And, from the very beginning of this religion there were the northern and southern traditions. And, what is remarkable, all the scriptures as listed above were heaped up one by one over the centuries, but none of them can be credited with perfect authenticity as being the original words of

Gautama Buddha himself. This may be compared with an example like the Bhagavad Gītā. We know its author as Vyāsa, but there must be interpolations in it not done by him. Most probably not all of the text we read now could have been spoken by Lord Kṛṣṇa on the battlefield of Kurukṣetra. But in this case all the Buddhist works are attributed to Buddha. They were not produced in one age, but came successively to light in different times.

Thus we have to suppose that all the Buddhist texts were forged by wise men in India, developing the doctrines propounded by Buddha. But what then is genuine and original Buddhism? This is still a subject of research. Answers in certain broad outlines may be given, but skepsis remains.

It is universally known that the worship of Jesus Christ as the son of God preceded the cult of Virgin Maria and other Saints; likewise the worship of Buddha was antecedent to that of many Bodhisattvas and finally of many Buddhas. This was a natural turn from monotheism to polytheism or from simplicity to multiplicity, as the German philosopher A. Schopenhauer once remarked, because the object of worship by the common people could not be permanently confined to one person or one idol alone. There is reason to believe that Mahāyāna was a changed form of the original Buddhism which, owing to both external and internal circumstances, underwent transformation. "All the Mahāyāna scriptures are the genuine and original sayings of Buddha" — this is a thesis held by every Buddhist since the introduction of the scriptures into China. And this was argued out by many famous masters. But the more they argued, the more they proved that it was merely hypothetical. In fact, only Mahāyāna Buddhism flourished in China ever since its introduction, though Hīnayāna texts were also introduced and translated. Genetically it was still tbe same Buddhism, but its outward forms and newly acquired characteristics and gradually modelled social conventions led it farther away from the original. At this point historical materialism may have its say. Because Dharma or religion always monitors and regulates life and can even be considered as part of life, and since the living conditions in different lands cannot be the same, so spontaneously the religion must change, adjusting itself to new environments and different circumstances, although its core or main principles may remain unchanged. Moreover, as Buddhism entered China, it was confronted at once with two great systems, both spiritual in nature, viz. Confucianism and Taoism. The struggle between them, especially their fight for power in the imperial court, has come down in history. This is a subject dealt with in all histories of religions. All in all, Buddhism has had to comply, to conform, to struggle for existence, for development and for permanence by absorption of foreign elements, by purging certain of its own elements, by amalgamation with other beliefs or even superstitions, in a word, by transforming itself. So it is reasonable to say that there was an Indian Buddhism and there was a Chinese Buddhism. The former in its Mahāyāna form gradually declined since the tenth century, yet survived along with Tantricism for nearly two hundred years until it became extinct. The latter still exists today.

At this juncture a brief remark must be made about the difference between the Lesser Vehicle (Hīnayāna) and the Greater Vehicle (Mahāyāna). Both were part of Buddhism, and the latter came out of the former with Nāgārjuna as its first patriarch. It was not Nāgārjuna who invented another system of his own called afterwards Mahāyāna, it was that its thoughts and beliefs fermented for nearly one hundred years before this master brought it to a certain systematization. Nāgārjuna's dates are uncertain: most probably he lived in the third century A.D. His works total 118 titles in Tibetan translation, among which there were nineteen in the form of *gāthās* meant to be chanted, fifty-one commentaries and elucidations on esoteric teachings, and forty-eight works on exoteric doctrines, together with other miscellaneous writings. Of these eleven are duplicated in Chinese translations. As to the existence of two masters with the same name Nāgārjuna, a theory held by Wassilijew, this is still an unsettled question awaiting further research.

The difference between these two Vehicles is significant. First of all there is the difference in aims. A follower of the lesser aims at becoming an *Arhat* who remains everlastingly in a state without birth and death that is *Nirvāṇa*. The greater has becoming a Buddha as its goal, which means not one's personal emancipation from all miseries and sufferings of life through entering into *Nirvāṇa*, but the salvation of all beings without regard to oneself. Next, there is the difference in doctrine. The lesser advocates that whatever said by the Buddha is real and hence all dharmas are real. The greater negates the reality of all in the universe, including oneself and all dharmas, and there remains only the Void which is real. The latter was also promulgated by the Āryasthāvirās, a branch pertaining to Hīnayāna, explaining that the voidness of dharma is the same as the voidness of *rūpa* or form, yet its explanation was not comprehensive. The real existence of all in the universe is denied in Mahāyāna thought, what is meant is that all is like *māyā* or illusion, and hence unreal. Such is the self-nature of dharma. Neither existence nor non-existence could be affirmed, which is how Nāgārjuna cut his Middle Path. Thirdly there is the difference in practice. The lesser recommends celibacy and renunciation. The greater does not recommend these practices to society, and its supporters in the initial stages were mainly householders. Finally the greater was further divided into three vehicles: the minor or Śrāvakayāna, the medium or Pratyekabuddhayāna and the greatest or Bodhisattvayāna. Many images worshipped in Buddhist temples are Bodhisattvas or Enlightened Ones, which are not prevalent in Hīnayāna, much less in the original sectarian Buddhism.

4

Thus the whole outlook of Indian Buddhism changed in China. Rules of conduct had to be changed because the living conditions were different. Many modifications had to be made in the *Śīla* (rules) due to the new circumstances. Vinaya further developed itself as time advanced as a separate sect in China with Dao Xuan (596–667) as its master. Among the various schools of Vinaya, only the Dharmagupta-vinaya was highly appreciated and generally adopted, with its 250 rules for *Bhikṣus* or monks and 348 for *Bhikṣuṇīs* or nuns. Dao Xuan was also famous for written works in which he finally resorted to the theory of Pure Consciousness as a philosophical support for his commentaries. This sect stood diametrically opposite to the sect of Tantricism. Normally the books on Vinaya, e.g. the *Rules of Mahāsaṃghikās*, are not shown to common people. They are kept classified in monasteries. We see nowadays a great store of materials for research on psychiatry in them.

A diversity of other sects also flourished, giving new impetus to the systematization of all the works of the *Tripiṭaka*. The Tian Tai Sect (Tian Tai being the name of a famous mountain) with its master Zhi Yi (538–597) taught Śamathavipaśyanāni or meditation, and held *Saddharmapuṇḍarika-sūtra* as its principal holy scripture. The Xian Shou Sect (name of its master), with Fa Zang (643–712) as its leader used only *Buddhāvataṃsaka-mahāvaipulya-sūtra* as its principal text. The Ci En Sect (lit. "the mother's love", name of a great monastery built by the third emperor of the Tang dynasty in commemoration of his mother) headed by Kui Ji (632–682) expounded mainly the theory of Pure Consciousness. The Jing Tu Sect (Sukhāvatī or "Pure Land") was first established by Hui Yuan (334–416) and afterwards enlarged by Tan Luan (476–542), with its followers worshipping only Amitābha Buddha — reciting the name of Amitābha all the time just as some Hindus do with their "Aum" — and having only its *Amitābha Sūtras*. Apart from all these noted sects there was another Dhyāna Sect, known as Chan Buddhism, which, though it venerated Bodhidharma (?–526) as its first patriarch in China, was far diverged from any Indian source, and formed almost a separate religion of its own which was again ramified into a northern and a southern school. There were also other minor sects that sprouted from these main ones and formed under the influence of either Confucianism or Taoism but mostly from both. They need not be treated here. It may be asked: as all these constitute

Buddhism, which represents the orthodox religion that one may follow?

Throughout the past ages many learned men entered the Buddhist order through this or that sect, and commentary after commentary on the translated texts of the piṭakas were written and heaped up and preserved. Through these endless writings, thoughts of other philosophies entered into this religion, all heterodox in a sense yet never rejected. There was oftentimes the tendency toward an amalgamation of the so-called three religions, though Confucianism could scarcely be called a religion. Taoism is a religion, but it has its philosophy standing apart from all its religious aspects. Confucianism or Neo-Confucianism of the Song dynasty and Ming dynasty has some very faint and distant resemblance to a religion in the modern sense. Traces of the effort made for the fusion of these three into one, though never successful, are often evident. It may be due to the fact that seekers of truths sometimes had glimpses or visions of this or that minor or major spiritual revelation first, and later on found and employed technical terms from these well established systems to express the same thing, and since identifications and equivalents could be found, a union was always thought to be possible. There must be universal spiritual truths in existence, just as there are material truths, that can be identified in essence but not necessarily in outward forms. But here again is a social factor that a scholar of Marxism would take into consideration. It is that the ruling classes of many dynasties always favoured such a union. A religion that claims to have millions of followers is also a great social force that cannot be ignored. The ruling dynasties could not abandon that, and further even craved for its support. In a negative sense, it was an attempt to avoid too much conflict between these religions, while positively it was to stabilize their own sovereign rule with the help of all three systems. Hence both conformism and eclecticism were appreciated and patronized. This imaginary union of the three systems furthered the transformation and the loss of identity of each, but on the whole, it was not of great consequence.

If we admit that Chinese Buddhism differed from its Indian original, as it certainly did, then we should not fail to notice another salient feature within Chinese Buddhism itself. Usually when a man enters into the Buddhist order, he has to pass through a certain period of preparation. This has been the practice in most religions ever since the ancient Greeks with their period of purification prior to their entering into the Mysteries. A Buddhist has to live several years in a monastery before he accepts the complete set of Vinaya and becomes an ordained Bhikṣu or monk. But in China there were believers in Buddhism who have done great services to the religion without first passing through any ritual of initiation. These were the *upāsakas* and *upāsikās* (man and woman lay believers). The *upāsakas* were generally householders, great intellectuals, distinguished members of society and influential persons in officialdom. They spontaneously formed a society or a class in society, and their achievements were considerable. To a certain extent the monastic order could not flourish or sometimes even subsist without their support. There was also a simple ritual to be performed for becoming a *upāsaka* or *upāsikā*, but that was usually not much heeded. In fact anybody can style himself as a *upāsaka* if he likes. Prominent *upāsakas* like Yang Wenhui (1837–1911), Ouyang Jian and their contemporaries like Mei Guangxi and Li Zhenggang were all great Confucian scholars. It was their effort that brought about a revival and development of Buddhism in this century. One can almost say, *cum grano salis*, that within Chinese Buddhism there is another Buddhism — that of the *upāsakas*. This view may be of some value in the academic field, especially for Western researchers, and it is with this that the present article is concerned.

5

Viewed from the cultural background stated above, it is easy to understand why difficulties would stand in the way of a complete comprehension of this Dharma. As said before, all hinged upon translations. However well versed in classical Chinese literature a scholar might be, he could not understand a Buddhist text if he had not rightly learned it from the beginning. It was as if everything was expressed in another language though the words were the same. Usually he would be perplexed by a number of transliterations. For example, the term *Nirvāṇa*, meaning a state of emancipation without birth and death, becomes the transliterated term *Nie-pan*. Such is the case with many other words like *Prajñā*, *Bodhi*, *Samādhi*, *Tuṣita*, *Yoga*, *Āgama*, etc., all important terms with deep connotations. Moreover, before Xuan Zang's time, i.e. the seventh century, especially at the first stages of the introduction of this religion to China, nothing was standardized. Every translator could just note down the pronunciation in his own dialect. This made the annotations from later dynasties indispensable. On a sidetrack, however, it left abundant materials for modern research on ancient philology, especially concerning changes in phonetics and euphonies.

In this respect Xuan Zang did a great service in bringing about a degree of standardization. His translations were called the "new translations" in contrast to the "old" ones. He set the rule that terms in the following five categories should be kept in transliteration: terms esoteric in meaning, like *Dhāraṇi*; terms with many meanings, like *Bhagavān*; terms denoting objects not found in China, like *jambu* tree; terms traditionally transliterated, like *Anuttara*, *Bodhi*; and finally terms that awake a certain sense of grandeur and respect above ordinary conceptions, like *Buddha*, *Bodhisattva*, etc.

It goes without saying that a native scholar could not immediately understand a Buddhist text because it was a special subject, a line of knowledge beyond his normal ken. Yet ultimately it was not too difficult for him because the language used in translations was far simpler than classical Chinese. And if he were familiar with the "old" translations, it could be so much the easier for him. Now here is a key point to be taken note of. As Xuan Zang did his new translations, he aroused a great turmoil among the conservatives. Orthodox believers who were used to the "old" translations could not tolerate his new corrections. This was a matter not only of language, but also of content. There must have been differences with regard to the original Sanskrit texts, and as history shows, improvements were made in the theories, including those on Voidness, during the several hundred years before Xuan Zang's time. The quarrel and revolt developed to such an extent that finally a royal edict was issued by the imperial court of the Tang dynasty that Xuan Zang should postpone his new translations of works that already had Chinese versions and proceed with works hitherto unknown. Purely from the point of view of the language, we see that the "old" translations were couched in proper expressions, easily understandable and pleasant to read, and suited to the Chinese mentality. Hence they are still very popular today. Yet the "new" translations done by Xuan Zang were more exact, neat, much closer to the original and unique, but sometimes just readable and without much regard to style. So in the academic field only the new translations are used for comparison and relied upon today whenever any Sanskrit original text is discovered and examined. It is interesting to note that the modern *Upāsaka* mentioned above, Mei Guangxi, knowing neither Pali, nor Sanskrit, nor even Tibetan, could make wonderful discoveries in his comparison of the texts of the "old" and "new" translations of the Lakṣaṇa school with respect to their differences. His pamphlet, though short, surpasses many a good dissertation in this field.

Here is another point worth consideration. We know that the basic human mentality is practically the same among all peoples, but the formulae of thought are different in different cultures. Akṣapāda's *nyāya* is very similar to Aristotle's logic in its use of syllogism, yet the processes of reasoning are incompatible with each other. After making a comparative study, Vidyabhusana concluded in his *History of Indian Logic* that *nyāya* is much less convenient than logic. In fact, there is a faint echo of dictatorship in Indian *nyāya* and a sense of democratic spirit in Greek logic. *Āgamapramāṇa* is not to be questioned, which is to say that words of the Guru command absolute faith and obedience. In an inferential formula, the proposition is stated first. One may stop there and satisfy oneself that it is true. The reason or "cause" comes next if needed, and if one still does not understand, an example either positive or negative is given in the third place. In this outward form, the Greek syllogism seems to be more liberal and convincing. Here again, an explanation in the light of historical materialism may also hold true. In ancient Athens, albeit slavery existed at the lower stratum of society, the free citizens developed and enjoyed a liberal spirit that can be traced even in their logic, convincing both by induction and deduction, whereas in ancient India, the caste system was long entrenched, with Brahmans at its top exercising their unquestionable authority over the masses in the spiritual field like dictators in the political. Practically speaking, *nyāya* is out of use in the modern world. But one has to understand it in its employment by ancient Buddhist writers.

Another fact which presented difficulty to translation is the whole construction of Sanskrit grammar. There is no lack of exactitude and subtleties and excellences in this language, but how distant it is from Chinese one can plainly see. Moreover, what appears peculiar is also the Indian treatment of numbers. Numbers such as those appearing in the *Avataṃsaka-sūtra* run many digits beyond the grasp of the ordinary mind. One may criticize these as fanciful, but one cannot deny that they are numbers. And, above all, there is always the peculiar mode of expression characteristic of ancient Indian thought, i.e. repetition. Oftentimes the same thing is stated in verse and again in prose. This can be considered a good point, because the contents can thus be checked over. In the *Saṃgha* or assembly, chanting usually preceded or followed the lecturing and discussions; it was a custom not too different from the singing of hymns before and after the sermons of the church services today, except that the *gāthās* were specially composed for the purpose on each occasion in accord with the contents of the speech which made up the whole work usually in prose. But in the prose alone the same idea was often repeated again and again like the turning of an ancient Egyptian noria, or in Buddhist terminology, "the turning of the wheel of dharma." This form was also preserved by the conscientious translators of the scriptures. It was an ancient joke in China that the words of Buddha were just like a bucket of water poured back and forth from one bucket to another, yet in the end it was still the same bucket of water. A sort of depressive or rather soporific monotony in turning round and round of the same words may not be inspiring or even interesting, yet one should be very cautious in reading the lengthy texts because the turning is often in a spiral form which offers the same view but with the ground slowly receding.

Such being the difficulties, one should know where to stand in relation to the sūtras. The great bulk of Buddhist literature is like a jungle forest in the tropics with several broad ways cleared. Many rare and precious species of vegetation can be found in it. If the simile of water is applicable, it is not just a bucketful but a big river. Probably nobody in the modern world aspires to be a master of the *Tripiṭaka*. For the lay person who believes in this dharma, has the faith which is the *sine qua non* for any religion and aims at his peace of mind or personal emancipation or *mokṣa*, the adherence to one or two sects would be sufficient. For instance, the Chan or Dhyāna Sect negates everything in the religion, while the Jing Tu or Sukhāvatī Sect affirms the legendary Pure Land beyond. If one manages to follow these two seemingly contradictory lines at the same time, he would be "like a tiger with two horns" as the traditional saying goes. One goes to drink water from a river in order to quench his thirst, but he need not pose as Indra trying to drink up the water of the whole river. The Sukhāvaṭi Sect still has its three short *sūtras* and one *śāstra*, while the Chan Sect has none. It has only a number of dialogues and even these can be dispensed with, since all depends on the master. If one wishes to be learned in Buddhism, he might look into several sects, in which case the works of those erudite *upāsakas* mentioned above are worth referring to. And there is much academic work left to be done in our present age. Above all the labour of Hercules is required to clean the stable, because too much has to be done away with.

6

The theory of Pure Consciousness pertains to the Lakṣaṇa school, but the late great master of Buddhism Ouyang Jian has sorted it out and designated it as a separate school. We need not go into details of his expositions, because ultimately this is only a matter of classification. As mentioned above, the Ci En Sect venerated Kui Ji as its master. Kui Ji was accepted as a disciple of Xuan Zang at the age of seventeen (648) and followed the master until the end of his life (682). Strictly speaking, Xuan Zang, as the chief proponent of this theory, must be considered as the founder of this sect. But Xuan Zang, the greatest leader of Buddhism of his times, who within nineteen years had translated 75 works in 1,315 fascicles, was too great to be called a sectarian chief. This disciple of his was also great in his achievements and was reputed as "the master of a hundred commentaries." The use of such titles, showing respect for a person according to how many *śāstras* he had mastery of, was a practice that originated from Nālandā. However, he wrote 43 works, only 31 of which are now extant. His commentary on the theory of Pure Consciousness was his masterpiece, and the Sect was famous for that.

On this theory, Xuan Zang had gone through the works of no less than ten Indian masters among whom Dharmapāla occupied the first place and whose views were taken as the final authority. It was Kui Ji who motivated his master to blend the different views of these teachers into a whole, and Xuan Zang complied with his demand to teach him alone. Kui Ji worked laboriously on his studies. Thus the famous Chinese version of the *Vijñāptimātratāsiddhi* with its *Commentary* came into being.

Two translations of Vasubandhu's *Commentary in Twenty Ślokas* (*Viṃśatikā*) were made before Xuan Zang: one in the north by Gautama Prajñāruci in 534–538 — not by Bodhiruci who was another Indian translator — and another one in the south by Paramārtha (499–569), both with the help of their Chinese disciples. Yet the theory became popular only after Kui Ji. Besides the *Viṃśatikā* there is the *Commentary in Thirty Ślokas* (*Triṃśikavijñaptibhāṣyam*) by Sthiramati which was mainly adopted and merged into Xuan Zang's work. The original Sanskrit texts of these two works were discovered at Katmandu in 1922, then edited and published by the French scholar Sylvain Levi, Paris, 1925. Thus there are three translations apart from one in Tibetan and the original in Sanskrit. By a comparison of these texts,[4] it can be concluded that most probably Prajñaruci had an original text slightly different from the present one, and all these three employed different sets of terminologies in translation. None could claim to be the best, though Xuan Zang's work was the last and the most exact. The content was of course the same. Strictly speaking, there was never any "standardized" original Sanskrit text in existence. Xuan Zang made use of several original copies which necessarily had variations in wording and in the arrangement of contents. There were probably interpolations, right or wrong corrections made by different masters, and all sorts of mistakes done by transcribers — all of which were unavoidable. It was he who put the works into fairly fixed form, and therefore his versions have always been regarded as reliable.

The Pure Consciousness theory constitutes the mainstay of the philosophy of the so-called Dharma-Lakṣaṇa school in Mahāyāna Buddhism. Its development seems to have been evolutionary, a gradual growth from simplicity to multiplicity with ameliorations toward completeness as a consolidated and independent system. The cardinal works upon which it is based are the noted six *sūtras* and eleven *śāstras*.[5]

4. This work was done by the present writer in 1948, and the results have been summed up in an article published in the journal *Studies on World Religions* No. 4, 1982, Beijing.
5. The traditional eleven *śāstras* can still be made up by adding the translation of the *Thirty Ślokas* by Vasubandhu, together with Sthiramati's commentary *Triṃśikavijñaptibhāṣyam* translated by the present writer.

In fact, there are only four *sūtras* in all, because two were not introduced to China, and the *śāstras* numbered only nine because one was known only by name and another was lost. They are listed here together with their translators and dates of translation:

The Sūtras

1) *Buddhāvataṃsaka-mahāvaipulya-sūtra*

2 trans.

a) Buddhabhadra 60 fasc. (418–421)

b) Śikṣānanda 80 fasc. (695–698)

2) *Saṃdhinirmocanavyūha-sūtra*

2 trans.

a) Bodhiruci 5 fasc. (514)

b) Xuan Zang 5 fasc. (647)

(One section by Guṇabhadra and another by Paramārtha, each in one fasc., are parts of a.)

3) *Laṅkāvatāra-sūtra*

3 trans.

a) Guṇabhadra 4 fasc. (443)

b) Bodhiruci 10 fasc. (513)

c) Śikṣānanda 7 fasc. (700–704)

Sanskrit original extant

4) *Mahāyānaghanavyūha-sūtra*

2 trans.

a) Divākara 3 fasc. (676–688)

b) Amoghavajra 3 fasc. (762–765)

5) *Tathāgata-abhyudgata-guṇa-alamkāra-sūtra*

No Chinese translation

6) *Mahāyānābhidharma-sūtra*

No Chinese translation; only quotations extant.

The Śāstras

1) *Yogācāryabhūmi Śāstra*

by Maitreya

100 fasc.

Tr. Xuan Zang (646–648)

Skt MS extant

2) *Āryavācāprakaraṇa Śāstra*

by Asaṅga

20 fasc.

Tr. Xuan Zang (645–646)

3) *Mahāyānasūtrālaṅkāraṭika*

by Maitreya

Commentary by Vasubandhu

13 fasc.

Tr. Prabhāmitra (630–633)

4) *Pramāṇasamuccaya Śāstra*

by Diṅnāga

4 fasc.

Tr. Yi Jing (711)

(Lost in the Tang dynasty, now extant only in Tanjur. An abridged translation from Tibetan done by the late Rev. Fa Zun appeared in recent years.)

5) *Mahāyānasamparigraha Śāstra*

by Asaṅga

3 fasc.

Tr. Xuan Zang (648–649)

2 fasc.

Tr. Buddhaśanta (531)

3 fasc.

Tr. Paramārtha (563)

Commentary by Vasubandhu

10 fasc.

Tr. Xuan Zang (648–649)

by Abhāva

10 fasc.

Tr. Xuan Zang (648–649)

15 fasc.

Tr. Paramārtha (563)

10 fasc.

Tr. Dharmagupta (609)

6) *Daśabhūmikasūtra Śāstra*

by Vasubandhu

12 fasc.

Tr. Bodhiruci

7) *Vibhāgayoga Śāstra*

by Maitreya

No translation

8) *Vidarśanā-alambanapratyaya Śāstra*

by Diṅnāga

1 fasc.

Tr. Xuan Zang (657)

1 fasc.

Tr. Paramārtha

9) *Antamadhyaviveka Śāstra*

by Maitreya

Commentary by Vasubandhu

3 fasc.

Tr. Xuan Zang (661)

2 fasc.

Tr. Paramārtha

10) *Mahāyānābhidharmasamuccaya Śāstra*

by Asaṅga

7 fasc.

Tr. Xuan Zang (652)

Commentary by Siṃhabodhi

16 fasc.

Tr. Xuan Zang (646)

11) *Viṃśatikā*

(mentioned above)

7

About the ten great masters of this theory from whose writings Xuan Zang gathered the essential ideas and blended them into one work called the *Vijñāptimātratāsiddhi Śāstra*, we have only vague accounts, mostly eulogistic in nature and without much information about their lives, as left to us by Kui Ji. Vasubandhu was regarded as the founder, but his dates remain uncertain. There are two records: the one holding that he flourished about 1100 years after Buddha's *parinirvāṇa*, and the other, about 900 years. The date fixed by B. Bhattacharya and generally adopted as 280–360 A.D. is highly probable if *parinirvāṇa* is fixed at 486 B.C. His biography translated by Paramārtha into Chinese, in which the second record is found, is still extant. Vasubandhu's contemporary named Bandhuśri (the fourth writer) made a very brief explanation of his thirty *ślokas*, and that led the later masters to make their detailed commentaries based upon it. Another contemporary of

Vasubandhu was Citrabhāna (410–490), who also worked upon this theory (the seventh writer). Another was Guṇamati (440–520 — the second writer), the teacher of Sthiramati (475–555 — the third), who was supposed to be the teacher of Paramārtha. Contemporaneous to Sthiramati was Śuddhacandra (the sixth). But the most prominent one among those Vijñānavādins or masters was Dharmapāla, who lived in about the beginning of the sixth century. He was the son of a minister in Kāñcipura, and after serving as the abbot of Nalāndā, left the monastery at the age of twenty-nine. Afterwards he settled at Bodhi Gayā and died there at the Mahābodhi monastery at the age of thirty-two. He was the guru of Śīlabhadra, the teacher of Xuan Zang. Dharmapāla had three great disciples, namely Viśeṣamitra (the eighth), Jinaputra (the ninth) and Jñānacandra (the tenth). Contemporaneous to Sthiramati and Śuddhacandra was Nanda (the fifth), who was the grand guru of Jinasena, another teacher of Xuan Zang who always lived outside the Nālandā monastery alone and equally famous as Śīlabhadra. We may count two centuries, the fifth and the sixth, as the period in which the Pure Consciousness theory gradually shaped itself into perfection until it reached its highest peak in the *Siddhi Śāstra* composed by Xuan Zang, a monumental work still very much appreciated today.

8

Consciousness is thought by some to be the one creative force in the universe without which there would be no existence. This is the view held by the Vedāntins in India, who described the universal reality as Being-Consciousness-Bliss (Sachchidānanda). For a correct understanding of that one may refer to *The Life Divine* written by Śri Aurobindo in English, which has been translated into French, German and Chinese. His exploration into this subject has been exhaustive and one could scarcely attempt to add a single word to that great work.[6] What may be discussed further on this subject are views traditionally held by systems other than the Vedānta.

Before entering into an analysis of this theory, a little digression may be in order. To be conscious, as far as our daily parlance goes, is

6. Śri Aurobindo himself called it his *magnum opus*.

understood by everybody. One most common story familiar to every Christian is that when Jesus was in the garden of Gethsemane, he found his disciples asleep and told them twice to keep awake, because something great was impending. There is also the parable in the Bible of the ten virgins meeting the bridegroom. In Greek mythology we find that the ingenious ancients invented all sorts of punishments, such as those inflicted upon Tantalus or Sisyphus or Danaides, or the wheel of Ixion, etc. But the one thing which even the gods dreaded most was the drinking of the waters of the Styx, which lulled them for one whole year into senseless stupidity and for the nine following years deprived of all their divine powers. The ancient Greek people understood very well what to be in unconsciousness meant. In the ethical teachings of ancient China, it was one of the main requirements in education that the children be trained to be always alert and mindful and vigilant in action.[7] Many references to this can be found in the *Book of Rites*. Probably every great spiritual system has taught something of the same nature.

There is one anecdote in Neo-Confucianism worth mentioning. As is well known, Neo-Confucianism and Buddhism were antagonistic to each other. There is an incident showing how the Confucians understood their opponents. Once Cheng Yi (1033–1107), the great master of the Song dynasty, was asked by a friend who the busiest man in the world might be. "The Chan Buddhist!" was the answer. This is indeed true, because the Chan Buddhist had everything to negate and nothing positive to hold onto, so he had to be conscious all the time, and therefore he is always mentally busy.

Probably this is the main point which all spiritual seekers have to realize if they are to avoid heavy thumps or even bad falls on the way.

These are the ordinary explanations of consciousness in the field of common rationality. But if we enquire into the Mahāyāna Buddhist theory of Pure Consciousness, we must at once go into rudimentary research of the sense perceptions, which pertains to the realm of epistemology. Senses are branches (or fruits) of consciousness, as the visual sense is called eye-consciousness, the auditory sense is ear-consciousness, etc. It is a fairly subtle and complicated system gradually built up in the *śāstras* mentioned above, a system that served as the kernel of the philosophy of the Lakṣaṇa school.

Probably every ancient system in India has its theory of sense-perception, because since very ancient times the study of five senses has always been a favorite subject that attracted the thinking mind and no system could afford to neglect it. In Alberuni's *India* (edited by Edward C. Sachau) it is stated:

7. To give another famous example: the great Neo-Confucian master, Shao Yong, did not touch his head to the pillow in a stretch of thirty years when he was engaged in his studies of the *Book of Changes*. Finally he acquired certain powers of foreknowledge and was venerated as a prophet.

> XV-XIX.
>
> The senses are five, called *indriyāni*, the hearing by the ear, the seeing by the eye, the smelling by the nose, the tasting by the tongue, and the touching by the skin.
>
> XX.
>
> Next follows the will, which directs the senses in the exercise of their various functions and which dwells in the heart. Therefore they call it manas.

And, in enumerating twenty-five categories relating to sense-perception, the author concludes:

> The totality of these elements is called *tattva*, and all knowledge is restricted to them. Therefore Vyāsa the son of Parasara speaks: "Learn these twenty-five by distinctions, definitions, and divisions, as you learn a logical syllogism, and something which is a certainty, not merely studying with the tongue. Afterwards adhere to whatever religion you like; your end will be salvation."

This is Sāṃkhya philosophy which is still a living system in India today. Certain Mahāyānists were also attached to it in the declining ages of Buddhism. Jainism has its philosophy dealing with perception similar to or rather based upon this, and maintains that knowledge of external objects through perception (*pratyakṣa*) is gained through the senses, but denies the separate existence of manas. Mahāvīra, the great prophet (*Tirthaṅkara*) of Jainism, might have been a contemporary of Gautama Buddha, but twenty-four patriarchs were supposed to have preceded him. Neither Buddhism nor Jainism can claim the priority in the investigation of sense-perception. In the Upanishads at a later date as well as in the Bhagavad Gīta, *indriyas* have also been treated somewhat in detail as related to the five elements — fire, ether, earth, water and wind. Thus it is reasonable to suppose that the study of senses was a common subject among the diverse systems in India since very ancient times, and each system had afterwards its own special developments and innovations.

The attempt is made here to analyze this theory in Buddhism, which has special characteristics of its own as understood by Chinese Mahāyānists, at the point of its re-introduction by Xuan Zang in the Tang dynasty (618–907).

9

As we proceed in our research, we find at each step that there are dogmas and hypotheses unacceptable to our modern mind. Nowadays perhaps only those who are converted Bhikṣus or Upāsakas would honestly believe such things as *asuras*, transmigration, world without forms, ten spheres of Bodhisattvas, etc. But one step further shows that sound doctrines are built upon them, if only we accept them as working hypotheses. If, on the contrary, we resolutely take the realistic view and argue at every step, then we cannot proceed and do not reach anywhere. If we station ourselves at a higher level in a state of unbiased impartiality and reconnoitre the windings of the way, we shall find the dogmas, hypotheses and unreasonable suppositions, however absurd or unimaginable they might appear, are ultimately within the field of human intellection and may lead us to a certain enlargement of the scope of our knowledge or even to certain new realizations. Truth in

Mahāyāna has always been divided into the secular or mundane and the higher or transcendental. The theory of Pure Consciousness deals with the former. There is much that is rational and realistic in it for us to appreciate. To a Western scholar it would probably be advisable to take this theory as a work of art, and then it becomes marvellously interesting to see how every element in it builds into a whole, where the traces of correction are noticeable and where an overall beauty lies.

Now, let us ask if this theory of Pure Consciousness was invented or forged by Gautama Buddha? The answer is definitely in the negative, so far as this theory in its present shape shows. Buddha in his teaching of the twelve independent links in relative origination (*dvādaśāṅgaḥ pratītyasamutpāda*) mentioned consciousness as the third link, name and form (*nāma-rūpa*) as the fourth and the six fields of contact as the fifth. This twelvefold chain of causality constitutes the core of original Buddhism, and it cannot but be authentic. Its deep-rooted historical background attests to this. In Hīnayāna as well as later on in Mahāyāna, we have the doctrine of the "Five Aggregates" (*skandhas*) which is the bulwark against Brahmanism's belief in the Self (*Ātman*), and it makes Buddha's teachings into a sort of "protestantism" — in the literal sense of the word — against that orthodoxy. The Five Aggregates can be roughly divided into two groups: first the four elements; the body, the senses, the sense-data — these are included in the group of *rūpa* that constitutes the first aggregate. Next comes feeling or *vedanā*, which is the second; then conceptual knowledge or *saṃjña* comes third;

synthetic mental states, synthetic functioning of compound sense-formations, compound feelings and compound concepts are the fourth; and consciousness or *vijñāna* makes up the fifth. In our modern way of thinking the first can stand apart as an independent category which belongs to the material world, and the fifth which is psychological may include the remaining three. In searching for the self or ego, one finds any or all of these aggregates but not the ego itself. Diverse schools built their theories upon the non-existence of ego, until finally the Vijñānavādins developed it to the fullest extent into a perfected system.

It is to be remarked here that Gautama Buddha the man had no idea of becoming a philosopher or even a religious leader. His main effort was focused on deliverance of suffering humanity from distress, and he found the causes of suffering to be a chain beginning from ignorance (*avidyā*) and leading finally to senility and death (*jarāmarāṇaṃ*), grief (*śokaḥ*), lamentation (*parideva*), pain (*duḥkhaṃ*) and mental affliction (*daurmanasyaṃ*). He seldom made other ontological or eschatological speculations; perhaps he was too busy for that. The ancient parable is of a man wounded by an arrow. The urgent need is to have the arrow removed and to heal the wound instead of discussing the character of the archer, the caste to which he belonged, etc. The contrary of ignorance is enlightenment, and Buddha taught ways and means to that such as the Eightfold Noble Path (*Āryāṣṭāṅgamārga*).[8] Consciousness remained as an important link in the chain, and no thinker since has improved on the idea of this chain of causation.

9

The chain of causality, otherwise called the Wheel of Existence (*Bhāvacakra*) begins with ignorance (*avidyā*). When ignorance is gotten rid of, then the *saṃskāras* are abolished. *Saṃskāras* is variously interpreted as "impression" or "operation" or "conformation", etc. and in Chinese it is simply interpreted as "action". Then consciousness (*vijñānaṃ*), the six fields of operation of the senses (*ṣaḍāyatana*) — in Chinese "six entrances" contact (*sparśa*), feeling (*vedanā*), desire (*tṛṣṇā*), being (*bhāva*), birth (*jāti*), and decay and death (*jarāmaraṇaṃ*) are annihilated as they are produced in this sequence. This seems to be a profound analysis based upon human experience. Obviously there is a lot to be explained about the second, third, fourth and fifth links, which the Mahāyānists made substantial use of in later ages.

8. The Eightfold Noble Path: *Samyagdṛṣṭiḥ* (right understanding), *Samyaksamkalpaḥ* (right thought), *Samyagvāk* (right speech), *Samyakkarmāntaḥ* (right action), *Samyagājivaḥ* (right livelihood), *Samyavyāyāmaḥ* (right effort), *Samyaksmṛtiḥ* (right mindfulness), *Samyak-samādhiḥ* (right concentration).

10

Now, we may proceed to examine the theories that were connected with the study of consciousness held by different sects at an early stage. Within the four hundred years after *Parinirvāṇa*, the Buddha's teachings ramified into different schools of thought forming a number of sects. In the northern part of India Buddhist sects numbered no less than twenty. In the seven hundred years that followed, they became even more numerous. They were all idealistic and were generally held to be Hīnayāna doctrines in contrast to Mahāyāna Buddhism. But ultimately the Mahāyāna doctrines grew out of them. We take the following concepts into consideration for our purpose.

The *Mahāsaṃghikās*, *Ekavyavahārikās*, *Lokottaravādins* and *Kaukkuṭikās* were agreed on forty-seven concepts, from which we gather only a few:

1) The body of the five senses is either with or without contamination.

2) In both the domains of corporality and incorporality (*rūpa-* and *arūpadhātu*) there are beings possessed of six senses.

3) The five different senses (*indriyas*) are physical organs, but the eye does not see, the ear does not hear, etc.

4) Intellect (*dhī*) is an added application (*prayoga*): it can dissolve all distresses and also lead to happiness.

5) There is no dharma of non-discrimination (*avyākṛtadharma*).

6) The principle of non-action (*asaṃskṛta dharma*) are of nine kinds:

a. *Saṃpramoṣa*

b. *Asaṃpramoṣa*

c. *Ākāśa*

d. *Ākāśānantyāyatanaṃ*

e. *Vijñānānantyāyatanaṃ*

f. *Ākiñcananyatyāyatanaṃ*

g. *Naivasaṃjñānāsaṃjñānāyatanaṃ*

h. *Pratīyayasamutpada-aṅgāni*

i. *Āryamārga-aṅgāni*

7) All *anuśayās*[9] belong neither to the dharma of mind (*citta*) nor to

9. *Kleśa* means psychological annoyance or afflications. *Anuśayās* is its synonym, such as greed, hatred, etc., according to *Sarvāstivādins*. For the Mahāyānists it came to mean the seeds of the twin obstacles of the affliction and of knowing, both dormant in the *Ālaya*-consciousness and always adding to the torpidity of the man.

that of mental properties (*caitasikās*); they have also no *ālambana*.

8) All *anuśayās* are different from *paryavasthānaṃ* (binding), the former do not correspond to *citta*, while the latter do.

9) *Antarābhavaḥ* — the vital being of a man after death and before his rebirth — does not exist.

There are points upon which the sub-sects of these four schools were not agreed. I mention only a few with which we are concerned at present:

1) Action (*karma*) and the indeterminate inner change in consciousness (*vipāka*) may take place in simultaneity.

2) Seed in the psychological field is identical with sprout.

3) Seeds of gross elements in *rūpa-indriyas* may change; *citta* and *caitasikādharma* have no import of change.

4) The mind pervades the whole body.

The main concepts of the Bāhuśrutīyas are agreed upon by its different subjects, and they are:

1) Buddha's five tenets are teachings of renunciation or *lokottara-dharma*, viz.:

a. *Anityā* or non-permanence

b. *Duḥkhaṃ* or suffering

c. *Śūnyatā* or voidness

d. *Anātmakam* or non-existence of ego

e. *Nirvāṇa* or the ultimate state of emancipation.

2) These five teachings can lead to the way of cessation of the

cycle of birth-and-death (*samsāra*). All the other tenets are of the world (*laukikadharma*).

All the other principles of the Bāhuśrutīyas are the same as those held by the Mahāsaṃghikās.

The Prajñaptivādins maintain that:

1) the twelve *āyatanas* are unreal,

2) *duḥkhaṃ* cannot be a skandha,

3) there is no untimely death, since death is the result of one's past karma,

4) and with the growth of karma as cause, the *vipāka* or ripeness of effect is produced.

Other principles of this school are the same as those of the Mahāsaṃghikās.

The Sarvāstivādās have sixty-two fundamental concepts agreed upon by all its adherents, and to mention only a few of importance here, they are:

1) Whatever dharma that exists must be included in these two categories, name (*nāma*) and form (*rūpa*).

2) All dharma can be grasped by or contained in the four memory ranges (*catvāri smṛtyupasthānāni*).

3) All *anuśayas* are *caitasikās* in correspondence with *citta*, resulting in the *ālambanas* or objects.

4) All *anuśayas* are grasped by *paryavasthānaṃ*, but not vice versa.

5) *Antarābhavās* certainly exist in *kāma-* and *rūpadhātus*.

6) The body of the five senses as the eye, etc. has contamination (*kliṣṭha*) and cannot be without contamination.

7) *Citta* and *caitasikā* dharma do exist substantially.

8) Both definitely have *ālambana*.

9) There is not a single dharma that can be transmitted from one life to the next; only worldly people claim there are transmigrations. [These statements mentioned above are taken from Vasubandhu's *Treatise on the Diverse Sects*, which has four translations: one by Paramārtha, one by Kumārajīva, one by Xuan Zang and one in Tibetan (gshuṅ-lugs-kyi bye-brag bkod-pahi ḥkhor-lo). The edition of the Institute of Inner Knowledge, Nanjing, 1930, made use of these four texts.]

11

Thus far we have seen that the subject of consciousness was being explored by diverse schools of philosophy in India since ancient times. Buddha himself made substantial use of it in his own preachings for the deliverance of humankind from suffering. From the sectarian views held afterwards by Hīnayānists developed the Mahāyāna innovations that gradually shaped this theory into an independent system represented by Vasubandhu. It was further brought to a state of perfection by the ten masters, culminating in Dharmapāla's interpretations, and was finally introduced anew to China by Xuan Zang. We cannot definitely say how far Shankarācarya, the Hindu sage, was influenced later on by this theory in promulgating his doctrine of Illusion (*Māyā*). But there certainly could have been influence, because his *Māyā* was not different from the *Māyā* of *lakṣaṇa* in Buddhism, both referring to the world phenomena regarded as mere Illusion. Obviously there was a great discrepancy between the doctrines of Shankarācarya and of Vasubandhu, for the latter could even be seen as an atheist in a certain sense. Within Buddhism we find that this system, though fairly sophisticated and complex, can stand by itself without any self-contradiction, though its method or form of expression employed many paradoxes in order to reveal certain transcendental truths as did the Śūnyatāvādins or the Chan Buddhists. It relies more upon rationality and intelligibility than upon mere faith and mysticism. Thus it is more of a philosophy than of a religion. With this historical background in mind we can approach the theory itself with greater facility.

12

We may begin with the five senses as they are first treated in every system. The eye sees and the ear hears. This is too simple to need any explanation. Yet the senses must be discussed here because they form the necessary and rudimentary parts of the whole system, and the five are usually grouped together because of their similar characteristics, namely:

1) They all depend upon the five inner organs of perception (*indriyas*), viz. organs of seeing, hearing, smelling, tasting and touching.

2) They are all related to the objects of senses.

3) They all function through direct perception (*pratyakṣapramāṇam*), which requires

a. that the object must exist — not like the hair of a tortoise which is non-existent;

b. that there should be no hallucinatory perversion on the part of the seer;

c. that it is limited to the present moment, thus excluding past and future moments;

d. that the object appears, as distinguished from the "seeds" of consciousness;

e. that the appearance is evidenced by the object;

f. that the appearance of subjective cognition is as yet distant from any discrimination, as yet without naming nor speculation; and

g. that the perception is intimately related to the object as different from the subject.

4) They are all intermittent, functioning not in a constant continuity.

These are the similarities of the first five senses (*vijñānas*). The explanation of the direct perception may seem quite superficial to a modern thinker, but it is important insofar as it paves the way for a deeper enquiry into the whole system. These four points about the five senses are also indispensable to a correct understanding of the remaining three — the sixth, seventh and eighth senses.

Now accompanying the five senses there must be the sixth, *manas* or mind. If one's mind was not there, one could still not see the object though with eyes wide open. The same is with hearing and the other three senses, as our ordinary experience shows. It is the awareness which is not the complicated thinking of the mind, yet it cannot but be called mind.

Objectively speaking, this *pratyakṣa* theory does not lead us far, simply because of its limitation to momentariness. A single unit of time in India is called a *kṣaṇa*, defined as 1/60 or 1/65 of a fillip or 1/900 of one turn of mind. As soon as there is the present moment, it is already past. Yet by the initial perception in this infinitesimal length of time, the features of a thing itself (*svalakṣaṇa*) can be touched. This is the foremost function of the five senses and also of the eighth sense. According to this theory, the self-feature of all in the universe is *tathātā* or suchness or thatness. It is above words and names, and no further knowledge can be said of it. In contrast to this is the general feature (*sāmānyalakṣaṇa*), a certain characteristic that is common to a group or a category of objects. It is with regard to general features that all words and names are employed, and knowledge is acquired through the channels of inference.

13

Simple as an act of perception is, it is yet divided into four parts in the analysis. Similar to the division of the knower the known and the knowledge in Vedānta philosophy, it is here separated into

1) the part of *lakṣaṇa* or objective appearance,

2) the part of *dṛṣṭi* or subjective perception,

3) the part of self-realization, and

4) the part of realization of the self-realization.

Lakṣaṇa means the phenomena of all objects in general. It is not limited to the appearance seen by the eye as colours or dimensions, etc. It includes the high and low tones in hearing, fragrances and odours in smelling, sweetness or bitterness, etc., in tasting, roughness or smoothness in touching and appearances of matter and mind or dharma. Thus whatever in the universe is, is included in *lakṣaṇa*.

Dṛṣṭi or seeing is the function capable of relating the subject to the object reflected in the mind.

Since every perception arises out of causal relationship, self-realization makes use of *dṛṣṭi* as its function outside of or external to its relationship, it is only related to its own function. With respect to the remaining three it is called the self. It must be noted here that this self has nothing to do with the Hindu belief in the Self, though the self is also included in that Self. It is the direct feeling of oneself like the touch of fingers on an object without any intervention in between. It is, according to Diṅnāga, the self-being of mind acting simultaneously with its own function. In other words, when the *dṛṣṭi* part is in action, this part approves of it.

Realization of self-realization, the fourth part, comes into relationship with the third. The second relates itself only to the first, the third relates itself to the second and the fourth, but this fourth relates itself only to the third.

To give an illustration, when the length of a piece of cloth is to be measured, the ruler is the measurer. The length thus known is the result of measurement. The same is the case with perception. *Dṛṣṭi* in relating itself to the *lakṣaṇa* is the measurer, and the result of this relationship is self-realization. Self-realization again poses as the measurer in relating itself to *dṛṣṭi*, and the realization of self-realization is the result. The third part in relating itself to the fourth has the fourth as the result, while the fourth in relating itself to the third has also the third as its result. The function of both the third and the fourth being the same, consequently there is no need to establish another part as the fifth.

The first two parts are easily understandable as they are external, the first being only the objective world. The next two are internal, both pertaining to direct perception. The measurement of knowledge by *dṛṣṭi* varies with the senses; that of the first five and the eighth is direct perception. That of the seventh sense is altogether false knowledge. That of the sixth sense comprehends all the three, namely direct perception, inference and false knowledge. *Lakṣaṇa* is outside of this scope: it is not included in these three measurements.

At this juncture something of the history of this theory may be noted in order to make it clearer. The first two parts of the perceptual act were established by Nanda, basing himself upon *Mahāyānasamparigraha Śāstra*, which divided consciousness into eleven kinds. After summarizing them into eight, Nanda made his division of *lakṣaṇa* and *dṛṣṭi*, making the classification more trenchant as a whole. According to him, *dṛṣṭi* is self-being, and the *lakṣaṇa* is the illusion which is produced or transformed thereby, and is thus unreal. This was in accord with the idea of Vasubandhu. As he denied the reality to *lakṣaṇa*, his theory was called "the theory of Pure Consciousness without *lakṣaṇa*" in later times.

There is then the functioning of *dṛṣṭi* or its application to *lakṣaṇa* and the resulting knowledge or understanding, which is called self-realization by Diṅnāga. This forms the third part. Diṅnāga the Nyāyaist had his resources in the Sautrāntikās. Regarding the causal relationship he admitted that the objects related to are within one's mind and are capable of inducing the sense faculties to a subjective clinging or hanging on. This clinging to or hanging on must have together with it the appearance of its functioning. That is to say, it must bring with it the *lakṣaṇa* of the objects in its action. This appearance of *lakṣaṇa* is like the image reflected in a mirror; it is the image of the object yet it exists only in mind. The capacity to produce an image lies with the mirror. Thus, in considering the first two parts, the objects must be regarded as internal or within the mind. The result of this function is knowledge in the superficial sense, or apprehension; it is also called self-realization. In later ages this theory was called one of "Pure Consciousness with *lakṣaṇa*" or the Theory with Three Divisions.

Here appears another exponent of this theory, Sthiramati, the disciple of Guṇamati. He followed the three divisions yet blended the theories of these two masters into one. He maintained that the first two parts are illusive discriminations and so unreal. Only self-realization is real. Thus the three divisions became in fact one whole again after his modification. His commentaries are now still extant in Sanskrit; the chief ideas were adopted by Xuan Zang in his *Siddhi*.[10]

10. Sthiramati's *Commentary in Thirty Ślokas* had a German tr. by H. Jacobi which has long been out of print. A selected tr. was done by Lu Chen. A complete tr. was done by the present writer in 1948. It is still in print.

The fourth part added by Dharmapāla was known by Xuan Zang, though it did not spread in India. Dharmapāla also died young. He maintained that the connection between *dṛṣṭi* and *lakṣaṇa* forms one line of relatedness that is still external with respect to the whole being of the mind. There must be another line of inner relationship between the subject and object or the actor and that which is acted upon. Now, to put all these again in pure Buddhist terms, *lakṣaṇa* is the feature or appearance of objects that must begin with the one real object that is "suchness" or "thatness" (*thatātā*). The objects which come into contact with the senses, the phenomena which are transformed and brought into being by consciousness, and the meaning of any subject — all these are meant by *lakṣaṇa*. It is comparable to the image reflected on a mirror, which is the example also adopted by Dharmapāla. *Dṛṣṭi* or seeing is related to things with forms or *rūpa-dharma*. Consciousness transforms itself into *lakṣaṇa* and thus enters into relationship, and this entering into relationship is what is meant by *dṛṣṭi*. It is comparable to the light of the mirror. In a higher sense it means also to understand and to reason out by inference. But, although the seeing can know the objective *lakṣaṇa*, it cannot know itself, just as a knife can cut but cannot cut itself. Here comes in the inner knower which is the being of the consciousness itself, and *dṛṣṭi* is no other than the function of this being, coming into relationship with an external world formed by itself. This part is self-realization, which is comparable to the mirror reflecting light and showing all images.

To realize is to verify or ascertain or to experience. As "suchness" is posed as the sole reality, all the eight branches of consciousness are not separated from it. The being of "suchness" can verify all eight. This is the part of realization of the self-realization. It can intimately experience the third part in its relation with the second part without error. It is compared to the back side of the mirror, bearing in mind that it is the ancient mirror made of metal.

Here the analysis of perception ends. A "part" is the part of the whole of an action. Normally one may understand the fourth part as the action of the inner psychic being, but that is not what is taught by this system. It is the part of action of consciousness which is, hypothetically, the sole reality.

14

We must now explore patiently into the senses. There is no doubt that for every sense there must be a basis, and this basis is called in Sanskrit "*indriya*", translated into Chinese as the "root" of the sense. It is the physical organ, as the eye, the ear, the nose, etc. Yet by this *indriya* a distinction is made between the "outer" and the "inner".[11] The eyeball and its nerves are called the outer organ, and if the outer organ is damaged or destroyed, then there can be no seeing. Yet it is not only the physical organ that sees or hears. In the layman's way of thinking, "life" will come immediately into consideration. When the life or life-breath is in the body, the sensory organs, if unimpaired, function well. But when life-breath is no longer in the body, these organs function no more. That is very plain. Yet the Buddhists of the Lakṣaṇa school have a different story to tell. There is apart from the outer physical organ another inner root called *rūpaprasāda-indriyaṃ* or the "root of pure form," a single root upon which the five senses depend. This may be called the subject of seeing and hearing, etc. It is only when both the inner and outer roots come into contact with the *viṣaya* or object that the consciousness arises.

If that be so, we may proceed to enquire further what *rūpaprasāda-indriyaṃ* (lit. pure-form root) is. Known by inference it is that which sees and hears by means of the physical organs, but unlike the physical organs, it is not subject to damage or destruction. We know that both the subject and object are transformations of consciousness as held by this theory, yet the outer nescient object cannot give rise to any perception while the conscious subject can. Unlike any perception produced which is liable to come and go, this *indriya* is not so, being free or being its own master. The specific perceptions may come and go, but this *indriya* remains unmoving. It gives rise to the five senses and serves as their *adhipatipratyaya* or "uppermost co-operating cause." All the five senses must depend upon it for perception.

Explained in another way, it is the function of the inner *rūpa* of the consciousness. *Rūpa* is simply form, and in the Lakṣaṇa school it

11. The tāntric theory of *Śakti* or power adopted this term without making any distinction between the inner and the outer. It is interpreted as a faculty of mind and used to explain certain supernatural feats of the yogi accomplished independent of the physical sense organs and certain phenomena in hypnosis. These matters are the province of so-called parapsychology, a science as yet not well established.

simply denotes every and any object that has a form. Substantial forms or external objects pertain to the so-called non-intimate part of *lakṣaṇa*. The inner pure-form *indriya* pertains to the intimate part of *lakṣaṇa*. Because of its being free from good or evil, it is called pure. This pure *rūpa* is also called the outer shell of ignorance or *avidyā*, which will be treated afterwards.

Thus without establishing any other true seer or hearer in the body, this explanation of perception fits remarkably well with what was taught by Buddha in the "chain of causation":

That which is conditioned by ignorance is action (sometimes translated as "will-to-action");

That which is conditioned by action is consciousness;

That which is conditioned by consciousness is *nāma-rūpa* (names and forms, sometimes translated as "psychophysical existence");

That which is conditioned by *nāma-rūpa* is the six sense fields;

That which is conditioned by the six sense fields is contact;

......

As a historical fact, masters of this school (Vijñānavādins) skillfully developed their own theories from the teachings of Buddha without any controversy. It seems that during the two hundred years after Vasubandhu, Buddhist thinkers were still capable of using their powers of rational thought in philosophy instead of relying merely upon blind faith, which in mixing itself with diverse beliefs can cause the production of endless superstitions. On the other hand too much rationalization and philosophizing helped the rise of Chan Buddhism in China, which remained altogether transcendental and aloof from words and theories and ignored in the end even Buddha the man. But the theory does not stop at the analysis of the five or six senses. The study must go further to the exploration of the hypothetical seventh and eighth senses that brought the systematization of this theory into perfection.

15

A

As is well known Mahāyānists uphold the doctrine of "dependent origination" (*pratītyasamutpāda*) which means that everything in the universe comes about through the combination or co-operation of a number of relative causes relying upon each other. Or, said in another way, things appear only by means of certain related factors or under certain conditions. First we begin with the sense of sight. It is produced through the co-operation of nine relative causes:

1) Seeing presupposes space. There must be a certain distance between the eye and the object. If the object is placed too near to the eye-ball it cannot be seen, or else the pupil of the eye may be cracked. This must be very clear to every ophthalmologist worth the name.

2) There must be light.

3) There must be the *indriya* or root, as mentioned above.

4) There must be the object to be seen.

5) There must be the attention (*manaskāra*) or making of the mind to see.

6) There must be the sixth sense,

7) and the seventh sense,

8) and the eighth sense,

9) and the seeds.

If "time" is taken into consideration, another factor must be added, i.e. *samanantarapratyayaḥ*, or the cause of sameness in a flow without interruption.

Next, by the sense of hearing, the same factors must prevail except light. We can hear just as well in darkness as in light.

Next, by the sense of smell, the first two factors are excluded.

The other causes are the same.

B

"Whatever dharma is produced through causation,
I say, that is void."

This is the first half of a famous *śloka* written by Nāgārjuna. Causation is action regulated by a principle of cause and effect: it is a term denoting the fact but no more than that. Yet everything in the universe is said to be involved in it. In the Buddhist phraseology here is a slight difference in emphasis which should be noted: instead of saying cause and effect, cause and auxiliary cause are generally juxtaposed, forming a compound which should mean causation rather than causality. *Hetu* in Sanskrit means cause, but *pratyaya* does not mean effect, it means auxiliary or relative or co-operating cause. Sometimes it is translated as condition. This slight tilt of emphasis makes the theory more spherical than lineal. Cause and effect, as expressed by the word causality, is usually understood as descension or generation in a straight line. On the other hand this *pratyaya*, meaning something that can be based or climbed upon or contacted or related to, is of four kinds:

First, *hetupratyaya* — For example, rice-seeds are the *hetu* or direct cause; soil, water, labor, etc. are the *pratyaya* or relative causes that must co-operate in the production of rice. The six *indriyas* or roots of consciousness are the direct causes, the six external objects are the relative causes and the six senses are the results.

Second, *ālambanapratyaya* — The support or attendant circumstance. A sick person, for example, needs crutches for walking because of his weakness. The mind and mental properties may be weak and must be supported. This is the object upon which they rest.

Third, *adhipatipratyaya* — This is the most powerful or ruling cause. It is compared to the field in producing grains. Thus the root of the eye is the ruling cause for seeing.

Fourth, *samanantarapratyaya* — This is the equal and unintermittent relative cause. It is merely *citta-dharma* based on the continuation of mind and mental properties. The first instant of thought gives place to the second instant of thought in succession. It is likened to a person walking over a single-log bridge who steps forward to give place to the next comer. The prior and the next instances of the mind or of the mental properties may be increased or decreased in number, yet their being must be the same or equal. The prior leads the next so that the next follows suit without any intermittence. All the functions of mind of any person have this condition except, it is said, that of an *Arhat* or liberated sage on the verge of *Nirvāṇa*, whose last mental state does not give rise to any following mental state.

Having made clear the four kinds of direct and auxiliary causes, we can easily understand analyses such as the eye-consciousness being produced from nine *pratyayas* and the ear-consciousness from eight *pratyayas*, etc. Yet there is an important point which we must bear always in mind: according to this theory both cause and effect are only hypothetically and relatively established. In order to explain the present condition which is the result of certain former conditions, the former cause or causes are established. Taking into account the present condition that may lead to future consequences, the present cause or causes are also presumed. Both are postulations that should only be taken relatively.

C

Next, we must turn away from the *rūpa-dharma* of the five senses and come to the *citta-dharma* or mental principles. The sixth sense — *manovijñānaṃ* — is sometimes translated as idea or mental consciousness. It is the sense of discrimination upon which the former five depend. It accompanies the five senses, taking their objects as its objects, but has also its own relationship with all other dharmas. For example, by the contact of the first sense with any object, it is at the very beginning direct perception, but at the next instant the idea of its color as blue or red, etc., or its dimensions as long or short, or its form as round or square, etc., comes about, and that is exactly the function of the sixth sense. Sometimes a single stray thread of imagination arises in our mind, also as part of its function, and this is called a "single-headed idea." This is brought forth by five relative causes.

1) *Indriya* or root — The root here is in the seventh, it is not

produced from the former five.

2) *Viṣaya* or object.

3) *Manaskāra*, as above.

4) A basis which is in the eighth sense.

5) Seeds.

We have stepped into the field of thinking. The sixth, seventh and eighth senses are all called mind, yet subtle differences can be made out. The seventh is that which perpetually thinks in formulating ideas and opinions. Both the sixth and the seventh are called *manovijñāna*, but the former is a determinative compound (*tatpuruṣa*) and the latter an appositional one (*karmadhāraya*). To a Hindu thinker this is very plain. The seventh is called *ahaṃkāra* or ego, or more appropriately, ego-consciousness. It is the seat (*āśraya*) of particularization for the former six senses in discriminating between things defiled and things pure. It arises through the combination of three relative causes:

1) Seeds produced by itself.

2) *Manaskāra*, same as above.

3) The fundamental abode (*āśraya*) which is the eighth sense.

It may be mentioned here in passing that thought *per se*, especially philosophical thinking as it is understood in modem times, had never occupied any important place in the oriental world. What was highly respected and aspired to is always spiritual enlightenment. This theory of Pure Consciousness also underrated thinking by attributing it to the sixth sense. In cultural history of course, Chan Buddhism afterwards tolled the death knell of thought altogether.

D

In the seven senses so far as mentioned above there is not much philosophy nor psychology to be talked about. But in the eighth there is something worth our consideration. In the ancient texts we find a number of synonymous terms for the eighth sense. To mention a few, counted in our present list, it is the eighth, but counted from inside outwards it is called the first sense. Its name in Sanskrit is *Ālayavijñāna* and also *Ādānavijñāna*. *Ālaya* has the meaning of storage, so it is called the Store-consciousness, or the All-conserving mind. What is stored up there are the so-called "seeds", or impressions formed by vāsanās or habits, through a process of "perfuming". *Ādāna* is interpreted as "seizing" or "upholding", because it keeps up or upholds all the seeds, which are like swift water currents and which should not be mistaken as the ego — so says the *Lankāvatārasūtra*. Both these names are retained in Chinese in transliterations. As it is that upon which all our knowledge depends, it is called the *Āśraya*, abode or seat of the known. Because it contains the seeds of all *dharma*, whether worldly or otherworldly, it is also called the seed-consciousness. Hīnayānists call it the root-consciousness, as it is considered to be the root of all dharma, though the name is somewhat vague.

"Seeds" must necessarily produce fruits under proper conditions. Generally speaking the law of causality is discussed in every philosophy, whether materialistic or idealistic. Here in this theory it also serves, in all its simplicity, as a backbone. For two things to serve as cause and effect mutually and at the same time is a misconception ("ein Ungedanke" according to Schopenhauer). A point is here to be made clear in order to avoid any confusion. The classical illustration of the diverse factors that make up sense as "a bundle of reeds" supporting each other so as to be able to stand on the ground, should not be, so often as it is, misunderstood as the relation of reeds mutually serving as cause and effect. It should be explained as a state of conglomeration in equilibrium. The mutual support is the cause and the standing is the effect. Effect is thus synonymous with fruits which are always in correspondence with seeds, yet effect is more often used in the sense of an action resulted from certain causes. In the Chinese language, the connotation of fruit comes through.

Here two terms are often to be distinguished: if the fruit is of the same species as its seed, which means a continuation of the species itself, the fruit is *Nisyandaphalam*. If the species is changed, the seed is called *Vipākahetuh*, a differently maturing or matured cause. Now, in the field of mental activity where the causes of a single action can be innumerable and the effect can be entirely different from the supposed direct cause or causes, the maturing of the fruit into one of a different species and at a different time is often the rule. As all this takes place in the eighth sense. it is also called *Vipāka*-consciousness. It leads from various causes to life and death, to good and bad results.

Another name for the eighth sense is *Amalavijñāna*, or the "dust-free consciousness" the abode of *anāsrava-dharma* — lit. "without leakage," i.e. pure and free from contaminations and afflictions — a name applied only to the Land of Buddha (*Tathāgata-bhūmi*). Certain ancient masters established it as the last or the ninth consciousness, which was redundant.

Each of these terms denotes something of its characteristic. The earliest translation of the term in Chinese is "the immortal consciousness" or literally "a consciousness ever-present or without extinction." This is inexact. According to the Mahāyāna tradition it is said to be exhausted in the "unmoving stage" (*acalābhūmi*) of a bodhisattva, or after the Vajrahood has been attained. This term was discarded by Xuan Zang in his "new translations."

As to the relative causes of this eighth consciousness, there are only four:

1) The root — which is the seventh, or *manas*.

2) The object — which comprises all beings, all worlds.

3) *Manaskāra*.

4) The seeds — the seeds inhering in the Eighth sense, formed since beginningless past by practices or usages (*samudācāraḥ*).

As the eighth sense serves as the basis of all the other seven senses, no other basis is required. It seems to correspond partly to what we call instinct in our modern psychology, insofar as it is formed through innumerable generations in the past before birth. As a fragrant flower diffuses its scent, one's activities constantly leave traces in the substratum of consciousness, thus forming the so-called "seeds" through a process of "perfuming". By this process activities give rise to seeds, and seeds again produce activities. The cycle goes on everlastingly until one has attained to *Nirvāṇa* or otherwise to the final stages of bodhisattvahood, as this theory maintains.

Now, if we search for the origin of this *Ālaya*-consciousness theory, we find that it is by no means an invention made by *Mahāyānists*; it is rather the result of a gradual improvement of a basic belief held by diverse sects beginning not long after Buddha's *parinirvāṇa*. Hīnayānists count usually only six senses, yet the Mahīśāsakās embraced as their esoteric teaching another sense called "the consciousness following throughout life and death" and held it to be a separate *skandha* or aggregate. Because the six senses are intermittent, so another subtle and constantly evolving consciousness is postulated as a basis. The Sarvāstivādās and the Hīnayānists held that there must be the "root of life" (*jīvitendriya*), and the generality common to all living beings (*nikāyasabhāga*) is the true *Vipāka*. The Mahāsaṃghikas call it simply the "root-consciousness", and the Vibhajyavādins maintain also that there must be this "separated sense." All these hypotheses point to the same phenomenon, which is ameliorated and embellished in the Lakṣaṇa school as *Ālaya-vijñānaṃ*.

16

Among us *homo sapiens* there are people, though few, who are absolutely lacking in *sapientia*. They are born without any physical defect, without any noticeable outward deformation. Apart from incredible stupidity there is also nothing abnormal. In the daily parlance in Chinese, they are said to be "without the root of intelligence." That, interpreted by this theory, must mean that they have less or no seeds of intelligence in the field of their eighth consciousness. Usually this consciousness is compared to a field where seeds are sown in the soil, and when external circumstances permit, these grow into diverse plants and also produce further seeds.

It is plain that what the ancient masters held as seeds are only what are called factors in psychology in modern times. In the *Yogācāryabhūmi Śāstra* it is stated that seeds are of two kinds: one is hereditary, formed since the beginningless past and born with the man, so to say, *a priori*;

another kind is acquired after birth, thus *a posteriori*. In modern education, the principle of developing the latent knowledge of a child is supposed to be better than "compulsory feeding" — to use a medical term — with knowledge. But, if the potentiality, or, in terms of this theory, the seeds of knowledge were not already existent in latency, then nothing could be developed. And, if there were no newly formed seeds added to the storage, then the reserves would likely be exhausted after a length of time, say, a few generations, just as one's savings and drawings in a bank. Mental images or impressions deeply sunk into the substrata of consciousness, designated here as *Ālayavijñāna*, may be lost to memory, yet when certain circumstances concur, they may come up to the surface, and this is what we call remembrance. But how many generations or aeons will it take for the newly acquired habits here called seeds to become a hereditary instinct, or to put the question in another way: how long will it take for an experience *a posteriori* to become *a priori*? — To this there is no answer.

Yet the theory of the formation of new seeds is noteworthy. Whatever good or evil done, said or thought of by a man is called *samudācāra*. Just as pure sesame oil can become fragrant if flowers are immersed in it, the Store-consciousness must necessarily retain the remnants of all these activities or *samudācāra* like the fragrance of flowers. These remnants are called *vāsanās*, another name for seeds or *bījas*. This process undergone is compared to "perfuming". The mind, so to say, is being perfumed with good or evil, or in Buddhist terms, undergoes defilement or purification. This perfuming consists in continuous contact or collision, and there come about *nāmavāsanās*, *rūpavāsanās*, *kleśavāsanās*, all formed in the sixth sense in cooperation with the seventh and the eighth. And these can be the newly formed or new seeds which are stored up in the eighth.

The distinction made here between the old and the new formations seems to us insignificant, yet in the context of Buddhist *sāsrava* and *anāsrava* dharma, it bears a great import. Moreover, we must think of a society with rigid and oppressive caste distinctions. Whether the lowest class people or outcasts of society are born with or without seeds of the right dharma in their consciousness is the question, and if without, could or could not new seeds of the right dharma be formed? The question boils down to the admittance into or exclusion from the *Saṃgha* of the untouchables.

17

We may take for granted the existence of seeds. Next, we have to examine the characteristics of the seeds as expounded by the Vijñānavādins. And these are enumerated by them as:

1) Instant extinction — There are distinct potencies in the seeds that make their appearance and disappearance in one instant. This is the so-called "transformation".

2) Co-existence with the fruits — Seeds are in harmony with activities at their present moment. Theoretically there must still be the priority of the one to the other, but that is not brought into consideration.

3) Constant in succession — Seeds must be of one species in a constant flux until they reach their ultimate end.

4) Definite character — Their nature or character must be definite so as to produce results in accord with the forces of causes, whether

they be good or evil.

5) Necessity of diverse relative causes in their production.

6) Conducing to the production of the fruits of themselves. If causes are different, the results must be equally different.

The seeds are indeed stored up in the eighth consciousness. They may also be properly called the distinctive functions of the eighth consciousness. Here comes in a sort of reasoning, common to the Mādhyamikas, which is very much like sophistry. The seeds are said to be neither the same nor different from the results they produce. It is argued this way: if the root-consciousness is considered as "being", then the seeds are its "becoming" or action of being. If seeds are the cause, what is produced is the effect. If the cause and the effect are one, then there need not be any principle of causality or any principle of being and becoming. If they were altogether different, then different productions would result, and wheat would produce something such as beans, or else the causative dharma would perish before there could be an effect, because both are entirely different.

Even though they are neither the same nor different, they do exist as two related hypotheses. If such a hypothetical dharma did not exist, then there could not be the law of causality. Here we see the application of an old formula in reasoning of the Mādhyamikā school, the "middle doctrine," used by Nāgārjuna and others. It is not to incline toward either side but to keep to the middle course or even to negate all without taking one's own stand. In its higher sense it is to keep aloof and transcend both sides, after having exhausted the reasoning of each side.

Such are the characteristics of seeds in broad outline. Seeds are generally grouped under two categories: those of mind (*caita-dharma*) and those of the mind connected with external objects (*rūpa-dharma*). Oftentimes they are simply called the inner and the outer. The *Mahāyānasamparigraha Kārikā* by Abhāva does not make any such classification, but places both in an inner category. Kui Ji and other Chinese Vijñānavādins adopted both, holding that the six common characteristics of seeds should cover both. Simple though as these things may appear, yet by taking a step forward in our investigation, we will find this theory of seeds has great implications in controversy with certain other doctrines.

First of all, *saṃskṛta-dharma* (composite things or, in Chinese translation, active principles) must have births and deaths, hence transformations. In any state of transformation there must be the potency or power that forms the seeds. This formation is at once accompanied by the potency's extinction. As such this characteristic overshadows the theory of constancy of the four stages from birth to death held by the Saṃmatīyās. Besides, this spontaneously cancels Iśvara's and Prakṛti's doctrine of Sāṃkhyas because of the non-permanence caused by transformation. Consequently the one supreme Cause or Creator is being negated.

Second, the co-existence of seeds and fruits should mean also their simultaneity, as pointed out earlier. Abhāva explains this as referring to the inner seeds. In our modern language this may be interpreted as the motive and its action appearing at the same time. This appearing at the same time seems to negate the precedence of cause to effect, a theory emphasized by the Sthāvirās and Sautrāntikās, and in fact also by modern thinkers. But here the motive is recognized through its action and therefore called the seed of the action, and thus both can be simultaneous in manifestation. Of seeds with respect to their own seeds, the production must be in the sequence of time, which means the cause must precede the effect. But of seeds with respect to fruits of another kind in the same mind, the production is said to be simultaneous. Even though they are simultaneously existent, they must be in harmony with each other in the mind of the same person. If seeds should produce seeds of their own kind at the same time, then the being of the producing seeds must be infinite and the seeds produced must also be infinite. But when the producer and the product are not of the same kind, as when new seeds are formed through "perfuming" while they do not as yet produce any fruits, the old seeds cannot be infinite. In that very instant of a single *kṣaṇa* there cannot be two fruits forming into one.

The Sanskrit word *samudācāra* (*sam*+*ud*+*ācāra*) is sometimes translated as "proper practice or usage" and sometimes as "purpose". Because it is related to seeds here it is put as "fruits", bearing in mind that it is the mental dharma or very subtle psychological motive (seed) which has its action as result (fruit). The *Ālaya*-consciousness or the store of seeds and the human afflictions (*saṃkliśta-dharma*, called also *sāsrava-dharma*, defilements or contaminations) always serve mutually as cause and effect. The example given is the wick of a lamp or-candle and its flame. The flame burns the wick. It is compared to the fruit producing new seeds through "perfuming". The wick producing the flame is comparable to the seeds producing the fruits. This example, however, is not exact, because the flame does not produce a new wick. Yet the simile of combustion is applicable here if we take not the wick but the gas produced in comparison. There is the cycle of the flame bringing forth more gas for burning thus increasing the flame. Nowadays we may use the electric spark as an example: the flash of light is produced by electricity but it is different from the electric charge. They are co-existent, appearing and disappearing at the same instant (*kṣaṇa*). The example would be perfect if the spark produced another new charge.

The human mind is volatile by nature and nothing in it can be stable unless it is trained to fall into silence. It is our normal experience that thoughts appear and disappear almost at the same time, sometimes actually comparable to sparks or flashes of lightning. This might have been the origin of the theory of instantaneous extinction from a simple materialistic point of view.

Third, seeds of the same kind must follow in succession till the end when they met their transformation (*pratikṣepah*) at the high stage of bodhisattvahood. As the first seven senses suffer changes and interruptions through feelings of pain, joy, etc., they do not correspond to the dharma of seeds. This surpasses the view held by the Sautrāntikās that the six senses can also maintain seeds. In fact, it is purely mental, not sensory.

Fourth, the certainty of nature means the effects are positively determined by force of the causes, either good or evil or neutral. In this view the seeds are formed not at random, but consistently and persistently following the causal force of *samudācāra* in the process of "perfuming". This negates the view held by the Sarvāstivādās that dharmas, whether good or evil or neutral as causes are of one and the same category (*sabhāgahetuḥ*), and there can be interrelationship between them. But it is understood in this theory that there must be the sameness of nature with regard to cause and effect, and that goodness does not produce evil and vice versa, which means contradictory natures do not follow each other in sequence. There must be seeds of goodness as causes of goodness.

18

Following this line of explanation we come to another point in this theory. It seems that causality should only mean the production of fruits of the same kind or of the same nature as the seeds (*niṣyandaphalaṃ*). How do we explain the "differently matured fruits"? The eighth sense is by itself neutral, which means being above and free from both good and evil, just as the first five senses. The first five do not make any such distinction in perception. But if an object is good or bad, it is recognized at once as such because the sixth (*manas*) comes into the field. It discriminates in conducing to the operation of a certain sort of seed. Fundamentally consciousness itself is pure or neutral, but being in correspondence with mental properties of different natures, it varies. The *Ālayavijñāna*, although neutral by itself, contains seeds of all descriptions. Evil and good acts (karma) bring forth distress and happiness respectively, but distress and happiness are not to be taken as vices or virtues: they are states of feelings, being neither good nor bad, and hence neutral. With respect to virtues they are different in kind or category. *Vipāka* means "differently matured" in the sense of transformation which makes a thing into something of a different kind at a different time.

Now, the iron rule of causality or karma is a thing dreaded even by gods according to Hindu belief, and it can only be obliterated by the saving Grace of the Divine. In Mahāyāna karma is not negated or neglected, but maintained and held to be transcendable through the realization of the Truth that is above good or evil karma. This realization can be attained through a sudden major enlightenment or a series of successive minor or gradual enlightenments.

In the fifth place, seeds are in need of diverse co-operating causes for transformation, that is, for performing the function of giving rise to present activities. In other words, seeds of the same kind without the co-operation of their relative causes cannot be called seeds. The theory contradicts other systems which advocated one primeval cause such as Nature, or *Prajāpati*, or *Brahman* in Vedanta philosophy, or Time or Space by the Vaiśeṣikhās which alone created the universe all on a sudden without any auxiliary agency.

Finally, the argument is extended by the sixth point — in the production of fruits, the fruits must be of the category of the seeds themselves or correspond to the seeds. This further implies that the effect cannot be various if the cause is one, or if effects are various their causes must be diverse. This again opposes the one universal Cause. It is also opposed to the view held by the Sarvāstivādins that *rūpa* and *citta* can mutually serve as cause and effect. According to this theory *rūpa* cannot be the cause of *citta*, and vice versa, since their functions are different and they do not harmoniously follow each other in sequence. Seeds are characteristically subtle and deeply immersed, while the fruits they produce are externally evident in manifestation. Hence, only if seeds exist in conjunction with the fruits are they called seeds. In other words, they must always be accompanied by *samudācāra*.

In a sense, all the seeds are only named arbitrarily, just as wheat and rice are, and they are all supposed to be transformations of our consciousness. We come to a causality of merely inner psychological dharmas, taking into consideration only the seeds of consciousness, which can be as countless as the microbes on our physical body which occupy space, while the seeds are related to time.

19

As just stated above, the eighth sense is also called the Seed-consciousness, because it is a big storehouse of all kinds of seeds, those of *rūpa-dharma* as well as those of *citta-dharma*. All actions arise therefrom, and hence comes all our karma. Seeds have the capacity to produce, yet they have no being of themselves. Since they are the *svabhāva* or *lakṣaṇa* or the object of *dṛṣṭi* of the eighth consciousness, they depend upon the eighth for their being. It is not that the seeds hold the eighth, it is that the seeds are contained in the eighth. The capacity of holding or containing seeds is the characteristic of this consciousness, and the capacity to produce the present action (*samudācāra*) is the characteristic of the seeds. Moreover, this consciousness is supposed to be the self-nature (*svabhāva*) of all dharma, without which there could be nothing in existence, neither divinity nor Buddhahood nor anything. That is to say, apart from our cognition of the universe there is no substantial reality of the universe, according to Vasubandhu. This is the reason why modern translators have designated this Vijñānavāda as "uncompromising idealism."

An illustration to this often employed is the ocean. The eighth consciousness is compared to an ocean which is tranquil and placid, filled with pure, limpid water. *Indriya* or roots, objects, attention and all seeds are compared to wind. When wind blows on it, waves are produced. As the external relative causes impinge upon its surface, the seven senses begin to function, and one begins to see, to hear, etc. The waves may be interrupted or sometimes cease in motion, but the water of the ocean suffers no interruption or cessation. The eighth consciousness always moves in continuity.

This sounds like our mind, but it seems to be more than mind. It has to do with transmigration, according to this tradition.

20

Now that this much has been said about the eighth sense and its contents, we may now return to the seventh, *manovijñāna* or ego-consciousness, and see how is it related to the eighth.

As the famous argument advanced by Śaṅkarācārya goes, nobody says "I am not." Yet self-denial or forgetting or obliteration of the ego is praised in every system since ancient times. The great spiritual master in India, Śri Aurobindo, argues out painstakingly the non-existence of ego, affirming only the centres of consciousness. In Buddhism, whether Hīnayāna or Mahāyāna, the ego is always being negated, regarded as an illusion that is innate, a notion or "grasping" that is born with the man *a priori* (*sahaja*). In this theory of Pure Consciousness it is the essencelessness (*pudgala-nairātmya*) of ego that is laboriously elucidated, and this together with the essencelessness of dharma (*dharma-nairātmya*) constitute the chief aims of Xuan Zang in composing his monumental work.[12]

"I am." This is only a habitual statement. Diverse labels are used in the interpretation of ego, such as activity-consciousness, evolving-consciousness, representation-consciousness, particularization-consciousness or succession-consciousness. Activity is interpreted as karma, or works done by the agency as the doer, which is self-evident in expressions like "I am the doer, the worker," etc. Evolving or turning (*pravṛtti*) refers to the cognition of the image of the external world created by consciousness itself, which can be said of the other six senses as well, but not of the eighth. By representation the reflection or mirroring of the external object is meant, though the so-called "mirroring knowledge" is another thing. Particularization means the differentiation between defilement and purity. Succession means the continuation of karmic forces throughout the three times, past, present and future. By each of these names we can understand this seventh consciousness to a certain extent.

In Pure Consciousness theory ego is negated. The lengthy refutations against the doctrines about ego held by the Sāmkhyās,

12. It is interesting to note here that a Neo-Confucian of the Ming dynasty (14th to 17th cent.) said exactly the same thing in China, although nothing of Śaṅkarācārya was known to him. This must be co-incidental, or else we have to suppose that thoughts travel everywhere in the world by themselves and are only picked up by certain people at different times.

Vaiśeṣikhās, Nigranthaputrās, Parivrājakās and within Buddhism itself, those held by the Sautrāntikās and Sammitīyās in Hīnayāna, and by Madhyamikās in Mahāyāna, are here omitted. Briefly summarized, this theory admits the ego as a false appearance that originated from the sixth sense. The self is regarded only as a conglomeration of the five *skandhas* or aggregates without self-nature, because of its production through numerous conditions. It is only seemingly existent, like Māyā. Memory, recognition and other psychological functions are explained by seeds, some newly formed through the process of perfuming and some already existent in the eighth consciousness since the beginningless past.

A person may be Māyā or illusion, just as everything else is. The question is how does the illusory ego-consciousness of the seventh sense take the eighth as its underlying, stable self? Here we find another example of the gradual development of this theory into perfection. Among the ten masters we find four who gave their different answers, and only the last answer given by Dharmapāla seems to be most convincing and final. The other masters might have given similar answers but we find no record. According to Nanda the seventh sense regards the mind proper as the ego (*ātmagrāhaḥ*), and when it comes into contact with the mental properties, it grasps them as everything which belongs to oneself (*ātmīyaṃ*). Next, according to Citrabhāna, the seventh is related to both the *dṛṣṭi* and *lakṣaṇa* parts of consciousness, and when it is related to the former, it takes it as the *Ātmā*, and when it is related to the latter it grasps it as *Ātmīyaṃ*.

To be related to means to come positively into contact with, thus producing a certain result. Here Sthiramati in his orthodox way of commenting on Vasubandhu maintained that the seventh relates itself to the eighth in its present activity thus holding it to be the ego, and relates itself also to the seeds of the eighth, thus grasping them as what belongs to the ego. This seems to be one step advanced in the interpretation of this theory. Finally, Dharmapāla in his analysis held that the seventh relates itself only to the *dṛṣṭi* part of the eighth, not to the *lakṣaṇa*, nor to seeds, nor to mental properties. *Dṛṣṭi* or seeing accepts the object, as is evident in its function, and hence there appears the ego or "I". If it is related to the *lakṣaṇa* part, then it is related to the external objects like the first five senses. It cannot be related to the seeds, because the seeds, such as those of forms (*rūpa-bīja*), belong to a class among the five classes of aggregates (*pañcopādāna-skandhās*) other than the class of the aggregate of consciousness. Moreover, it cannot be related to the mental properties (*caitasikā*) because the properties are not masters of themselves, not abodes to be resorted to or relied upon. Hence, the seventh sense, the I, is related only to the *dṛṣṭi* part of the eighth. Comparatively speaking, this explanation given by Dharmapāla seems to be most satisfactory.

At this juncture it is fitting to ask: how is life to be explained? According to the Sarvāstivadins of Hīnayāna there is a principle pertaining neither to *rūpa-dharma* nor to *caita-dharma* that sustains the warmth and conscience of the body for a certain length of time. It is called the "root of life" (*jīvitaṃ*). But according to this theory, it is to be also explained by seeds. By the action of one's past karma, seeds in the eighth consciousness bring forth two results, first to produce fruits or activities, and next to temporarily sustain the fruits in consciousness. This sustenance of *citta* and *rūpa* in continuity is then called Life, an assumption of something without any real separate entity. This pertains to the category of dharma not in correspondence with mind (*viprayuktasaṃskāra-dharma*).

Life then hinges on karma. To the question of who has created his karma and who reaps the fruits if there is not the ego, it is answered in this theory that the dharma of *citta* and *caitasikā*, being always in continuity and propelled by forces of causes and auxiliary causes, forms the karma, with its results experienced by the eight branches of consciousness of a falsely created ego. And it is the force of karma that brings about the rotation in a cycle of deaths and rebirths.

To come to the conviction that one is not someone, or to have one's ego dissolved, which is never an easy task, means the loss of his identity. The person in the present, be he a sage or a criminal, is no longer the same person as in the past, and if he does not attach himself strongly to his past karma, he may have certain peace of mind and live peacefully with others in society. Here lies the beauty of most religions: to hold forth the promise of a new person growing out of the old one and beginning a new life, as if becoming someone else. The dharma of this Lakṣaṇa school is no exception. But it is even more radical than other systems, because again not only the ego but also dharma itself is held as void.

21

With regard to the sixth sense a few words more must be said. It is sometimes translated as idea, and sometimes as mind, and in modern Chinese, the term has been taken to denote "ideology". Accompanying the first five senses and also relying upon them, it relates itself to the five kinds of objects and thus grasps the object distinctly. Its functioning goes through direct perception or inference or error in the measurement of knowledge. When separated from the five senses, it comes forth individually as a single-headed idea in our mind. It is the obscure idea which pertains to direct perception in meditation. In its scattered condition, it is our ordinary mind in the waking state, coming into contact with every dharma as it goes through all the three measurements of knowledge. In dreams and daydreams it is the single-headed idea which gains precedence when many such ideas are jumbled in confusion. In these two conditions no correct knowledge can come about. In consideration of the qualities (*guṇa* or merits), this sense depends upon the first five in going thoroughly through the three natures of being good or bad or neutral. Yet this applies only to the mental state of an ordinary man or the mental state with certain hindrances (*kleśa*), i.e. in the *sāsrava* state. In the *anāsrava* state or freedom from any hindrance, only goodness remains.

Ordinarily this sixth sense is taken as the master of the mind and the seventh and eighth senses are neglected. It distinguishes itself from the other seven by always remaining in a state of present activity. It is the most powerful and the most swift in action. All our actions of mind and speech and body are caused by it because it discriminates, determines and motivates them all. Action is karma. All the karmic forces, whether good or bad or neutral, issue from this source. Whatever good or bad is done, it is preceded by idea. If the idea is good, then the action or speech can be good. So it can be said that because karma has no individual being of its own, it takes only this sense as its nature; this is the same as to say karma is idea and idea is mind.

So far this refers only to the thinking mind. As to the feelings (the five *vedanās*) opinions vary. One group of ancient masters held that this sense has only sorrow, joy or indifference, but no pain. Another group held that pleasure and pain, both of which pertain to the bodily senses, are also acknowledged by it. In utmost pleasure there is no root of joy, and likewise in utmost pain there is no root of sorrow. Perhaps one must be able to make sharp distinctions between the emotional and physical feelings before one can make a judgment on those two groups.

As outlined above, this sixth sense does not depend upon many relative causes to come about. There are certain conditions under which it does not arise, for example, in the states of *asaṃjñāsamāpatti* and *nirodhasamāpatti* where all thoughts cease to exist and when one is in a state of perfect silence similar to *Nirvāṇa*. These can be reached only after life-long practices. Also when one is in a state of coma or falls into a profound sleep caused by exhaustion of physical energy, then this along with the first five no longer functions. When it does function, it is instrumental in initiating the action of the first five. It helps them to rise.

22

Now, if we turn to the side of objects, we may perhaps gain a clearer understanding of this theory. All objects in the universe are regarded as features or appearances (*lakṣaṇa*) of consciousness that brought them into shape, or in a technical term here, "transformed" them. They are divided into three categories:

First, natural objects — these include the total *lakṣaṇa* of the first five senses and of the eighth, together with the partial *lakṣaṇa* of the sixth. They are produced from their proper seeds in the *Ālayavijñāna*, possessed of their real nature or maintaining to themselves their own nature. Thus nature here is an equivalent to reality. *Rūpa* is real *rūpa* and *citta* is real *citta*. Since all objects are transformed by the *Ālayavijñāna* into *lakṣaṇa*, and since this *Ālayavijñāna* is formed by *tathātā* or Real Suchness under certain relationships, so the *lakṣaṇa* is originally the real being of *tathātā* without *lakṣaṇa*. Although this being is now being deluded and has transformed itself into the false or apparent dharma of physical objects, its nature is yet real. And this nature is understood as appearance in itself (*svalakṣaṇa*), only to be approached by direct perception regardless of the past or future. By itself it does not follow the *citta-dharma* in being good or bad or neutral.

Summarizing all that has been said by ancient masters of this school, natural objects include

1) *sāsrava* seeds,

2) the physical body with all its organs,

3) the material world of five senses, and

4) *rūpa* appearing in *dhyāna* (not included here in our discussion).

And, all these objects are "transformed" by the *Ālayavijñāna* or Root-consciousness and thus come into being.

Second are imaginative objects: this category is in Chinese translation the "singular-image objects."

The image is synonymous with *lakṣaṇa*. It arises singularly without any productive seeds, nor has it any reality upon which it establishes itself. It is the perversion of *dṛṣṭi* that comes about along with the sixth sense. The examples are the hair of the turtle or the horns of a rabbit. The *rūpa* of the most minute atom (*paramāṇu*) or the *rūpa* of the farthest distance are supposed to belong to this group, since they do not have their own seeds in the mind.

Third are substantial objects, or in Chinese, "objects carrying their own substance." This category involves two kinds:

1) the real which denotes objects brought forth by the mind (*citta*) in coming into relationship with mental principles (*citta-dharma*), and

2) the seeming which denotes objects brought forth by the mind (*citta*) in coming into relationship with matter (*rūpa-dharma*).

What is immediately transformed by consciousness is the substance. Which means the seeds of all external objects in our mind are formed by the eighth sense. This process of formation is "transformation". It is immediate, instantaneous, and by it all objects, or rather all images of objects, come about. The image is the simile of the object, the appearance of *lakṣaṇa*. The material object is nescient and does not produce the image of itself, its image is only produced from and in the mind or, the sixth sense in its *dṛṣṭi* or seeing capacity. Thus it is only one end of a rod as related to the other, so to speak.

When the seventh sense (*manovijñāna*) relates itself to the *dṛṣṭi* part of the eighth or the root-consciousness as its object, it carries with it the self-feature (*svalakṣaṇa*) of the *dṛṣṭi* in the relationship. Its *lakṣaṇa* is not produced from any special sort of seed, it is arisen merely from the relating end and the related end, that is to say, half of it is produced from the seeds of the active relating *dṛṣṭi*, and another half of it is produced from the passively related root-consciousness. That which relates and that which is related are both in the mind, and in this juxtaposition the appearance of the ego is formed. The ego has no being of itself; it is merely a seeming or illusory appearance of self produced from both ends of the *citta-dharma*, as when beams of light produced from two lamps shine upon each other.

But in the second category, the imaginative, there is also the non-substantial imaginative object. How is this real *citta-dharma* to be distinguished from that? The non-substantial imaginative object does not rely upon the related substance, it is simply that which all of a sudden appears in the *dṛṣṭi* of the sixth sense. The real substantial object arises from the substance of that which is related to. That makes the difference. The substantial imaginative object is also the seeming substantial one. If the object is the image of the moon in water or any image in a mirror or images of the past in remembrance, then though the transformation relied upon a substance, both the image and the substance are unreal and both depend upon the seeds of the *lakṣaṇa* of the sixth sense. So both non-substantial and substantial imaginative objects follow the *dṛṣṭi*, having no seeds of their own.

This seems to be fairly complicated. Yet this is still a systematic and reasonable analysis of the whole process of perception. What here given is only a very brief sketch in broad outlines, without going into a large bulk of details. But it may be asked: physical matter (*rūpa*) is something tangible, having its dimensions and qualities, etc. How can it be transformed by consciousness and thus brought into being?

The answer is that the eighth consciousness itself does not create *rūpa* by transformation. The eighth holds in itself the seeds of the *lakṣaṇa* of *rūpa*, and by force of causation of the "inner perfuming," it forms the *lakṣaṇa* of *rūpa*, such as the five *indriyas* of the eye, the ear, etc., and the five attributes of color, sound, etc. The five senses use the transformed five *indriyas* as "ruling causes" (*adhipatipratytya*) and their five attributes as "objective causes" (*ālambanapratyaya*) — by causes here the relative or co-operating causes are meant. If the five senses were not supported by the transformations of the eighth, then they would have no objects. That would be the same as to say there would be no existence. Here existence is not denied, but only the reality of existence is being denied. *Vijñāna* alone is.

23

If consciousness is the last word for the universe, how is life and how is matter to be explained? This theory does not pretend to be able to explain the origin of life or matter. Certain spiritual masters in modern times advocate that there can only be gradations of consciousness, and the world is not to be divided into one spiritual and another material, maintaining that apart from all living beings including those of the vegetable kingdom, even minerals are endowed with consciousness in a latent form, as the molecular structure of certain precious stones or even the crystallization of water into snowflakes in beautiful symmetrical forms show. Moreover, there can be such wonders as materialization performed by some mystics. No doubt, supernatural feats such as materialization or levitation should not be brought into discussion in the field of dialectical philosophy. This theory is also in its own way distant from mysticism. On the whole, in China at least, Buddhism did not greatly deviate from the original teachings of Buddha, which were factually a movement of enlightenment which cleared away all sorts of superstitious beliefs in the ancient Brahmanical world and was very much against the performing of wonders or miracles. This theory is greatly inclined toward intellectualism and rationalism. Thus in order to explain matter, knowledge (*vidyā*) and ignorance (*avidyā*) are brought into consideration.

The world is involved in ignorance. This universal ignorance is divided into two kinds: the conscient or cognizant, and the nescient or incognizant. The eight branches of consciousness and the six states of mental properties are arisen from the former, and all material objects such as mountains and rivers and all material elements are arisen from the latter. Both co-operate in forming the inner root of the senses. This inner root insofar as it is of matter, is conscient and able to reflect the object. The five senses are the products of this inner root, which is one, while their respective physical organs are separated. Fundamentally there is one essence of knowledge (*vidyā*) which is spiritual. Yet the very first movement of mind or consciousness is ignorance. The essence must be taken as a spiritual whole which in this theory is denoted as the real mind of *tathātā*, but it is covered by ignorance. Conscient ignorance covered or wrapped up for a long time produces the essence of consciousness. The essence of *dṛṣṭi* reflects *rūpa*, and *rūpa* develops into the physical organs. When the ignorance, though thick, has not yet formed the *rūpa* of the four physical elements, it is called the outer crust or shell of *avidyā*. The original spiritual essence in the universe is understood as the real, subtle and brilliant mind, but being wrapped up in the shell, it has become individualized, and forms the abode or dwelling of ignorance. This results in the formation of the five *skandhas* or aggregates and all living beings. And, one argues, if it were not by the force of *avidyā*, what else could wrap up the spiritual mind? All the eight senses and mental properties must have a certain place upon which they depend before they can come about, and the *rūpaprasāda-indriyaṃ* is their *adhipati-pratyaya*.

According to the philosophy of Śri Aurobindo, there is *vidyā* involved in *avidyā*, and there cannot be evolution without involution. On this point there is a great resemblance between these two systems.

As this theory goes, the root can develop out of senses which reflect the objects but is incapable of relating itself to *rūpa*. Only the senses, as the offspring of this development, are capable of coming into relationship with *rūpa*, owing to their ability of discrimination.

The five senses together with the sixth are said to be the essence or rather the spiritual light of the eighth passing out through the six outlets in its radiation. If it passes through the eye, it can discern *rūpa*, hence it is called eye-consciousness. Likewise if it passes through the ear, it can discriminate *śabda*, and hence it is called the ear-consciousness. The same is the case with the other three up to the sixth, which takes cognizance of all dharma and is called the *manas* or mental consciousness. By way of illustration, it may be compared to a chamber with six windows in which a monkey is confined. If one calls the monkey through any of the windows, the monkey answers through that window. This is a metaphor for perception.

A word about *Manaskāra* may be said. It is translated as "attention", the first of the five overall pervading mental properties (*pañca sarvatragaḥ*), and that on which depend the feeling, thinking, will (*vedanā, saṃjña, cetanā*) which are present in every perceptual relationship. *Manaskāra* awakens the mind and leads it toward the object. It may be asked: does it lead the mind in its state of seed or in the state of present activity? The answer is that the nature of *manaskāra* is clear and sharp. Even in its seed state it alerts the mind and other mental properties to start their present activities. A simile for this is many people sleeping in a big dormitory, among whom one is by nature an insomniac. And when a thief has entered the hall, this man rouses up all the others. The seeds of *manaskāra* awaken the mind when the mind is asleep, and by their action it leads the mind to take action when the mind is awake. It must be present with all activities of the senses.

24

So far all the eight branches of consciousness briefly stated above pertain to the principle of mind (*citta-dharma*). The term mind is synonymous with heart in ordinary Chinese, but differently interpreted in different systems. Usually mind is said to be connected with thoughts with the physical brain as its basis, and heart is connected with emotions and feelings, with the corporeal cardia as its centre. It seems to be a proven truth as advocated by many spiritual masters that thoughts do not have their seat in the brain, but belong to another plane in the cosmos. In Buddhism in general thoughts are almost obliterated; in any case they occupy no such important place as in modern philosophy. According to this theory, mind is simply the eighth sense as it assembles all seeds in producing their present activities, but it includes also the remaining seven and their present activities in forming and assembling seeds by "perfuming". Mind relates itself to objects and discriminates and contemplates ... in all, it thinks. Thus discrimination and contemplation and thinking are functions of mind, and they are grouped under *citta-dharma*. Yet that which ever depends upon, corresponds with and pertains to mind is the mental property (*caitasikādharma*). It must be noted here that correspondence means the condition of existing at the same time, depending on the same basis and being in equal relationship and equal in fact.

Mental properties are numerous, generally held to number fifty-one in all[13] and classified under five categories. The Sarvāstivādās held that mental properties are different from mind proper (*citta*), but the Sautrāntikās maintained that they were the same. By this theory it is held that as the mental properties are produced by the potency of mind, it is reasonable to give the first place to the powerful mind and ascribe to it the name of pure-consciousness, and this as mental-consciousness must necessarily include its properties. But ultimately in a transcendental sense mind and mental properties can be spoken of as one or two, or neither one nor two. They are just like the sun and the sunshine: they appear at the same time.

13. See Appendix.

25

The whole theory revolves around the problem of seeds. Seeds are said to be of two kinds: those originally existent in the store-consciousness, and those that are newly formed. Formation comes about after long periods of "perfuming". A distinction is here made between the perfumer and the perfumed. What is perfumed is no other than the eighth sense, and those capable of perfuming are the remaining seven senses. With regard to this point, two ancient masters were not agreed. Nanda insisted that all seeds are newly formed, but Chandragupta held that all seeds are originally inherent in our consciousness. The argument against Nanda is that there is no reason for the seeds of the highest grade of *anāsrava* nature and the seeds of neutral character — that is to say, being neither good nor bad — to be newly formed, and if these were not originally existent, from what could they be produced? The opposition to Chandragupta is that if only the aboriginal seeds were existent without any new formation, what would the results of formations by the remaining seven senses be? The question goes further: if water is wet in and of itself, it does not need objects to moisten to prove its wetness. If that were the case, then fire should not burn and wind should not move. Finally a third master, Dharmapāla, came to the conclusion that both kinds of seeds are existent in the store-consciousness. And that was the solution of the key issue of this theory.

This reasoning did not go any further. Obviously there is here the question of the origination of the already existent seeds, but it remains understandably unanswered.

Next, the process of perfuming offers certain difficulty to our understanding and needs further explanation. The eighth is being perfumed, and is hence passive. The first seven senses are the perfumers, hence active. The perfumes are goodness, evil and neutrality. Like tiny particles of a scent they usually remain. But why are the remaining seven senses not being perfumed?

To be perfumed there are four conditions that must be fulfilled. First, the object must be stable, that is, persisting in maintaining its own nature from the beginning to the very end, and hence capable of retaining the scent. The other seven senses are never stable, so they cannot accept any perfuming. Second, the object must be neutral or indifferent, so as to be able to adopt or form new habits. Just as musk and sandalwood have too strong a smell and so are not neutral and cannot be perfumed, so are goodness and evil. Third, there must be receptivity on the part of the object. It must be free unto itself and soft by nature, and then it can be easily perfumed, unlike stone. None of the mental properties are masters by themselves, all are too stubborn, and so are also the *asamskrtadharmas*. Fourth, there must be harmony between the two. The perfumer and the perfumed must be present in the same place and at the same time, being neither separated nor combined. (This is also different from the doctrine of the Sautrāntikās that the former moment of the mind perfumes its next moment.) By this point it is meant that the seven senses of one person cannot perfume the eighth sense of another. One may make some impression on somebody else, but the retaining of this in memory must be done by the person impressed.

Only the eighth sense can fulfill all four of these requirements. But on the active side of the first seven senses, there are also requirements for them to satisfy before they can perfume so as to form new seeds. First, they must be inconstant, or to have origin and end, in other words, formation and destruction. Only in this way new habits can be brought to shape. This eliminates the *asamskrtadharma* which are eternally the same and incapable of any action. Second, they must be possessed of power. Goodness or evil or indifference must be strong enough to generate movements. This excludes the eighth which is not powerful. Third, there must be waxing and waning in the action and thus an ability to promote the growth of habits. As the result of becoming a

Buddha the formations of the senses are always fulfilled in perfect goodness without any increase or decrease, so they cannot perfume. Then the fourth requirement is the same as the fourth mentioned above, that is, the active and the passive must always be in harmony with each other, which means always in good correspondence. Hence the perfumer and the perfumed appear and disappear in simultaneity.

26

A

As far as this theory goes, it appears to be a very well organized and meticulously elaborated system of philosophy or rather psychology within the field of Mahāyāna Buddhism. Yet it is a dharma and a dharma with a purpose of its own. In the final analysis this dharma is neither philosophy nor religion in the European sense. Its purpose is plainly stated in the first paragraph of the opening chapter of Xuan Zhuang's famous treatise, the *Vijñāptimātratāsiddhi*. It runs:

> This treatise is now written for those people who are misled and who have misconceived the double voidness. It tends to bring them to a correct understanding by breaking through their double obstacles. Owing to their grasping of *ātmā* (ego) and dharma (religion), both obstacles arise. If the double voidness is realized, both the obstacles can be removed as a consequence. By the

removal of obstacles, two excellent results can be achieved. By removing the obstacle of afflictions which perpetuates births and rebirths, one attains to *Nirvāṇa* or final emancipation. By removing the obstacle of knowing which hinders correct understanding, one attains to *Mahābodhi* or the Great Wisdom ....

Thus it can be seen that this theory has a pragmatic purpose. The volumes of words which follow are intended to carry out this aim.

If all dharma are taken together they are a hundred in number, according to Vasubandhu, ninety-four *saṃskṛta-dharma* or dharma with activities and six *asaṃskṛtadharma* or dharma without activity. In enumerating the hundred items, he ended with two terms: *pudgala-nairatmya* and *dharma-nairatmya*. In Vasubandhu's times it was perhaps not necessary to give any explanation to these two terms because they seemed to be too self-evident. Yet this led to the annotations made by later Vijñānavādins.

The Vijñānavādins do not lag behind the Vedāntins in their use of etymological analysis, and the later Tantric masters followed the same method. They all employed a method which was a sort of mnemonic device for the purpose of propagating one's own creed without any regard to philological or etymological truths which, however, were not entirely discarded whenever they could suit their special purposes. For example the word "*pudgala*" here, was analysized this way:

pu = often or again and again;

dga = to take, to go through;

la = spheres of beings, as these of gods, men, and animals.

The word means ego.

Sattvas or individuals, being always deluded, must perform actions as long as they live. All actions large or small are summed up as karma. Owing to their past karma they go to or pass through diverse spheres of existence in cycles of births and rebirths. Yet they are not masters of themselves, and there is no self-will. This means *pudgala-nairatmya.*

It has been naively questioned whether *pudgala* or ego is the mind. If it is, then egos must be eight in number. Is the ego the mental properties? If so, egos must be fifty-one in number. Is the ego a material principle? As the five inner roots are not visible and the five outer roots are the same as external matter, and as both appear and disappear without cessation, whereupon is the ego to be established? ... In this way every item of the hundred dharma may be enquired into, yet nowhere can any real *pudgala* be found.

The word dharma is explained as coming from the root *dhṛ*, which means "to hold" or "uphold" in regular tracks. This is the correct etymological analysis. *Dharma-nairatmya* means dharma without any real essence to itself. Which is the same as to say that dharma is not. According to worldly truths (*saṃvṛtisatyaṃ*) all the hundred dharma are established together with their distinctions, yet in transcendental truths (*pàramārthasatyaṃ*) they are said to be all illusory like magic images. Thus non-existence appears as existence, and existence is non-existent. All are like airy nothing or flowers seen in hallucination or the moon in water or a drop of dew or a flash of lightning. Viewed in this scope the world is nil or void. And following from this all human sufferings and distresses are wiped out, as they must also be nil or void.

By a broad division, dharma is only of two kinds as just mentioned, that of action and that of non-action. As everything in the universe undergoes changes and nothing is everlasting, so the universe is considered to be one of movement or changes or action. In recording the results of observation of this phenomenon, ancient Chinese made their *Book of Changes*, which is still widely studied. Buddhism views the same universal phenomenon but expresses it in a different way. Whatever exists is seen as the result of certain factors or conditions combined or related together, and this combination or relation must mean action. All the principles of mind and matter are thus included therein. This is then the theory of "dependent origination" (*pratītyasamutpada*). Besides this there is also the opposite dharma of non-action, which comes ultimately to a Suchness.

As everything in the universe is dependent in origination, it must be then devoid of any real being of itself. Only its outward appearance which is called *lakṣaṇa* can be reached by mind. Hence all things are only seemingly real, and one step further in reasoning brings us to the conclusion that all are transformations of our mind.

Next to the appearance there is the "name" which is applied to the appearance. If we say something is unnamable, we are still attaching a label, and thus becoming even more distant from the thing-in-itself.

A third kind is the dharma of distinction. This comes in with the mind's function of distinguishing objects as positive or negative, subject or object, etc.

A fourth kind of dharma is that of right knowledge. This is the knowledge involving the first three and the knowledge of Buddha and Bodhisattva, or the knowledge of *anāsrava*, explained as "no leakage." Leakage is the condition of affliction and annoyance of our ordinary mentality, with all its feelings of sorrow or happiness, etc. This is *kleśa*. It signifies suffering but also enjoyment. One may experience something enjoyable and be happy, and this happiness is also leakage.

All these four kinds are grouped under *samskāradharma* or principle of action. The fifth is the *asaṃskṛtadharma* or principle of non-action. These five dharma and the three *svabhāva* or self-natures are the main subjects which the Lakṣaṇa school studied deeply and finally annulled.

B

Before we inquire further into the details of this theory, one point of some importance should be made clear. This theory of Pure Consciousness including the doctrines of the ten masters belonged to the Lakṣaṇa school, otherwise also called the Yogācāra school, in opposition to the Mādhyamikā school. The Yogācāra and the Mādhyamikā schools were antagonistic to each other; their controversies will be treated at the end of the present work. But to understand their quarrel, one should first understand that Yogācāra stood as a school different from *Yoga* in general.

The word *Yoga* used in Buddhism bears a different sense from what is now generally understood as *Yoga* in India. In Chinese the word remains in its transliteration. It should not be misunderstood as the system of *patañjali*. As Buddhism is often and rightfully placed in the category of atheism, the Buddhist *Yoga* does not mean the merging of oneself into or identification with the Divine. It is interpreted as "accordance" or "conformance" or "correspondence", and applied to the self-nature of all dharma as being not contrary to and hence in correspondence with objects. It is used with subjects such as *dhyāna* and *mati* to indicate conformance to practice. It is also applied to the establishment or non-establishment of right reasoning regarding mundane or supermundane truths, and also obtaining of spiritual fruits such as *Bodhi*. If the divine virtues are in accord with each other, they are also said to be in *yoga*. When the right medicine has worked upon a disease and cured it, it is also *yoga*.

Yogācāra or the "conduct of yoga" is not what is now known as yogic exercises. Yogācārya was not an ordinary *yogi*. He was a Buddhist master well versed in theories of diverse schools but also expert in *dhyāna*. *Saṃgharakṣa*, for example, was a yogi but belonged not to the Yogācāra school. The famous work of this school is called *Yogācāryabhūmi Śāstra* by Maitreya (actually by Asaṅga) which was delivered three times over by Śīlabhādra in lecture form to Xuan Zang and thence introduced to China. Its original in Sanskrit and its translation in Chinese are now extant.

It does not seem that Haṭha Yoga and Rāja Yoga as independent systems were ever introduced to China. Similar practices can be found in Taoism, but it is difficult to say which was influenced by which, and equally difficult to say they were purely parallel developments without any knowledge of each other. In later times as Mahāyāna declined, Buddhist Yogācāra gradually deteriorated. *Yoga* still remained and flourished in India in the Tantric school, which is another story.

27

A

Details of the contents of Pure Consciousness theory cannot be fully given here, but certain main points may be mentioned. The negation of the essential reality of external objects gives rise to doubts. The argument over these doubts deals with the definiteness of the place and time occupied by objects and the indefiniteness of the perceptions and their functions. There are four questions advanced by the Sautrāntikās and answered by Vasubandhu in his *Treatise of Twenty Ślokas* (*Viṃśatikā-vijñaptimātratāsiddhiḥ*):

1) If apart from real external dharma as the really existent *rūpa* the consciousness of *rūpa* arises without being conditioned by it, why then does this consciousness arise only at certain places and not at all places?

2) And, in the same manner, why does this consciousness arise at a definite time and not at all times?

3) At the same place and the same time there can be not only one

person but many. Why should the consciousness of one person be a definite criterion for the appearance of an object? For example, some people with eye-trouble see certain hairs or bees at places where there are none, while other people with good eyes do not have such visions.

4) The fourth question consists of three questions all connected with function:

a. Why the illusion of hairs, etc. does not have the use of real hairs, etc.

b. Why drinks or food, etc. taken in dreams do not have the use of real drinks or food, etc., and

c. Why airy cities (*gandharvanagara*) do not have the use of real cities?[14]

All these four points of doubt are explained away by Vasubandhu using the simile of dreams. In dreams objects are perceived at definite places and times and not at all places and times. Beings of the same constitution and of the same karma do see the same objects. Men may see the river as a river, but hungry ghosts may see it as something different from a river. Thus things perceived depend upon the perceiver. As to the "use" or function of unrealities, these are also possible, as evidenced by the fact that a man may have emissions in dreams.

Here we see plainly that the limit of human reasoning is transgressed, however convincing these explanations might have been in Vasubandhu's time. The argument eventually shows itself to be still a matter of faith, or in a slightly derogatory sense, a matter of superstition. Descriptions of hungry ghosts and of hell as a realm of moving iron mountains and flaming iron ground or of the guardians of hell and all sorts of torture present a grotesque picture frightening and threatening enough to serve as material for fine literature but too fantastic to be included in the field of philosophy. Yet we may still extract a certain essence out of the crude minerals of ancient thinking.

14. The original Sanskrit text for the English interpretation of these four questions is as follows:
yadi vijñaptiranarthā niyamo deśakālayoḥ Saṅtānasyāniyamaśca yuktā kṛtyakriyā na ca kimuktam bhavati yadi vinā rupādyarthena rupādi vijñaptirutpadyate na rupādy-arthāt kasmāt kvaciddeśa utpadyate na sarvatra tatreva ca deśe kadācidutpadyate na sarvadā taddeśakālapratiṣ ṭhitānām sarvesām Santāna utpada na kevalamekasya yathā taimirikāṇām saṅtāne keśādyāhhāso nānyeṣām kasmādyattaimirikaiḥ keśahhramarādi drśyate tena kriyā na kriyate na ca tadanyairna kriyate gandharvaṇadāreṇāsattvān nagarakriyā na kriyate na ca tadanyairna kriyate tasmādarthābhave deśakāla yadan-napānavastraviṣāyudhādi svapne dṛśyte tenānnādi kriyā na kriyate na ca tadanyairna kriyatc niyamaḥ saṅtānāniyamaḥ kṛtyakriyā ca na yujyate

B

The argument is taken a step further by another theological question: if apart from consciousness there are no real external objects as the eye and things seen by the eye, why has Buddha himself talked about the twelve stations, i.e. the six sense organs and the six sorts of sense data (*cakṣurāyatanaṃ*, *rūpāyatanaṃ*)?

The answer: These are transformations of the consciousness and not independent realities. The eye-consciousness is produced by its own seeds through the combination of diverse relative causes, and it is by this that the *lakṣaṇa* or appearance of an object is formed. Buddha talked about the station of the eye and the station of visual form as being based upon their seeds and their formations, but he did not say that apart from consciousness there could be such external realities. Moreover, Buddha said this for the purpose of bringing people to the realization of the voidness of the ego, just as he taught the existence of an inner being of man after death called *antarābhava* in order to refute the theory of absolute nihilism, which claims that there is nothing left after a man's death. But Buddha also did not mean that these beings are external realities; they are merely illusions as well.

C

Now another question arises: if voidness of the ego is intimately accompanied by the voidness of dharma, is this theory of Pure Consciousness not void, as it is also dharma?

The answer: No.

Why?

It is not something grasped, so it is. This means that if any real existence of dharma is grasped in *dṛṣṭi* and *lakṣaṇa*, which are transformations of consciousness, it is then wrong. For treating this malady of grasping the non-reality as reality, the voidness of dharma is prescribed. It is not that what the correct knowledge above words realized as the nature of consciousness is also void. What is grasped in *sarvakalpita* (universal discrimination) as *paratamtra* (dependent for origination) is non-existent, and therefore void. What is realized as *pariniṣpanna* (perfect and accomplished reality) is existent, and therefore not void. If this correct knowledge is also void, there will be no more worldly truth. And if there is no worldly truth, then there will also be no more transcendental truth. This would lead to an absolute nihilism which Buddha calls an incurable disease. Such nihilism was greatly denounced by Nāgārjuna and Vasubandhu and nearly all Mahāyānists.

D

Now another question arises: if consciousness is the being at all states of *rūpa*, how is it that the similitude of *rūpa* appears, for example, the substantiality of matter, in its persistence without changes?

Answer: The appearance with its persistence is due to the influence of the perfuming action of names and forms in man's mind formed as perpetual habits since beginningless past. It serves as the abode upon which the pure and impure dharma reside. If there were no such appearance, then there would be no perversions or false clinging of the senses to the unreal *rūpa* as real objects. There would be also no impure dharma or contaminations, and hence also no pure dharma.

Put in another way, the question is simply this: if no real external *rūpa* is admitted, how can there be the appearance of a similitude of *rūpa*? The answer is: because of the false appearance and false being, one must admit the existence of *rūpa*-consciousness and non-*rūpa*-

consciousness. If there is no transfigured similitude of *rūpa* as the cause, there will be no transfigured false being as its effect, because causes and effects are related in mentality.

E

Another question: As the external objects of senses are perceived through *pratyakṣa* or direct perception, how can they be negated as non-existent?

Answer: At the very moment of direct perception, the object is not understood as external. Only when the sixth sense comes into play is the conviction of something external produced. And this is false. What is produced through *pratyakṣa* is the part of *svalakṣaṇa* self-appearance, which is the product or transformation of consciousness, and that can be held as existent. But any real external *rūpa* grasped by the *manas* must be held as non-existent. It is in the nature of *sarvakalpita*.

As to this point, there are different opinions. The Sautrāntikās admit the continual existence of the external objects instant by instant (*kṣaṇa*) without interruption. The refutation is: as the *manas* after the five senses comes into the scene in contact with *rūpa*, at that very instant the perceiving *pratyakṣa* of the five senses disappears, and therefore that can be no longer direct perception. The Sarvāstivādās hold that *rūpa*, etc. are also extinguished instant by instant. Then as the *manas* comes to the field, the five senses and their objects must have disappeared too. How can there be then direct perception?

Here Mahāyānists made a very subtle modification by saying that the sixth sense accompanies the first five at the moment of perception and also has its grasping as in the next moment.

If it were not so, the Mahāyānist argues, then by hearing a sound there would be no grasping of the sound. Thus in the sixth there is also *pratyakṣa* in accompanying the first five. From any given initial moment it has grasping as its next moment, and thus the further distinction arises. Then the object is held as external. And, seen in this way, objects perceived in our daily life are not real objects. They are not external yet beheld as external. All is like a dream: no objects should be grasped as real external objects.

Now it is again questioned: if in our waking state all objects are like those in dreams and not separated from our consciousness, how is it that when we are awakened from dreams we remember what we have seen in our dreams as purely our mental images, while in our awake state we do not know objects seen by ourselves as purely creations of our consciousness?

The answer is that when one is in dreams, one does not know himself to be dreaming. Only when one is awakened can one remember his dreams. The same is true with the objects we see in our awake state. Until we reach the state of true awakening which is Enlightenment, we cannot know ourselves to be dreaming. So the Buddha regarded life and death as a long dark night. On this account we do not know the creations of our consciousness.

F

Here another difficulty poses itself, namely, the phenomenon in Buddhist psychology called *paracittajñānaṃ*, meaning the knowledge of the mind of other people, which is sometimes a proven experience. If one's mind can be related to the mind of another person, is this not the same as the mind grasping something external?

Answer: Who says that the mind of others is not the object of one's own consciousness? It is only not admitted that the mind of others is the object intimately related to one's mind. The function of consciousness is not like the holding of any object by hand, nor like the sun, moon or fire shedding light intimately upon objects external to itself. It is only like a mirror reflecting the image of an object. Mind reading is not that one's mind could intimately take hold of the other's mind. What consciousness knows is the part of appearance transformed by itself. This is so with mind reading, just as it is with the cognizance of *rūpa*.

Another question: The theory of Pure Consciousness advocates that there is nothing existing outside our mind. As there are minds of others outside our own mind which can be known, what then ... ?

Answer: Does this theory hold that there is only the consciousness of myself? If so, how can there be the distinctions between the high and the low, the sages and the common men, *citta-dharma* and *rūpa-dharma*, etc.?

It must be understood that this theory of consciousness holds that all human beings are possessed of eight senses, six groups of mental properties, the division of the perceived and the perceiver in transformations, the twenty-four non-corresponding dharmas, the twofold Voidness and the ultimate Suchness — *tathātā* — revealed by it. Because all the self-nature, the correspondence, the divisions, the transformations, etc. are not separated from consciousness, so it is called the Pure Consciousness theory. Conviction of the existence of any real matter apart from consciousness is relinquished.

Now, all the doubts about this theory seem to have been dealt with by these questions and answers interpreted above. But the most powerful attack came from not different sects in Hīnayāna or other systems outside Buddhism, but from Mahāyāna itself.

28

Much has been said about the *Ālaya*-consciousness. One question remains unanswered: how is it connected with the belief of transmigration?

We know that nearly all the ancient systems in India, with the exception of Carvakas perhaps, believed in different spheres of existence and the cycles of birth-and-death. One may be born after death on the same plane as human beings or on another higher or lower plane, in a paradise or in a hell. Buddhists believe in a ladder of six planes from the highest, the gods, to the lowest rung, the hungry ghosts. Human beings occupy the second rank, next to the gods. But even a god is subject to transmigration. He must descend to the human plane after his merits are exhausted in paradise and work for his own salvation in becoming a Buddha. It seems that man alone is privileged to Buddhahood. If one has not yet attained Buddhahood, then his cycle of births and deaths would roll eternally onward within the six spheres. That a human being should ever be reborn as an animal is the most fantastic absurdity produced by the human mind. Any student of Darwin's theory of evolution would laugh at it. It seems to be no other than a relic of the primitive belief in metamorphosis, a natural phenomenon beheld but not understood by primitive man, such as a caterpillar's turning into a butterfly. But even the comparatively more enlightened Mahāyānists hold transmigration as truth.

The *Ālaya*-consciousness contains all the seeds of one's good or evil dharma so that they are not dispersed or lost, and upholds the *rūpa-indriya* and the physical body so that they are not corrupted. Thus it forms one's karma and conjoins his lives in continuation. It constitutes the being which is believed to be still living after a man's death and before another birth. It is called *antarābhava* and has been a point of argument among the different sects mentioned before. This is the fruition of a living being, and its psychological seeds produce their activities beginning in the embryo.

After a man's death, it is said, his *antarābhava* wanders about in the cosmos seeking for a resting place like a traveller looking for an inn. This seems to be very much like the vital being of the Hindu belief or the soul of the West. If it chances to see — because owing to its past karma it has the visionary power — the sexual intercourse of a male and a female, it is at once attracted to the couple and becomes attached. If it is a male being, it is attached to the mother, and if female, to the father.

Being jealous of the couple, it identifies itself with its beloved and enters the womb like iron attracted by magnet. This is the process of a normal conception and the first stage of the formationn of an embryo. The male and female sex cells may unite, but when the *antarābhava* is not present, no new embryo can be formed. It leaves the body last when a man dies and enters the womb first when a man is to be born. What and how the future man will be is then largely determined by the karma of the good or bad deeds of his past life or lives, transformed into karmic seeds stored in the *Ālaya*-consciousness.

As a theory of rebirth this sounds almost scientific. Yet deep-rooted and widely spread in the Indian tradition as it is, it met strong opposition in China. Ancient Chinese people were devoted to their parents and nearly worshipped them as gods. Filial piety was considered a basis of all high virtues. The attachment of the *antarābhava* to the father or mother was regarded as a repugnant heresy to be repudiated. This belief greatly influenced or handicapped the spread of Buddhism in general. There is a great discrepancy in social and ethical conventions between these two peoples indeed.

29

In the light of this theory something more about conversion may be said. A principle formed within one's being with no outward expression is called *avijñapti-rūpa*. It is the latent karmic cause that gives rise to results of happiness or distress. By itself it is not any substance, yet it is produced from the four great elements that conserve the substance of the body, so it is still called *rūpa* as the teaching of the Sarvāstivādās has it.

This is a special phenomenon that deserves some attention because it has something to do with what we call spiritual training in education. With initiation the novice goes through certain ceremonies for accepting the code of conduct, *Śīla* or *Vinaya*, by answering questions of his guru, by making certain gestures and postures such as bowing before the Buddha image and repeated salutations to his guru and other participants, by reciting certain precepts, etc. Thus through the karma of the body, of the speech and of the mind a special formation comes about in the person of the novice which is supposed to be a new sheath of *Śīla*. It has no external form, yet it has the power of stopping the man from doing evil ever afterwards. As if by magic or any hypnotic force he is led to observe the rules and shielded from committing crimes. This is the *avijñapti-rūpa*.

According to the Sautrāntikās this formation has no mentation, so it does not pertain to *citta*, and as it has no substance, it does not pertain to *rūpa-dharma* either. Being neither of these, it is yet a principle that is formed within the body.

The *Abhidharmakośa* states that the *avijñapti* has karma or *rūpa* as its nature just as *vijñapti* or patent karma do. Because it does not express itself in order to be made known to others it is called *avijñapti* or non-expressive.

According to the explanation given by this *lakṣaṇa* school it is a function of the seeds of mentation in the *Ālaya*-consciousness, so it is still a *citta-dharma*. It is of two kinds — good and bad. The good *avijñapti* has the merit of stopping one from doing evil and of conducing to happiness, but the bad one has effects just the reverse. By accepting the *Śīla*, the power of mentation of the sixth sense creates new seeds in the eighth sense of the person, seeds of mental properties which have the merit of checking the person from breaking the rules. Hence it is regarded as a "body" of *Śīla*.

This seems to be what we call the shaping of a new character. Surely it cannot be done in a day or on the occasion of a single initiation. A new habit cannot be formed in a short time. A guru worth the name must necessarily infuse something new into the consciousness of a disciple. If he has great spiritual power, his impression made on the disciple can be permanent and the influence everlasting. The sowing of new seeds into the field of consciousness is the best explanation.

30

As seen from above, a distinction is always made between relative or worldly truth (*saṃvṛtisatyaṃ*) and transcendental truth or true reality (*paramārthasatyaṃ*). The latter is often referred to as being above words or speech and beyond the thinking mind. Unfortunately this has been often used by mystics and others as a last resort for all illogical reasoning, a sort of *deus ex machina* that saves the situation of defeat or embarrassment in debates. In this theory, however, Buddhist *nyāya* (logic) is everywhere employed to demonstrate its propositions, making it most appealing to high intellectuals who have no deep faith in the religion. In Kui Ji's *Commentary* each of the two categories of truth is said to be fourfold, in typical *nyāya* fashion.

Satyaṃ is truth. In fact, there are truths and truths. The most famous ones are those proclaimed by Gautama Buddha such as the Four Noble Truths—*Duḥkhaṃ*, *Samudayaḥ*, *Nirodhaḥ* and *Mārgaḥ*. These have always been exalted and never contradicted because they are statements of real universal phenomena. In the field of philosophy the distinction of these two truth categories has to be made for the sake of clear thinking. The word *saṃvṛti* as been well interpreted by Kui Ji, in fact by his master, as "covering", "appearing", "destructible" and "flowing along with worldly currents," etc. all correct. The term *saṃvṛtisatyaṃ* is explained simply as "worldly truth" or "truth of the laity." It is treated here as "A".

A

1) The worldly truth of names without reality—All names of things are arbitrarily given by man. From the viewpoint of designation they are truths, as a jar is called a jar, a basin is called a basin, etc. These are concrete objects. There are abstract objects also given names. Both kinds are included in this category of worldly truth.

2) The worldly truth established following each and every fact — According to a certain fact, the dharma of each fact is established, such as *skandha* or aggregate, *dhātu* or sphere, etc.

3) The worldly truth established following proven hypotheses — For example, *duḥkhaṃ* or distress, *samudaya* or collection, etc. are universally acknowledged, experienced and proven.

4) The worldly truth of unreal and unestablished names — This refers to the theory of twofold voidness as being the true nature of the world. This truthfulness is merely inwardly realized but inexpressible

outwardly in speech. It relies yet upon the unreal names given.

As to the transcendental truth, it is also divided into four kinds. It is treated here as "B".

B

1) The truth of the manifestation of being and its becoming — Like *skandhas* or *dhātus*, it is possessed of real being and nature surpassing the worldly, hence transcendental, and named according to different facts. It is spoken of as manifest.

2) The truth of the differentiation of cause and effect — This refers to *duḥhaṃ*, *samudaya*, etc. In knowledge, in the removal of ignorance, in spiritual practices and in realization causes and effects are evident and play a great part, surpassing even that of normal rationalization, hence they are called transcendental.

3) The truth of reality manifested by relying upon theory — This refers to the theory of twofold Voidness which is realized by surpassing conventional ideas. The Voidness is being relied upon and the reality is manifested as a consequence. It is transcendental.

4) The truth of reality with its names obliterated — This refers to

the one real Suchness (*tathātā*) which is above words that characterizes it as transcendental, and also above all conventional truths, which makes it again transcendental.

As this theory holds, all worldly or conventional truths (A. 1) are without reality, since they are established merely in accord with empty names, which nonetheless cannot be obliterated. The last of the eight is not established in names and words, and therefore it cannot be regarded as conventional: it is alone real in transcendence. All the rest (A. 2, 3, 4; B. 1, 2, 3) are at once conventional and transcendental. Now, we can only conclude that all in all truth is a matter of relativity. The true truth cannot be by itself true. It awaits the conventional as its counterpart to appear true. The conventional truth also awaits the true truth as its opposite to be true. Thus both are relative.

Such a classification has always been highly appreciated by the intellectuals among Buddhists. And it seems that this detailed analysis has not been found in any other ancient Indian system.

31

The foregoing has some connection with another question of certain importance: Are the eight senses of the same nature (or self-nature *svabhāva*)? The answer is yes and no. Their nature cannot be definitely said to be one because:

1) the relationships upon which their functions depend and their corresponding results are different, and

2) the perfumers and the perfumed — the first seven and the eighth — cannot be one and the same.

Yet all these eight branches cannot be spoken of as different from self-nature, because all are like waves in the ocean of consciousness, and waves are not different from water. If all eight were different in their self-nature, then they could not all come into causal relationship and would be like magical illusion without any definite nature.

The differentiation depends upon worldly truth and not upon the real transcendental truth, because in the latter words and names and thinking are no longer existent. This is A. 2 in contrast to B. 4 in the previous chapter. In it both subjectivity and objectivity are obliterated.

Of all things only consciousness is. All things are false appearances, and this includes both the ego and dharma, because there is no essential reality to either, and both are said to be void. But utter voidness cannot be. With the voidness which should be without anything, there is still the false appearance. This brings us again to the point that both worldly and transcendental truths must be co-existent and related to each other, i.e. without this one the other one cannot be. This is therefore also a middle path between and beyond existence and non-existence, a doctrine of the Middle Path of the Pure Consciousness theory.

32

The unreality of names needs further elucidation.

Here a distinction is always made between *svalakṣaṇa* or self-feature and *sāmānyalakṣaṇa* or common feature, in other words, between the specific or particular and the general. *Lakṣaṇa* means feature or appearance and means nature or characteristic as well. Names and words make up speech (*vāgvikalpa*). It is not that apart from the appearance formed in the mind there is any other object held to be real; the unreal knowledge and designations are not objects themselves. As the being and *lakṣaṇa* of the dharma grasped by mind are beyond the reach of words and unapproachable by unreal knowledge in forming any causal relationship, so they are said to be real. They are known through *pratyakṣa* or direct perception, being above words and discriminative knowledge. What revolves around *sāmānyalakṣaṇa* is the unreal knowledge in forms of designations and denominations. For example, fire has its heat, water has its liquidity and matter has its substantiality as its *svalakṣaṇa*. These can be proved and known, yet they cannot be achieved by words. The sixth sense arises after the function of the first five senses, and by its knowledge words or speech come about. Speech or words are related to the *sāmānyalakṣaṇa* of these things.

If, as the argument goes, words are related to the self-feature of any object, then by saying fire, the mouth must be burned, or by saying John everything about the person John must be known. John the person is an aggregate of diverse dharmas or elements which is his *svalakṣaṇa*. In calling him John, only the person is known, not all the elements of the person are known. So words are said to revolve around the *sāmānyalakṣaṇa*. And, *sāmānyalakṣaṇa* cannot be obtained by words at all.

On the whole it is a process of bi-partition or elimination. By specifying color of any object, the appearance as color is denoted to the exclusion of any other quality such as its dimension, its weight, etc. It is then the particular in the general. The name of a color, say red, is again a general feature. while red flowers, red fruits and red paints are particulars. The generals are the common feature, and the particulars are the self-nature. If an object is composed of numberless atoms, the object is taken to be the common feature while the atoms are its self-feature. In this way bi-parted, it reaches the point of the unnamable as *svalakṣaṇa* and the limit of the namable as *sāmānyalakṣaṇa*. All the unreal knowledge and designations and denominations can reach the *sāmānyalakṣaṇa* but no further.

It may be questioned why by saying fire, water is not understood, since the self-feature of water is equally unobtainable? It is not so. The distinctions of all designations and denominations have been made since ancient times through human habits or conventions in general. This cannot be considered to be on a par with the present case. For example, the perception of a red color and understood as red is the knowledge arisen through inference (*anumānaṃ*). Through direct perception the consciousness of the eye relates itself to the color, yet it does not understand it as such a color. Only the *manas* or the sixth sense understands it as red when it comes into relationship with the general feature of colors but not attaching itself to this particular color. But neither the name red nor the knowledge of redness correspond exactly to the red object. To the exclusion of other colors such as blue and green it is indeed red, but this is another matter.

And yet apart from the names and unreal knowledge there is also no other contrivance for hypothesizing a *svalakṣaṇa*. Knowledge is unreal in the sense that it is only similar to *svalakṣaṇa*. That is as far it can go. In causal relationship it cannot be the intimate one, and even in an intimate relationship it cannot take hold of the *svabhāva* or self-nature. On seeing a color as red, for instance, it is not the *svabhāva* of the red color that is obtained. Even if it can be obtained, it is not understood as such. The names and unreal knowledge reach only a similitude and do not depend upon the *svabhāva*. It can only be said that *svalakṣaṇa* is that upon which the unreal knowledge depends.

Yet the names and unreal knowledge must depend upon vocal sounds in coming to be. These things originate speech. Where the sound of speech does not reach, these do not come about. Sound is apprehended by the auditory faculty; it has no meaning by itself. It is through the combination of names, phrases, sentences all related to by the *manas* that meaning arises and in relationship with which understanding grows. That which designates and that which is designated are not the *svalakṣaṇa*. Moreover, there is no separate being of the *sāmānyalakṣaṇa* or common feature, because it is unreal. As a consequence this unreal dharma as speech does not depend on any real fact. It revolves only around a similitude of fact. A simile is something added or superimposed upon. The *sāmānyalakṣaṇa* is added to the *svalakṣaṇa*. A general characteristic covers many individual characteristics, so it is something superimposed. And speech is the sound revolving around the superimposed simile. Therefore it cannot be said that the unreal must necessarily depend upon the real to be established. (This can also answer the question posed in 27 D above.)

According to this theory everything in the universe resolves into transformations of consciousness, and both the ego and dharma are said to be unreal, only similes. Both have no being, both are only names. In the *śloka* of Nāgārjuna quoted above (15 B), the second half reads:

> It is also the unreal name.
> This is the meaning of the Middle Path.

33

A very important epistemological topic much discussed among Mahāyānists and especially among Vijñānavādins is the three characteristics of perception. From the idealistic point of view these characteristics constitute the world-nature. This nature denotes the *svabhāva*, which is interpreted also as the *svalakṣaṇa* of our existence, equating nature with characteristic. These three are:

1) *parikalpita* — lit. "the nature of overall discrimination and speculation in the grasping of objects." "Grasping" here means perception and implies attachment.

2) *paratamtra* — lit. "the nature of depending upon others in origination."

3) *parinispanna* — lit. "the nature of all around perfect and accomplished reality."

About the first there are different interpretations. According to Sthiramati, the mind is capable of grasping with attachment. The first five and the eighth senses grasp only dharma, the seventh grasps the ego and the sixth grasps both. But according to Dharmapāla, there are two masters of *parikalpita*, namely, the sixth and the seventh senses grasping dharma and ego respectively. By the grasping of both, distinctions and speculations arise pervasively. The first five senses and the eighth, not being accompanied by intelligence (*mati*), do not have such grasping. They are also too weak, different from the powerful *manas* capable of attachment to dharma and therefore able to perfume and form habits or seeds of good and evil. As long as the mind does not realize reality, all the false discriminations and speculations arise, owing to the habits of falsity formed since beginningless past. And the one of self-realization is divided into the perceived (*lakṣaṇa*) and the perceiver (*dṛṣṭi*), called the grasped and the grasper. These two are only factually true but not rationally true. This phenomenon is that of *parikalpita*, and its forms are innumerable.

The second characteristic refers to the objects grasped. The word "others" in the term "depending upon others in origination" means causal relationships. This is again differently interpreted by two teachers and their followers, who formed into two groups.

The first group holds that mind and its properties, owing to the perfuming of falsity, appear to be separated into two divisions in perception, the *dṛṣṭi* and the *lakṣaṇa* — the grasper and the grasped, though fundamentally there is only one thing, i.e. self-realization.

These two parts are factually true but not really true according to proper reasoning. This phenomenon is the "overall discrimination and speculation in grasping."

The abode upon which these two divisions depend, which includes the being and acts of consciousness, is formed by causal relationships. This characteristic is called *paratamṭra* because it is produced by the seeds of false discriminations in causal relationship.

How is it known to be so? It is known through *āryavāda* or what the sages taught. It is stated that the false discriminations are dependent upon others in nature, and the grasping and the grasped are discriminative overall.

The next group holds that mind and its properties and the two parts transformed through the influence of perfuming are also of the nature of *paratamṭra*, because they are produced by causal relationships. But speculation about the fixity using a fourfold truth-table formula on the basis of these two parts with regard to existence or non-existence, sameness or difference, oneness or multiplicity, accompaniment or unaccompaniment, etc. is then *parikalpita*. The fourfold formula is:

1) it is;

2) it is not;

3) it is both is and is not;

4) it is neither is nor is not.

It is also known through *āryavāda*. What the sages taught about measurement of knowledge, about the division into two parts, etc. all belongs to *paratamṭra*. And the first four dharmas among the five taught by the Lakṣaṇa school are also included in this category.

The second group also argues: if it be held that there is only self-realization that is in the nature of *paratamṭra* and the *lakṣaṇa* part is not, then the two parts transformed in the *anāsrava* mental state of Buddha must also be in the nature of *parikalpita*. If this is admitted, then the divine knowledge could not have arisen therefrom, because coming into relationship with *parikalpita* is not the way to truth. If this is not admitted, then it should be known that the *sāsrava* mental state has also the two parts as well. Again, if the two parts in the *sāsrava* mental state are of the nature of *parikalpita*, then they must be like the horns of a rabbit or the hair of a turtle, non-existent and not the object of causal relationship because *parikalpita* as a characteristic has no being of itself. And again, the two parts grasped cannot form any seeds, because they are non-existent, like the son of a sterile woman, and the continuing consciousness produced must also be devoid of these two parts. Moreover, all the habits are included in the *lakṣaṇa* part, and since that is non-existent, how can there be any causal relationship formed by it? Furthermore, whatever is produced through causal relationship is not separated from consciousness. If the inner two parts of *lakṣaṇa* and *dṛṣṭi* produced from causal relationship are not of the nature of *paratamṭra*, then the being upon which these two depend must also be produced from such a relationship, because there is no other cause. Hence a syllogistic formula of inference can be established thus:

The two parts produced through causal relationship are of the nature of *paratamtra*

because they are produced from the seeds of causal relationship, like the part of self-realization.

And, if there is only the part of self-realization, then how can the seeds be related to, and how can there be the realization of self-realization? How can the correct and incorrect measurements of knowledge be self-related in one mind? Now, if the *dṛṣṭi* part is admitted, then there can be no such difficulties.

Therefore, according to right reasoning, all the mind and mental properties, the parts of *lakṣaṇa* and *dṛṣṭi*, either in the *sāsrava* or in *anāsrava* mental state, are *paratamtra* in nature, as they are all produced from diverse relative causes.

As to the third universal nature, *pariniṣpanna* or "all around perfect and accomplished reality," it is no other than the truth revealed by the twofold voidness which is fully and perfectly established as the reality of all dharma.

It is real, meaning not vain. It has no perversion in its being. It is ubiquitous or all pervading and constant and eternal which means it is accomplished. This contrasts with ideas of voidness and eternity held by the so-called heretics and Hīnayānists. The terms are the same, yet their interpretations are different and hence they are regarded as perversions by the Vijñānavādins.

This third universal nature is no other than the Real Suchness (*tathātā*).

These several attributes do exclude certain things such as *svalakṣaṇa* which cannot be all-pervading, and also *sāmānyalakṣaṇa* such as transience, voidness and egolessness which might be all-pervading yet without any self-being. Self-being with its effectuation of the Real Suchness is always talked about as one.

In the characteristic of *paratamṭa* a distinction is made between the pure and impure. All dharma produced through causal relationship are discriminative and so called impure. The pure *paratamṭa* is included in the category of *parinispanna* because it is also devoid of perversion, not contaminated in its being, and especially because it is thoroughgoing in its effectuation, which is like all *anāsrava* dharma, also all-pervading and broken off from every contamination. Therefore it is regarded as perfect and accomplished as well. This truth of *parinispanna*, being on that part of *paratamtra*, is permanently devoid of the nature of *parikalpita*, without any grasping or speculation. It is thus the nature of the Real Suchness as manifested by the twofold voidness.

34

As just mentioned, *pariniṣpanna* rests on or constitutes a part of *parataṃtra*. By this it should be understood that both are not separated from each other, yet not combined together. If they were combined together, then the Real Suchness would also have its destruction, or else *parataṃtra* would have no origination. They are not separated because within the very characteristics of *parataṃtra* there is Real Suchness. As one rests on the other, no separation can be talked of. Yet they are not one.

Here is a fairly subtle point to be noticed. *Tathātā* in Chinese is literally translated as "the real as-if." This "real as-if" indicates the nature of voidness, but it is not the void itself. Void is the condition revealed by the "as-if", or the reason for the "as-if". It is then the very Real Suchness, distinct from the appearance of being and non-being or existence and non-existence. As it is said to be void, it is of course distinct from the appearance of being, yet it is not distinct from the appearance of the void. It must be realized as transcending both.

In the same way, the characteristic of *pariniṣpanna* is neither different from nor identical with the characteristic of *parataṃtra*. If both were entirely different, then Real Suchness could not be their common feature, and if completely identical, then Real Suchness would also be as transient as *parataṃtra*. Also both would be subject to purity and to impurity, and the effectuation of root-knowledge (*a priori*) and acquired knowledge (*a posteriori*) would not be distinct.

An example may be given to illustrate such a condition of being identical yet not being one, as for instance impermanence. If the nature of impermanence were entirely different from the nature of our ordinary actions, then our actions should be permanent, and the difference would be just like the difference between the color blue and yellow or any other color. If both were entirely identical, then impermanence could not be the common feature, just as the common feature of all colors cannot be one color. The general is not identical with the particular or specific.

This shows that *pariniṣpanna* is neither identical with nor different from *pararaṃtra*. Dharma and the nature of dharma should also be so understood in right reasoning. *Parataṃtra* is taken as the dharma and "as-if" as its nature.

The same it is with *parikalpita*. As said by Vasubandhu, the overall nature of *manas* is speculation and discrimination. *Parataṃtra* is the nature of the objects related to or grasped by it, and is thus capable of bringing about overall speculation and discrimination, and hence can also be called *parikalpita*. But according to Abhāva, another master of the Lakṣaṇa school, identity is meant in the sense of not capable of being different; it is present with *paratamtra* but absent from *parikalpita*. Existence in respect of existence can be said to be identical or different, but in respect of non-existence, what can there be to be identified or differentiated? Moreover, existence and non-existence cannot be one: *paratamtra* is impure while *parinispanna* is pure, which shows the difference. Hence these three universal characteristics are neither identical with nor different from each other. According to another explanation, *paratamtra* serves as the resting place for distinguishing of ego, *rūpa*, etc., so it is also called *parikalpita*. This is slightly different from the idea of Vasubandhu but comes to the same conclusion.

Much has been discussed on this subject in the commentaries. All in all, it comes to a matter of relativity, that is without the one there cannot be the other, and vice versa. If, for example, there is no *samvrtisatyam* there can be no *paramārthasatyam*, as stated above.

Finally, a last word may be said: it is a matter of realization. If one has not realized the voidness of *parikalpita*, one cannot readily understand the nature of *paratamtra*. Or, one should have realized *parinispanna* through the awareness of the voidness. Said in another way, it is through the root-knowledge of nondiscrimination that the Real Suchness can be realized. Which is the same as to say *parinispanna* can thus be made clear to oneself. Then the knowledge of the *paratamṭra* nature of everything in the universe arises, and one regards everything as an illusion (*māyā*), as a mirage, as dreams, as images in a mirror, as shadows of light, as echoes, as the moon reflected in water, etc. — all transformations of the mind, all seemingly or falsely existent but really non-existent. And consequently, the ego of oneself and other selves and the dharma of existence and non-existence, identity and difference, presence and absence, etc., all wrongly grasped as real by laymen, would be like airy flowers without reality and also void of self-nature, and all are regarded as vain speculations and discriminations. Ultimately this induces to enlightenment.

35

Immediately following these three universal characteristics there are established another three universal characteristics in negation or nullity. At first sight this seems to be absurd, because what can be distinguished or categorized if it is null? Yet this is negation based upon position. Even in the philosophy of the Vaiśeṣikās, "nothing" (*abhāva*) is stated to be of four kinds: the nullity of something that is not yet produced (*prāgabhāva*), that of something already extinguished (*pradhvaṃsābhāva*), that of mutuality or interrelationship, i.e. "if A is, then B cannot be" (*itaretarābhāva* or *anyonyābhāva*) and the ultimate nothingness (*atyantābhāva*). All these four are established in relation to the positives. Now, by this theory of Pure Consciousness, the three negatives are posited as an elucidation of the three positive characteristics.

As it is well known Buddha preached his dharma to all the classes in ancient India, to people of all grades of intelligence in society. This doctrine was meant for the novices or the laymen. Just like the positive characteristics, negation is relative. First, in correspondence with *parikalpita*, as ordinary people are firmly attached to it, the negation of all phenomena is preached. Next, in correspondence with *paratamtra*, as everything in the world is a conglomeration of numerous diverse factors in relationship, the negation of natural origination is stated. Thirdly, in place of *parinispanna* which is completely devoid of *parikalpita*, the negation of even the most sublime truth is emphasized. This is the nullity of *paramārtha*. It is likened to the empty space which pervades all material objects, yet revealed by the absence of all material objects. Even the second characteristic, not being the most sublime truth, can be referred to this kind of negation, because it is devoid of the first. In any case, it is not that the most sublime truth is nothing, it is that the most sublime truth is that of nullity or nothingness.

Paramārtha is of four kinds: the worldly, the philosophical, the realized truth of the twofold voidness and the sublimity of the sublime truth. The last is the one reality, or the essence of Pure Consciousness, or in one word, the Real Suchness.

This is then the most transcendental truth which, however, can bring forth tremendous untoward effects if misunderstood.

36

It must always be noted that Buddhist dharma is not like modern philosophy, although it contains all sorts of theories. In terms of *yoga*, it is the way of knowledge or Jñāna Yoga, an intellectual approach to that final goal of *Nirvāṇa*. The worship of Bodhisattvas which is to be relegated to Bhaktiyoga, especially the worship of Avalokiteśvara, also has its place in Mahāyāna, but it is not much discussed. There are ten states of Bodhisattvahood in an ascending scale, which though well discussed in the *Treatise*, need not be brought into consideration for our present purpose. The five stages of practice based upon this theory, from initiation to enlightenment and all the landmarks along the way, also need not be treated here. The grouping of people born with genetic tendencies toward Mahāyāna beliefs, important though it is in India with respect to its caste system, is not of much value to us in our modern world. Nevertheless, there are several points in this very elaborate, concise and compact system that should not be neglected.

First, there is the discussion on meditation. Meditation is said to be of three kinds:

1) that of remaining in a comfortable state of pure dharma without any relaxation,

2) that of conducting to the development of diverse supernatural powers, and

3) that of accomplishing things for the benefit of all beings.

All these are said to be done in the state of Samādhi which can be reached after years and years of practice. One must have a strong will in this energetic effort, the right mental and physical force that enable him to follow the grand path and especially the wisdom that would lead him to his fulfillment.

Next, *tathātā* of Suchness or the "real as-if " is another important topic brought into discussion. It is divided into ten kinds:

1) The overall *tathātā* — It is covering all, "going everywhere," the truth revealed by the twofold voidness.

2) The most excellent *tathātā* — At the summit of all dharma, it possesses innumerable merits.

3) The excellent outflowing *tathātā* — "Outflow" refers to the spread of these doctrines.

4) The *tathātā* without commitment — It is not involved or committed to ego or to dharma.

5) The *tathātā* without differentiation — It is a state of equanimity

regarding *Nirvāṇa* and life-and-death as one.

6) The *tathātā* above purity and impurity — Its nature is radically pure; it is not the recovery of purity after defilement.

7) The *tathātā* without discrimination of dharma — Though teachings and descriptions of *tathātā* may vary among different systems; it is fundamentally the same.

8) The *tathātā* which does not wax and wane — If any contamination is removed or if any perfect purity is attained, it is neither increased nor decreased.

9) The *tathātā* on which free knowledge depends — If it is realized, then the liberal comprehension of whatever dharma without any obstruction can be obtained.

10) The *tathātā* upon which all free actions depend — If it is realized, then all supernatural and godly actions can be achieved.

Suchness being one is yet in this way divided into ten different kinds by distinguishing its merits. If any remark is called for here, one may say that this is a typically Indian way of thinking, formed under the influence since Vedic times of sacrificial rites, the performance of which affords great care in details. The meticulous niceties are remarkable.

37

By such a deep analysis into the perceptions of man we learn that the one consciousness may be divided into eight branches or parts, which are its results. There is nothing specially profound in this theory that baffles our understanding, as it rests entirely on the doctrine of *pratītyasamutpada* (dependent origination). We may suppose that there is such a fundamental principle of the universe as fire, as sung in the very first verse of the Ṛg-Veda. Now, by lighting a match-stick fire may be produced if all the conditions or factors of causal relationship are present. In the same way, the fundamental consciousness can be revealed if the proper conditions are present. It is as simple as that. Yet this theory has its own purpose — the removal of the double veiling of one's firm attachment to his ego and to dharma. The brilliancy of the sun appears after the dispersion of the obnubilation of clouds. After the removal of veiling, the Great Wisdom can then shine forth in its full glory. The way to becoming a Buddha would then be straight and smooth. Wisdom must be distinguished from consciousness, yet it relies solely on consciousness. In the *anāsrava* state, one's consciousness is weak while his wisdom is strong; in the *sāsrava* state, the opposite is the case. As a logical consequence it is necessary to convert and transform the consciousness as a whole into wisdom in order to be enlightened. Wisdom is knowledge, but it is supposed to have no veiling effect. This is called Mahābodhi. It is fourfold. These four aspects are not intended as kinds or categories. They are separately treated only in respect of their corresponding mental states.

Common people are of different types. The one general distinction made here is whether or not one is born with *anāsrava* seeds in his *Ālaya*-consciousness, whether or not he has in his nature the inclination (*a priori*) toward becoming an Arhat or Buddha. This point was endlessly discussed as a great problem because in ancient India the caste system prevailed. This tradition seemed to be so deep-rooted as to defy any abolition, sudden or gradual. Rama, the hero of the race, had to decapitate a *śūdra* saint doing *tapasya*, because he felt himself abashed at the sight of such a person of the lowest caste performing certain acts only Brahmans were privileged to perform. In this respect, however, Buddhism seems to be more benign and benevolent, insofar as it permits everyone to enter the Saṃgha without any caste-distinction. This implies that the nature of man is held to be informed by seeds of good dharma and everyone can be enlightened. Yet this also became a point of vulnerability which exposed Buddhism to attack by other systems.

As the seeds of the Great Wisdom are also existent in one's *Ālaya*-consciousness, the right thing to do is to carefully nurture them for their growth. So long as they are covered by the thick coating of ignorance of the double veiling, they cannot properly grow and develop. Now, by the force of divine Truth, that veil can be cut open, and if rent asunder, *Mahābodhi* may appear, grow and flourish splendidly in all eternity.

The first description of *Mahābodhi* is *ādarśajñānaṃ* — the wisdom like a great round mirror. This is merely a metaphorical way of expression. The wisdom is the mirror itself. It is devoid of "me" or "mine", of the grasper and the grasped, of the subject and object. Being free from all defilements, it is pure both in its essence and its outward expression. As it contains and upholds seeds of all virtues to the fullest extent, so it is said to be "round". And as it is capable of producing forms and images of all objects created by mind irrespective of time and space, it is compared to a great round mirror reflecting all images. It is the result of transformation of the eighth consciousness of the *sāsrava* state into that of *anāsrava* state.

The second is *samatājñānaṃ* — the wisdom of equality. All dharma and oneself and other selves and all beings are regarded as equal and beheld in a great compassion. It is the knowledge of Bodhisattvas manifested to them each according to his station (*bhūmi* or "land"). This is established in *Apratiṣṭhitanirvāṇaṃ* — an abode of Real Suchness revealed both by compassion and wisdom. This is attained by transforming the seventh sense into the *anāsrava* state.

The third is *pratyavekṣaṇājñānaṃ* — the wisdom of subtle observation. It comes wholly into causal relationship with the *svalakṣaṇaṃ* and *sāmānyalakṣaṇaṃ* of every dharma without any obstacle in its observation. This comprehends virtues of numberless *dhāraṇīs* and displays infinite activities among men, making them happy by showering the great dharma like rain. This is achieved through the transformation of the sixth sense into the *anāsrava* state.

The fourth is *kṛtyānuṣṭhanajñānaṃ* — the wisdom of accomplishment. For the benefit of all beings as they undergo all their transformations, things are achieved in accordance with the original great will of the Bodhisattva. That great will is to convert beings of all worlds into Buddhas, and the Bodhisattva vows not to become a Buddha before the hells are empty. This wisdom is obtained through the transformation of the first five senses into the corresponding senses in the *anāsrava* state.

A man possessed of the Great Wisdom or *Mahābodhi* is a Bodhisattva. The changing of the eight branches of consciousness into the fourfold wisdom may be beyond the reach of a layman. Even if it actually takes place, it is not evident. In our modern age we can think of a wire charged with electric power: outwardly there is nothing to be seen yet internally there is a great difference. That seems to be a fitting simile. Consciousness is there but its use or rather its effectuation is entirely changed. It is totally wisdom. Perhaps one is no longer in his normal status as man or self-imagined superman. One must have elevated himself to the status of a Buddha or Bodhisattva. A man as Tathāgata is imaginable.

38

This fourfold wisdom is intimately connected with a trinity in Buddhahood, as advocated by this theory. First there is the *Dharmakāya*, literally "the body of Dharma." What is called "*kāyaḥ*" here can better be interpreted as "an aggregate." Mahāmuni, because of his accomplishment in the supreme dharma of silence, is also called *Dharmakāya*, but that is only eulogistic usage. Here it signifies the real and pure dharma state of all Tathāgatās, an abstract state of perfect silence without any external feature, full of boundless constant virtues, yet unapproachable by means of words or thoughts. As an aggregate of supreme dharma, it is achieved by Tathāgata through his first "mirror wisdom." It is called also Svabhāvakāya, or the aggregate of self-nature.

Second, there is the *Saṃbhogakāya*, or "the body of enjoyment." What is enjoyed is the happiness of Dharma by Tathāgata himself, and also the happiness in the Pure Land manifested by him and enjoyed by

Bodhisattvas of the ten *bhūmi* or states. This "body" is an aggregate of wisdom, performed through the "wisdom of equality."

Third, there is the *Nirmāṇakāya*, or "the body of transformation." Bodies or aggregates of merits of the living incarnations on different planes or worlds are meant. They may appear on any plane and preach dharma for the benefit of others. This is done through the third wisdom and the fourth.

The above is a brief statement of the connection between consciousness and the fourfold wisdom and the trinity in Buddhahood. Trinity is a favorite subject often mentioned among ancient Indo-Aryan peoples. Christianity also has its Trinity. Perhaps *Dharmakāya* here may be compared to the Holy Ghost. In the field of Buddhism the three bodies of Buddhahood have remained as something of an ideal and often three statues are installed in the temple representing these three "*kāyas*" to be worshipped. Viewed from the standpoint of cultural history, the division of one into three and the merging of three into one seem to have been a social convention formed long before the shaping of such an elaborate theory of the three "*kāyas*". The three "*kāyas*" are much talked about in Mahāyāna, but for our present purpose these endless discussions are omitted. Objectively speaking, it is doubtful whether this sort of transformation has ever taken place by anybody at all, with perhaps the only exception of the legendary Gautama Buddha himself. But as Buddhists are used to talking in terms of aeons, probably there may be some day in the infinite future when certain people will actually come to such a transformation. Compared to the period since the formation of our planet earth till now our historical period of civilization is still too young.

39

The theory of Pure Consciousness as briefly stated above seems to have been firmly established after gradual amelioration by ten masters in succession. It grew into a tightly organized and almost irrefutable system as it climaxed in Dharmapāla's interpretation. After Dharmapāla no other master distinguished himself on this subject, but it was transmitted by Xuan Zang to China and flourished.

The theory stood so irrefutably that attacks on it by other religions and Hīnayānists were all to no avail. The truly forceful attack came from inside Mahāyāna itself, namely, from the Mādhyamikās, followers of the Middle Path formulated by Nāgārjuna. As is generally known, the Middle Path was first taught by Gautama Buddha himself. But that was a middle course between the two extremes of self-affliction and self-indulgence. Tormenting the flesh does not lead to the salvation of one's soul, it leads as surely to one's destruction as intemperance. But this teaching of Nāgārjuna was purely a philosophical ratiocination of opposites such as existence and non-existence, coming into being and going out of being, "cause and effect are one" and "cause and effect are two," identity and difference, birth or origination and death or destruction, etc.

About Nāgārjuna ample materials for translation and research are available. The famous Russian scholar W. P. Wassilijew conducted studies of Nāgārjuna before the Soviet Revolution. There is one thing specially noticeable in Nāgārjuna's writings which has not been enough appreciated, which is his division of the periods of Buddha's preaching according to the contents of the sermons — a work of re-construction of history. It was reasonably convincing and has been endorsed and adopted by every Buddhist scholar in China ever since. The periods were four. In their sequence, the first consisted of the teaching of existence (*sat*), represented by the four *Āgama sūtras*; the second, the teaching of voidness (*śūnyatā*), expounded by the *Prajñāpāramitā sūtras*; the third, the teachings of both existence and non-existence (*sat* and *asat*), including all the Mahāyāna *sūtras*; and finally the fourth, the teaching of the negation of both *sat* and *asat*, which was the Mādhyamikā theory. This made Nāgārjuna's doctrine stand supreme as a vertical uplifting when reasoning about two opposites on a horizontal plane had reached both limits and could not proceed any further.

The debates between the Yogācāras and Mādhyamikas took place in Nālandā for a very long time. Among the protagonists of the

Mādhyamikā doctrine, several eminent ones may be mentioned. The first one was Bhavaviveka. Both Bhavaviveka and Buddhapāla were followers of Saṃgharakṣa whose origin was somewhat obscure, but as a follower of Mādhyamikā he was well known. In those ancient debates the method used by Buddhapāla corresponds to what we may call a sort of negative or destructive criticism. It proceeded by merely pointing out the mistakes of the opponent without establishing anything positive of one's own. But Bhavaviveka did otherwise. His criticism was constructive as well. He made a positive contribution in the form of a *nyāya* formula of his own which embraces both negation and affirmation. He attacked the *lakṣaṇa* theory of the Yogācāras in three aspects:

First, about the three universal characteristics, Bhavaviveka questioned whether *paratamṭra* and the remaining two were identical or different. Generally dharma could be separated into two groups, the pure and impure or the contaminable and uncontaminable. The Yogācāras maintained that *parikalpita* was contaminable and *parinispanna* uncontaminable, being perfectly pure, but about *paratamṭra* nothing was said as it was neither, and hence thought to be located somewhere between the two. But according to Bhavaviveka, *paratamṭra* and *parikalpita* must be identical as both are different from *parinispanna* and both are contaminable. It is then redundant and of no use to establish *paratamṭra* as a separate characteristic of depending upon others.

Next, he questioned whether the three characteristics were established in conventional truth (*saṃvṛtisatyaṃ*) or transcendental truth (*paramārthasatyaṃ*). According to the Yogācāras *paramārthasatyaṃ* is approached through divine wisdom, and what is approached through divine wisdom cannot but be established. The three characteristics exist in divine wisdom as transcendental truths. But Bhavaviveka held the opposite view. The three exist only as conventional truths, while in transcendental truth they do not exist.

The argument necessarily extended to the interpretation of these two truths. Generally it was understood that conventional truth pertained to laity, while transcendental truth pertained to divine wisdom. And divine wisdom comprised both root-indiscriminative-knowledge (*a priori*) and acquired knowledge, which is obtained *a posteriori*. Here also Bhavaviveka had his modification: only the root-indiscriminative-knowledge can be *paramārthasatyaṃ*. As to acquired knowledge, it cannot be divine wisdom, although it may be guided by it.

It may well be supposed that Bhavaviveka who was not educated at Nālandā was close to the Sāṃkhya or even Vaiśeṣikā philosophy. Basically he admitted the existence of real external objects outside mind and of atoms composing matter. These views were opposite to those held by Vijñānavādins.

40

After Bhavaviveka there was another powerful critic on the Yogācāra school, a second generation disciple of Buddhapāla named Candrakīrti. He was on the side of Bhavaviveka but went farther in criticizing him. He again resorted to the destructive method of reasoning cherished by his master's master.

What Nāgārjuna taught about origination through causal relationship meant the negation of birth or production, which can be of four kinds: production by self, by others, by a common cause and production without any cause. In explaining this, Buddhapāla said that if anything could be produced by itself, it would be senseless to say production because the produced is there already, or else the production would be infinite. Bhavaviveka was opposed to this kind of reasoning. But Candrakīrti again supported it. He went so far as to negate *nyāya* itself. His position was that because the fundamental principle of Mādhyamikā is that everything in the universe is empty of self-nature, the same must be the case with the reasoning and examples in *nyāya*. By establishing a syllogism in *nyāya*, Bhavaviveka must have first asserted the self-nature of his reasoning and examples. And to explain the theory of the voidness of self-nature by syllogism would be self-contradictory. Hence, even *nyāya* has to be dispensed with, lest it would lead to confusion.

Next, Candraīrti criticized the theory of three universal characteristics by pointing at the first, *parikalpita*, which the Yogācāras held as possessed of self-nature. He maintained that *parikalpita* expresses *pratītyasamutpāda* or the origination through causal relationship, thereby nullifying self-nature. If such origination is admitted, self-nature cannot at the same time be admitted. And, regarding the theory of voidness upheld by Yogācāras, he criticized it as not thoroughgoing. According to the Yogācāras, if there is no *parikalpita-dharma* on *paratamtra dharma*, it is then void. In the classical example of the rope and snake, it is the image of the snake that is understood as void, but still the rope exists. But according to Candrakīrti, in this case it is not the voidness of self-nature but the voidness of other-nature or foreign-nature. If voidness is to be established, it should be the voidness of self-nature.

Candrakīrti further attacked the theory of Pure Consciousness. This theory was firmly based upon the eight branches of consciousness with *Ālaya*-consciousness as its fundament. The bulwark of this theory is its fortification of karma, works or actions. The seeds of one's past karma are stored in the *Ālaya*-consciousness, and as they grow up, fruits or rewards are to be reaped. But Candrakīrti regarded this as merely a fanciful hypothesis, not real fact. Karma as it exists is ever in continuity. The outward action might be obliterated, but its inherent power could not be, and its character would remain in latency, There is only the difference of dormancy and manifestation. Unless and until the workings are fulfilled with all their internal power exhausted, it would continue in existence. There is then no need of setting up a specific store-consciousness for its preservation. And together with the negation of the eighth consciousness, all the remaining seven are negated.

Furthermore, the Yogācāras laid stress on the part of self-realization, which they used to explain man's memory. By one's memory one remembers what he has seen or heard. While he is seeing or hearing, he explains to himself what is being seen or heard. That is self-realization. And by means of this self-realization, one comes to the awareness of oneself. Candrakīrti opposed this idea. He maintained that a thing cannot be at the same time the subject and the object of an action, and so no self can be realized by self. He argued that a knife can cut or a hand can touch, but a knife cannot cut itself, and a hand cannot touch itself.

Finally Candrakīrti argued also about the non-existence of real objects outside the mind. Vijñānavādins used dreams as an example.

What one sees in his dream state is purely the formulation of the mind, as the same is true of what he sees in his waking state. So the difference between the dream state and the waking state is merely a matter of degree. And until one has come to the Great Awakening, one cannot know his life as one long dream. Candrakīrti also refuted this idea. He held that both mind and the objects of mind are equal (from the idealistic point of view). If there is no real object in dreams, there must also be no real mind. Thus in dreams there must be real objects as well.

These are the vital points of the Pure Consciousness theory attacked by Candrakīrti. And there was no counterattack from the other side. One is led to think that the stronghold of this theory is ultimately not so impregnable. Candrakīrti's view developed later into the reversed idea that because of the voidness of self-nature, there could be origination of all things through causal relationship, with the Mādhyamika view held in priority.

Debates and arguments like these between the Yogācāras and Mādhyamikas were carried on for many years in Nālandā before Xuan Zang's arrival, and after probing deeply into the grounds of both sides, he thought of effecting a certain reconciliation. Eventually he composed a treatise entitled "A Synthesis of Truths" in three thousand *ślokas* which was approved by Śīlabhādra, and this somehow cooled down the heat of the fight among those upholders of truths, including the powerful Hīnayānists, and brought them to a temporary and naturally unstable compromise. Unfortunately that treatise was lost, and the quarrel continued. In the history of a Tibetan source, it is stated that afterwards a long public debate held at Nālandā between Candrakīrti and Candragomin, a noted Vijñānavādin, lasted for seven years. On the one hand the Middle Path was interpreted in terms of the non-existence of self-nature, and on the other, in terms of pure consciousness. The audience consisted of learned men and also villagers and herdsmen. In the course of such a long debate, these common people also learned something of these two doctrines. No final conclusion could be reached, but the general impression was that the doctrine of Nāgārjuna was like medicine, efficient in curing diseases but also containing poison, while the teaching of Maitreya was the ambrosia for all human beings. Thus Candragomin was to a certain extent victorious. He might have made certain slight modifications in the theory, but how the debate actually took place is not clear. And the wheel of time and the wheel of dharma together rolled on and on till the rise of the Tantrics in the end of the tenth century when both parties fell into silence.

41

After passing over much of the material in Xuan Zang's Treatise which seems to be of less importance to us, there remains one topic which should be treated, as it is held to be the highest goal of life not only in the Yogācāra or Lakṣaṇa school but in Buddhism in general, that is *Nirvāṇa*. It is of four kinds:

1) *Nirvāṇa* of the original self-nature in all its purity — This is the *Nirvāṇa* realized internally by sages, the nature of which is perfectly silent, a state where names and words do not reach and with every way of mentation to it cut off, thus separated from all distinctions and all phenomena. It is transparent like the void space without production and destruction or birth and death. It is neither one with nor different from all dharma. Being equipped with numberless subtle merits, it is possessed by all human beings. This is the truth of Real Suchness of the Dharma Lakṣaṇa, pure in its self-nature though not free from

defilements. This is in accord with the general saying that all beings since all eternity are abiding in *Nirvāṇa*, as taught by Gautama Buddha.

2) *Nirvāṇa* with remaining reliance — This is the realization of Real Suchness free from all covering or veiling of afflictions. Yet there is still the remaining slight suffering of that upon which it relies, i.e. the physical body which is not extinguished, though the veiling may be permanently removed. This shows that one can still be living after having attained *Nirvāṇa*.

3) *Nirvāṇa* without remaining reliance — This is the realization of Suchness with all afflictions permanently extinguished together with the body. The ocean of life-and-death is thus crossed, and no future life is possible.

4) *Nirvāṇa* without abode — This is the realization of Suchness by which one is relieved from all his knowledge, including even his saintly knowledge. Then being flanked by great Compassion on one side and by great Wisdom on the other, one does not take his stand either in life-and-death or in *Nirvāṇa* and works for the welfare of all beings for all eternity. As his work is being done everlastingly in unbroken silence, it is also called *Nirvāṇa*.

The first is latent in all human beings. The second and the third may be attained by adherents to both Vehicles. Bodhisattvas may enter the second and the fourth, but Buddha alone has access to all four.

How is Buddha or Tathāgata to be regarded as possessing any remaining reliance? He only appears to have certain sufferings remaining, though factually this is not so.

Now, since *Nirvāṇa* has been taken by Buddhists since ancient times to be the highest goal of life, certain observations may be permitted to be made here by the present writer.

From a cultural-historical point of view it is to be noted that the conception of *Nirvāṇa* together with the theory of transmigration and the quite pessimistic view of life so prevalent in ancient India never existed in ancient China. These ways of thinking became known through the introduction of Buddhism. At the early stages, the word "*Nirvāṇa*" was wrongly translated as "inaction", the keystone of the philosophy of Lao Tze, which actually meant "spontaneous action," but afterwards corrected and left in transliteration as "nie-pan". This was some time before the Christian era. We cannot say that ancient Chinese people in the archaic dynasties were any happier than in later times, but there was as yet no such pessimistic *Nirvāṇa*-consciousness among them. Yet in ancient Greece we can find some traces of a similar if not identical conception in mythology. The answer of Silenus to King Midas is: "Poor species of one day, children of vicissitudes and distresses, why do you compel me to tell you that which would be most beneficial for you not to have heard of? The best for you is entirely unattainable by you — not to have been born, not to be, and to be nothing! The next best for you is to die sooner rather than later."

This then is *Nirvāṇa*-mindedness expressed in another land. Further, there is the story of Apollo's reward for Trophonius and Agamedes, the two architects who built the magnificent temple for him. And again, there is also the story of two brothers of admirable filial piety who had drawn the carriage of their mother instead of the cow, and whose mother prayed for them to receive the best boon that the gods could give. This was granted, and what was given was a swift departure from mundane existence; and as life was so swiftly abandoned, it could be inferred that they would not be born again on earth. This is *Nirvāṇa*, though not so named.

The whole problem hinges upon the belief in transmigration. This belief was not known in China but was popular among the Indo-Aryan people. The famous Pythagoras was a devout believer in it. From the time of Pythagoras (died in 497 B.C.) or even before him to the time of the Catholic Convention held at Constantinople in 553 A.D. when this doctrine was condemned as heresy, more than a thousand years passed. That shows the belief persisted for quite a long period. If it were not influential and had not had results, it would probably not have been condemned. Even today most people in the oriental world still maintain blind faith in this doctrine. When a Buddhist master dies, people euphemistically say he enters *Nirvāṇa*.

If *Nirvāṇa* is set up for humankind as its highest goal, then evolution would lose its significance. All in all, this is an abominable existence and a lamentable life, and the sooner one gets out of it the better, according to the advice of the wise Silenus. But this is also not a solution. If one believes in Karma, then suicide or euthanasia cannot put an end to it even if life is ended. Again there is no other way out. Yet it is not so disappointing. In the final analysis as Mahāyānists pointed out, *Nirvāṇa* has its basis of realization on the manifestation of the real phenomenon or the discovery of the Real Truth in everything. One has then to strive insistently with all beings toward that end, hence the journey is a lofty and perpetual one. The work transcends both life and death and stays aloof from the problem of human suffering. Put in dialectic terms, the real phenomenon of the world is a great Void, and this great Void is also the content of *Nirvāṇa*. Thus both the world and *Nirvāṇa* can be identified in the one real phenomenon. The drive toward *Nirvāṇa* cannot stop so long as the progress of the world does not stop. And it was the vow of Samantabhadra Bodhisattva that unless and until hell is emptied of all souls, he would not become a Buddha and enter *Nirvāṇa*. This is a great determination which all Mahāyānists aspired to. The aim thus is not to get out of life as soon as possible.

42

At the end of such a dry and fairly long treatise, any summary or conclusion would be redundant, as enough repetitions have been made. Yet a few words more may be added as an observation on the whole.

In the final analysis this theory is still a very simple one of certain limited psychological speculations interwoven with religious beliefs common to all Indian systems. The division of universe into six planes or spheres (*dhātus*) is an ancient one not limited to Buddhism. Heaven and hell are part of the scheme just as in Christianity. Next to human beings there is the world of asuras. The name "asura" (lit. being without light) had no bad meaning in Vedic times, but it gradually changed and came to mean something like a monster. Apart from the beings of the hell there is another category of "hungry ghosts" which occupy another sphere forming a world of their own. Of all these nobody could give any definite description, and they had no important place in this system. What is remarkable is its theory of karma, but this too is found in Hinduism in general. It is something mechanical connected with the theory of causality and can scarcely be called a religious belief. Otherwise there is nothing of mysticism or of magic in it. Comparatively speaking, this Lakṣaṇa school in Mahāyāna Buddhism is the most enlightened one among the many schools. And it was because of its rationality that it was so attractive to the Chinese intelligentsia and lasted for more than a thousand years.

Undoubtedly many parts of the world are now undergoing a period of revolution in which great and sudden social changes take place. In our modern society it is easy to brush aside any ancient belief as superstition if one is an atheist, or as heresy if one holds certain orthodox faith. But generally one cannot discard or condemn things so lightly. It makes good sense to examine carefully things inherited from the past, and if they are found usable, they can be made use of, or if unusable, they can be shelved and carefully preserved for our future generations who may yet utilize them for purposes we cannot foresee. This is natural in the economy of things. If, for example, to level the Great Wall — a useless and lamentable relic from today's perspectives — with the ground would require not much less effort than to build it, then why should it not be preserved as a monument and memorial of our past civilization? Only in the most recent period of restoration and restitution have people awakened to the necessity and adopted this attitude toward ancient things.

Historically China is a country of religious tolerance. Now, the freedom of religious belief is enjoyed by every citizen, as is clearly stated in its Constitution. This is an advanced policy of scientific socialism in the spirit of true democracy.

There is often the misrepresentation in certain parts of the world that where materialism prevails, everything pertaining to idealism should be thrown overboard. That is a very unfortunate misunderstanding. Fundamentally Marxism, deep and broad as it is and now justifiably held high as the guiding principle of the nation, is never so self-contained as not to permit its scope to be enlarged nor has it ever advocated that any and everything traditional should be overthrown. Misinformation and incorrect interpretation caused confusion as to its nature, which was considered the illness of the time. China also suffered from that illness for a short period but very soon recovered. Now social conditions have improved by themselves. Most of the old Buddhist temples, lamaseries and monasteries have been rebuilt and renovated. So is it with ancient Taoist and Confucian buildings. The *Tripiṭaka* is well preserved, and a new and enlarged edition of it has been made. So it is also with the Taoist scriptures. Perhaps no nation can afford to lose the treasure of its cultural heritage, which must not only be material but spiritual. A trivial bit of evidence is that this theory of Pure Consciousness, considered one of the subjective and "uncompromising" doctrines of idealism, is still studied and here presented to English readers.

As to the work itself, it is purely an exposition without any new discovery. This study in general has been comparable to the gleaning of gold particles from sand along the banks of a river. Much time and effort was unavoidably spent in vain. And the result as this seems still far from being satisfactory. One principle in this sort of research is to know how to extract, that is how to eliminate all the unnecessary material accreted throughout the past ages in order to uncover and reveal the original substance in its true light. Only in this way, it seems, can ancient Indian thoughts be justly treated or correctly evaluated.

Perhaps anyone who has some experience in translation knows well that to find an English equivalent to a term in another language, and in this case, Sanskrit, is oftentimes very difficult. Only with the help of ancient Chinese annotations can the precise meaning still be largely ascertained. But English is not the mother-tongue of the present writer, so the outcome is necessarily imperfect. If there is any mistake, it is his own, since he works single-handedly as an academic. Therefore any comment or criticism by the sagacious reader would be welcome and highly appreciated.

附 录 一

百 法

Appendix I

One Hundred Dharmas

由世亲所列的“百法”，其梵文均被译成了不同的现代语言，然而因为词语有多种或多层含义，它们在任何一种翻译中都不曾被标准化。因此，下文只列出了梵文原文。[1]

The Sanskrit terms of the "Hundred Dharmas" arranged by Vasubandhu have all been translated into various modern languages, yet in none have they been brought to any standardization, as the words have many meanings and shades of meaning. So only the original Sanskrit terms are listed here below.

I.	Citta-dharma 心法	8
II.	Caitasika-dharma 心所法	51
III.	Rūpa-dharma 色法	11
IV.	Cittaviprayukta-saṃskāra-dharma 心不相应行法	24
V.	Asaṃskṛta-dharma 无为法	6
		100

I. Citta-dharma 心法

1. Cakṣur-vijñāna 眼识
2. Śrotra-vijñāna 耳识

1. 为方便读者，此处根据 Dan Lusthaus 的总结（http://www.acmuller.net/yogacara/outlines/100dharmas.html）给出汉译，并订正了梵文中的一些错字，将一些不标准的用词改成现在通行的说法。

3. Ghrāna-vijñāna 鼻识

4. Jihvā-vijñāna 舌识

5. Kāya-vijñāna 身识

6. Mano-vijñāna 意识

7. Manas 意

8. Ālaya-vijñāna 阿赖耶识

II. Caitta/Caitasika-dharma 心所法

Pañca-sarvatraga 五遍行

1. Manaskāra 作意

2. Sparśa 触

3. Vedanā 受

4. Saṃjñā 思

5. Cetanā 想

Pañca-viniyata 五别境

1. Chanda 欲

2. Adhimokṣa 胜解

3. Smṛti 念

4. Samādhi 定

5. Prajñā 慧

Ekādaśa-kuśala 十一善

1. Śraddhā 信
2. Vīrya 精进
3. Hrī 惭
4. Apatrāpya 愧
5. Alobha 无贪
6. Adveṣa 无嗔
7. Amoha 无痴
8. Praśrabdhi 轻安
9. Apramāda 不放逸
10. Upekṣa 行舍
11. Ahiṃsā 不害

Ṣaḍ-kleśa 六烦恼

1. Rāga 贪
2. Pratigha 嗔
3. Māna 慢
4. Mūdhi 痴
5. Vicikitsā 疑
6. Dṛṣṭi 恶见

Viṃśati-upakleśa 二十随烦恼

1. Krodha 忿
2. Upanāha 恨
3. Pradāsa 恼
4. Mrakṣa 覆
5. Māyā 诳
6. Mada 骄
7. Śāṭhya 谄
8. Vihiṃsā 害
9. Īraṣyā 嫉
10. Mātsarya 悭
11. Āhrīkya 无惭
12. Anapatrāpya 无愧
13. Aśraddhya 不信
14. Kausīdya 懈怠
15. Pramāda 放逸
16. Styāna 昏沉
17. Auddhatya 掉举
18. Muṣitasmṛtitā 失念
19. Asaṃprajanya 不正知
20. Vikṣepa 散乱

Catvāro'niyata 四不定

1. Middha 睡眠

2. Kaukṛtya 悔

3. Vitarka 寻

4. Vicāra 伺

III. Rūpa-dharma 色法

1. Cakṣu 眼

2. Śrotra 耳

3. Ghrāṇa 鼻

4. Jihvā 舌

5. Kāya 身

6. Rūpa 色

7. Śabda 声

8. Gandha 香

9. Rasa 味

10. Sprastavya 触

11. Dharmāyatanikāni rūpani 法处所摄色

IV. Citta-viprayukta-saṃskāra-dharma 心不相应行法

1. Prāpti 得

2. Jīvitendriya 命根

3. Nikāya-sabhāga 众同分

4. Visabhāga 异生法

5. Asaṃjñi-samāpatti 无想定

6. Nirodha-samāpatti 灭尽定

7. Asaṃjñika 无想果

8. Nāma-kāya 名身

9. Pada-kāya 句身

10. Vyañjana-kāya 文身

11. Jāti 生

12. Sthiti 住

13. Jarā 老

14. Anityatā 无常

15. Pravṛtti 流转

16. Pratiniyama 定异

17. Yoga 相应

18. Jāva 势速

19. Anukrama 次第

20. Kāla 时

21. Deśa (dik) 方

22. Sāmagrī 和合性

23. Saṃkhyā 数

24. Anyathātva 不和合性

V. Asaṃskṛta-dharma 无为法

1. Ākāśa 虚空

2. Pratisaṃkhyā-nirodha 择灭无为

3. Apratisaṃkhyā-nirodha 非择灭无为

4. Āniñjya 不动灭无为

5. Samjñā-vedayita-nirodha 想受灭无为

6. Tathatā 真如

附 录 二

肇 论

Appendix II

Three Theses of Seng-zhao

序言

逻辑和辩证法都有助于清晰的思考。“智辩术”（Sophistry）最初以逻辑和辩证法为基础，含涉修辞学，这种似是而非的推理术兴盛于古希腊以及其后的希腊—罗马世界。智辩术曾对古代哲学的发展有过不小的推动，然而发展至末期，职业智辩师（Sophists）对这门艺术的使用达到了滥用的地步，以至于无论一个命题对于常识而言是多么荒谬和矛盾，他们都可以给出合理的论证。约略在同一时期，在中国的战国时代（约公元前475—前221年），也有同样的情形出现，亦有智辩师，能言善辩，在中国通常称之为唯名论者，属名家。所论者如“白马非马”，“镞矢之疾而有不动不止之时”。他们推论说理，遣词造句，尤其是含糊其词的能力，使人钦佩。然而能胜人之口，却不能服人之心。现代学者或许会欣慕于照相术，可以轻易地见到“飞矢不动”，进而赞叹古人的玄思。然而依照常识，白马还是马。弓箭手深知自己力量有限，不能射出“不动之矢”。即便知道“飞矢不动”，面对迎面而来的飞矢，任何人都会本能地躲闪。于是，此类推理就不能久行于世了。墨学堪称非凡，极具宗教色彩，重“兼爱”，却因持有奇特的逻辑，如称“杀盗非杀人”，而终究行之不远，兴盛也不足百年，就从古代中国文化的舞台上隐退了。

或许有人认为，寻求真理应当排除常识或生活实利的不当干扰，为了真理自身而寻求真理。然而我们仍须知道，一旦有真理之发现，此真理应当可以实现于我们的内中有体和外部活动。否则，正如一位现代精神大师所言，这真理将无异于思维游戏的答案，或一抽象的非真实，或一纸空文。常识哲学或有范围的限碍和狭隘的缺点，但仍不失为人类生活的良好支柱与根基。

在历史上，唯名论者所取得的成就不可小觑。因为宇宙万物都有其名与形（梵文称“名色”），正确地处理名形关系极为重要。唯名论者在刑名学上对法家有巨大的帮助。然而他们的逻辑推理，无论能否引出任何知识真理，一旦走向极端，就引出了荒谬。客观地说，荒谬可笑并无大害。然而有这样一些高妙的推理，在本质上貌似玄学，其所思不为不深，论证严谨，其所表述之真理亦属正确，那么我们当如何看待呢？笔者以为，这些推理不独是荒谬的，而是有害的了。

古代智辩师或许应该为希腊文化的没落负有部分责任，正是他们的误用，贬低了逻辑和辩证法的地位。与此相较，自商羯罗（788—820）开始，幻有论（虚幻主义）以及此前的空论（虚无主义）在印度的发展，造成了更为严重的后果，二者长期迟滞了社会的进步。与佛教一同进入中国的空论，蔓延之势如森林大火，给中华民族带来巨大的损害。在印度，损害甚至更为明显。因为自佛陀时代之后，就有空论和幻有论的流行，逐渐悄无声息地侵蚀和削弱了这个民族的创造力和生命力，使其过度地衰老了。持守此种信条的皈依者或信徒对于空论的误解和误用，连同视人生如幻之态度，导致了享乐主义不顾一切的大泛滥，继而堕入极度的悲观主义的深渊之中。个人如此，民族亦如此。其逻辑是，如果尘世间的一切都如梦，如溪水之浮沫，为空，为不真实，为徒劳，那么行害人害己之事，有何不可呢？积极进取，又所为何事呢？如果生命自身为空无，那么生命中的一切一定也是空无。信仰业报轮回不可能阻止情命的大爆发和间歇性的心理沮丧。在社会中，腐败深入了骨髓，在生命里，颓废潜入了肌肤，所有充满希望的事业都有破坏性的失败主义情绪紧随其后。不无遗憾地说，印度的现状，亦如人类的一切不幸，其发生并非偶然，溯其最远最深的源头，都在此类观念近旁。

笔者无意在此做道德的说教。但是我们无法否认，在此类高妙的玄学推论中，甚至连社会上最残暴的罪行也等同于虚无。彼世成为此世彻底的虚无。这些理论并非无可辩驳，我们可以在其论域中予以驳斥。我只是想说，沉溺于高妙的推理是何等地有害和危险。纵览整部世界历史，其失远大于得，虽然必有所得。《肇论》的内容是公元5世纪初的一位中国僧人对于若干玄学问题的探讨，正是智力游戏或说"思维技艺"的绝佳例证。

* * *

佛教在印度的出现犹如一轮升起的太阳。远在阿育王时代之前，佛法的种子就已经撒遍北印度，进而茁壮成长，生机勃勃地繁茂于中亚，最终抵达中国。世界历史见证了三次伟大的征服：罗马帝国的征服，佛教的征服，以及随后的基督的征服。佛教未能进入非洲，在欧洲的传播也失败了，却成功进入东方，并且在中国扎根一千多年，这其中有何缘由呢？过去的一百多年以来，许多东西方学者都在思考这个文化史上最使人痴迷的问题。

此类问题已经有了许多答案，还会有更多的答案。现代中国学者从历史唯物主义视角探索和思考这些问题。中国人能理解佛教，如果有其必然，或许在于佛教进入中国之前，道教已经为其铺平了道路。我们现在知道，物理层面的真理是属于普世的，而生命层面的真理亦是属于普世的。古代中国人和印度人都具有高度的文化，伟大的学者在心思层面也有相似的发展，在更高的层度上或许还会有相似的体悟，这是再自然不过的事了。在佛教传入之时，中国人发现这新法与自己的文化如此相似，乃至相同，于是毫无意外地理解并轻松地接纳了她。土壤已经施好肥料，一切都准备妥当，于是这朵取自"西天"的新葩顺利地生长，开花，并结果。

佛教与道教的比较研究是一个专门课题，限于篇幅，无法于此详述。不过，笔者可以简述几点相似之处。从根本上说，它们都具有一种弃世的精神，都有对超出世俗存在的高上追求。它们都认可圣贤言教的权威性——在印度，"圣言"

是正理内甚至高于正理的知识标准——这也正是二者区别于现代科学的地方。因为科学认为，除其自身以外，就没有更高的权威了。而且它们都认为，最高真理超出文字、名相以及思维形式，只能体悟，不可表述。它们都认为，所有人类的知识，包括它们自己的言教，都属外在的，而其内在知识却另有所在。道家有寓言，得鱼忘筌，得兔忘蹄；佛教有筏喻，登岸应弃舟。老子所言之“无”，尽管至今仍被极大地误解，却能很好地相应于从佛教而来的新范式“空”。我们可以想象，佛道之间在大体上多有重合，二者初遇之时，定当会有良好的默契的。佛教初入中国时，碰到了一些抵触，但是很快就受到欢迎和兄弟般的款待。佛教和道教在最终分道扬镳之前，携手走过了很长的一段路程。

正是在佛教与道教临近分手之前，佛教学者僧肇（384—414）撰写了这几篇以道释佛的论文。僧肇是鸠摩罗什的弟子，辅助老师翻译佛经。南梁慧皎《高僧传》撰有“僧肇传”（512 年），至今仍在。很显然，僧肇精通老庄之学以及当时流通的大部分佛经。《易经》《老子》和《庄子》是中国的三部主要玄学著作，僧肇熟谙其中的两部，《易经》可能是个例外，他几乎没有引证过。僧肇不喜欢《易经》，可能是由于两者之间的宇宙观和人生理想不相一致，也可能是他还没有成熟到理解《易经》的年纪，他离世时只有 31 岁。

有两点或许应该引起研究宗教史的现代学者注意。第一，虽然僧肇的论文是用一种当时流行的精致文风撰写而成的，但是相较于同时代的作品，僧肇的文字并没有达到应有和能有的完美程度。我们能够看出某些文字表述的稚嫩和生疏。或许他专心于将外文翻译成汉语，以致影响了自己的思维和表述方式。僧肇所用的语言现在已属古旧，加之以稚拙的行文，使其思想显得比实际上更加深奥晦涩。许多读者难解《肇论》，此为缘由之一。第二，从僧肇作品中的引文来看，至少所有确定由他撰写的作品全都基于道教和佛教经文。经文属“圣言”，是衡量知识的权威。不同于德国汉学家李华德（W. Liebenthal）所言，在僧肇的文字中没有任何迹象显示，他曾有精神师一样的证悟。认为僧肇基于其证悟而主张神秘主义、神悦或如此之类，更是牵强之论。因为僧团贬斥此类行为，禁止僧人展示个人成就之超能力，无论是中国的还是印度的僧人，如果违反，都会被逐出僧团。这等同于基督徒被罗马天主教廷逐出教会一样。再者，就我们所能见到的文字而言，僧肇的思想，皆有所本。

· · ·

众所周知，现存的僧肇作品并非全是真作。开篇有“奏秦王表”的《涅槃无名论》或许是伪作，原文已经佚失。《答刘遗民书》或许不是伪作，但内容不重要。还有其他若干文章，或只存篇名，或虽有文本，但真实性可疑。因此，笔者从著名的“僧肇四论”中仅取三论，译为英文。中文原文取自北宋僧人净源撰《肇论中吴集解》，书后“题辞”言成书于公元1058年，近年有据宋版翻印的石印本，可见刻板边缘的若干轻微损坏。

《肇论》有两种更早的译本，一种是英译本，一种是现代汉语译本。英译本的作者是19世纪40年代生活在北京的德国教授李华德，所译书名为“The Book of Chao”，这个译本并不普及，只有少数几位身在中国的学者知道（《华裔学志丛书》第13册，北京辅仁大学1948年出版）。现代汉语译本的作者是中国社会科学院世界宗教研究所所长任继愈先生。任继愈亦只翻译了三论，置于不同篇目下，其中两论收于其《汉唐佛教思想论集》（1974年，北京），第三论发表于本研究所杂志《世界宗教研究》（1979年，北京）。关于这两种译文，我略作评论。

在文学领域，任何有过写作尤其是诗歌创作经验的人都知道，在灵感迸发或创作力极高的情况下书写的文字，同一位作者几乎不可能在其他时机，以其他形式加以更改或重新创作。将古文改写为现代文与此类似，即使皆属同一种语言，其难度并不比翻译成另一种语言要低。如鸠摩罗什对一般翻译的评价，两者都“失其味”了。虽然如此，现代汉语译文对初学者是大有帮助的。

评价李华德的《肇论》译文，应该区别于他的《肇论》研究。李华德在其译著《肇论》中收集了完善的辞书资料，并将大量术语译回梵文，广泛征引汉语古典文献，这些都是极其值得尊敬的工作。中国学者很可能会省略这些研究，而正是这些工作让我们了解到，为了让西方读者更好地理解所谓“前禅宗”时代的中国佛教，李华德做出了多么大的努力。李华德的研究工作如果不是完全，也一定是部分地得到了已故学者汤用彤教授（1893—1964）的指导，两人当时都在北京大学任教。汤用彤教授是研究佛教的著名学者，他的中国佛教史研究举世闻名。然而无论是否得到了他的帮助，李华德都做了大量工作，其成果是一部非常值得推荐英语读者阅读的译著。

但是，李华德的译文本身不算出色。正如他自己曾说：“译文基本属直译，但是有些地方，如果不改变行文句式，就无法达义。有那么一两处译文，太过随意，只能算作是原文内容的概述。”我们确实发现，李华德的翻译完全改变和重建了原文的结构，几乎所有行文形式都被转换为欧洲“模式”(Denkform)。古代推论喜好“词句轮转”，反复使用相同甚至同义的表述，忠实的翻译应当予以保留，但是李华德却用自己的模式替换了原有的形式，而在新的形式推论中，其所使用的几乎所有的术语都有待于商榷。于是，为了尽量贴近原义，译者除了使用大量脚注之外，还在译文中添加了许多插入语，一般说来，好的翻译应当尽量少用插入语。

从总体上看，李华德教授的译文给人这样一种印象：译者深陷在一大片荆棘丛中，无法脱身。他的问题并不出在方法，他的方法很好，而问题是出在视角上。从根本上说，李华德看待和处理《肇论》，视其如同某种欧洲的哲学系统，而这正是他的失误之处。但是李华德原本可以避免此类视角的，因为他已经从欧阳竟无大师那里学到了“体”“用”之别（即普遍意义上的“存在”与“生成”），为什么没有同时学到“佛法非哲学非宗教”呢？

笔者的译本所采用的翻译方法是直译，不增不减，不加修饰，止于可读。译文旨在帮助读者清晰地了解，佛教初入中国时，正如中国僧人僧肇的阐释，怎样在理论层面被道家接纳。译文意在服务普罗大众，不仅只为了若干学者。

通常，新译应当优于旧译。就本书而言，则未必如此，因为每位译者都有自己的处理方式。有关本书的内容，笔者最后想说的是，语言上的机巧、争论和辩驳之类，有着悠久的历史，在欧洲起于苏格拉底，在印度起于佛陀时代，在中国稍晚于孔子。

徐梵澄 1981年2月15日 北京

（李文彬 译）

INTRODUCTION

Both logic and dialectics lead to clear thinking. Sophistry, the specious art of reasoning originally based both upon logic and dialectics and also involved in rhetorics, flourished in ancient Greece and later on in the Graeco-Roman world in general. It helped in no small measure the development of ancient philosophy. At a final stage of its development, the professional sophists used yet further abused this art so much so that for any proposition, however absurd and contradictory to good sense, they could find sound arguments. In about the same period, at the time of the Warring States in China, (circa 475–221 B.C.) the same thing happened. Sophists, usually called Nominalists in history were not lacking and, indeed, very competent debaters they were. It was argued that, for example, "a white horse is not a horse," or "swift as the arrow is, it has its moments without motion as well as moments of ceaseless motion." Well, the skill in the exposition of causes and reasons and in the employment of words specially in their ambiguity is admirable. The opponent can thus be defeated in debate but nobody is convinced. A modern scholar might become enthused if he is told that pictures of a motinoless arrow can readily be seen on a photograph and might appreciate the ancient metaphysical mentality. But a white horse is still no other being than a horse according to common sense. The archer knows well that his strength is limited and cannot set his arrow in ceaseless motion. Everyone will instinctively shun the arrow shot at him in spite of his whole knowledge of its being motionless. Hence this sort of reasoning had not lasted long. Not much better fared the philosophy of Mo Tze, otherwise a remarkable system rich in religious colouring with Universal Love as its core, also because of its singular logic which maintained, for example, "to kill a robber is not to kill a man." It flourished for less than a hundred years before it retreated from the stage of ancient Chinese culture.

At this point it may be argued that one must seek truth for his own sake without any illegitimate interference of common sense or life-utility. But still the truth, once discovered, must be realisable in our inner being and our outer activities: "if it is not, ... it would be no more than the solution of a thought-puzzle or an abstract unreality or a dead letter."— as a modern spiritual Master pointed out. The philosophy of common sense may be blamed for the limitation and narrowness in its scope, but it is still a good support and foundation for life.

Yet, the achievements of the Nominalists in history were not inconsiderable. Since everything in the universe has its name and form (nāma-rūpa in Sanskrit) , the right handling of names and forms is of primary importance. Their service thus rendered to the Legalists in the field of jurisprudence was immense. Yet their logical reasonings which may or may not lead to any intellectual truth become ridiculous when carried to the extreme. Objectively speaking, being ridiculous or laughable is not much of an evil. Now, there are high reasonings that appear metaphysical in nature, apparently deep in their thoughts, sound in their arguments, true in their specific formulation of truths, what can be said of them? They are no longer ridiculous but harmful.

Perhaps the ancient sophists were partly responsible for the decline of Greek culture since they misused and hence degraded both logic and dialectics. Compared with this the development of Illusionism (Māyavāda) in India since Shankarācarya (788–820 C.E.) and that of Nihilism (Shūnyavāda) earlier had even greater consequences. Both retarded the progress of society for ages. Together with the introduction of Buddhism into China, the Shunyavāda spread like a forest fire had brought great destructions to the race. In India the ruin was even more evident, because both Shūnyavāda and Māyavāda prevailed ever since Buddha's time. The creative impulse together with the vitality of the race was gradually and silently sapped and weakened, and senility unduly crept in. By the devotee or any professed follower of such a creed, a misunderstood and misapplied theory of the Void together with the view of life as Illusion usually resulted in a great outburst of reckless hedonism for a certain period immediately followed by a steep downfall into radical pessimism. As it was so with the individual, so it was with the race. The rationale is if everything in our mundane existence is unreal or void or vain like a dream or a bubble in the stream, what is then the harm of doing evil sinning against oneself or against society, and what for is the achievement of anything positive? As life itself is void, so everything in life must be void. Beliefs in past actions (karma) and rebirths are by no means secure safty valves for preventing the vital explosions and the spasmodic psychological depressions. Corruption goes into the heart of society, decadence creeps into every walk of life, and a destructive defeatism treads on the heels of every hopeful enterprise. It is regretful to say that the present condition of India as a symbol of all human misery cannot be incidental but had its deepest and remotest source somewhere here.

It is not intended here to boost moral principles. It cannot be denied that in those high metaphysical reasonings, even the most atrocious crimes in society are regarded as nil. The otherworldliness comes to a perfect nothingness of the present world. We know that these theories are not irrefutable and they can be defeated on their own grounds. It is meant here only to say how the high reasoning can be harmful and dangerous if indulged in. Viewed in the whole history of the world, its demerits greatly outweigh its merits, though merits there must also be. The discussions on several metaphysical subjects written by a Chinese Buddhist monk in the beginning of the fifth century are translated here. In the opinion of the translator a very good example of a play of the intellect or "mental acrobatics" it is.

* * *

Buddhism rose like a sun in India. The seeds of this Dharma were widely sown all over North India even before Asoka's time, grew gradually into large plants and flourished exuberantly in Central Asia and finally in China. History tells of three great conquests in the world: the conquest of the Roman Empire, the conquest of Buddhism, and the conquest of Christ that followed. How and why Buddhism could not penetrate into Africa and failed in spreading to Europe but succeeded in coming to the East and held the field for more than a thousand years in China are the most fascinating and enthralling problems in cultural history that engaged the keen intellects both in the East and the West for the last hundred years or more.

To these questions many answers are found and can still be found. Modern thinkers in China tackle these problems from the historical materialistic point of view. It cannot escape their perpiscuity perhaps that before its introduction to China, the way was paved for it by Taoism. Now we know that the truths on the physical plane are universal, and no less so are the truths on the plane of life. Since both the Chinese and Indian peoples were highly cultured in ancient times, it was natural that great intellects had similar developments on the mental plane and probably similar realisations on the higher planes above. When the new Dharma was brought into the country and found to be very much akin or even the same as the native one, inevitably it was appreciated and easily accepted. In a sense because the soil was already well prepared and fertilised, so this new flower transplanted from the "Western Heaven" could easily grow and bloom and bear fruits.

A comparative study of Buddhism and Taoism is a special subject too large to be dealt with in this small space. Yet a few points of their similarity may be mentioned here. Fundamentally there is a spirit of renunciation and a pursuit of higher things above the mundane existence common to both. Both believed in the authority of the saying of the sages, — in India, Āryavāda is taken as a measure of knowledge in or even above Nyāya, — and this is the point where both must differ from modern Science, because Science believes in no higher authority other than its own. And in their pursuit of truth both claimed that the supreme Truth stood above words and names and forms of thought, inexpressible yet realisable. Both regarded all human knowledge including the verbal teachings held by themselves as external while their internal knowledge lay somewhere else. In Taoism the parable is the hare-trap or the fishing-net, which can be abandoned if the hare or the fish is caught. In Buddhism there is the classical example of the raft which must be dispensed with when one has crossed over the ocean and landed on the younger shore. A great Void, unfortunately very much misunderstood even nowadays, taught by Lao Tze could very well fit into the new pattern of the thought of Shūnyata in Buddhism. On these broad lines of coincidence one can well imagine how these two great systems could have come to a nice understanding at the first stage of their meeting. The newcomer met some resistance in the very beginning, but was very soon welcomed and entertained like a younger brother by his elder brother and both walked a long distance hand in hand before they quarelled and finally parted company.

It was at this stage just before their separation when the Buddhist scholar Seng-zhao

(383–414 C.E.) wrote these treatises elucidating the doctrines of Buddhism in the light of Taoism. Seng-zhao was a disciple of Kumārajīva who helped his master in composing the texts of the Chinese translations. His biography is extant, included in the "Biographies of High Monks" by Hui Zhiao of the Liang Dynasty (in 512 C.E.) . Obviously he was conversant with the philosophy of Lao Tze and Djuang Tze, and most of the Buddhist texts then current. Thus among the three principal Chinese metaphysical works he was supposed to be well versed in two, with probably the exception of the first, the Book of Changes, which was scarcely utilised by him either because he disliked it owing to the discrepancy in the cosmic views and the ideals of life between these two systems, or because he was not yet too mature for that as he died at the age of only thirty-one.

Two points perhaps should not escape the notice of modern researchers in the history of religions. First, though what Seng-zhao wrote was in a style well elaborated as it was fashionable to write in that manner in his times, it was yet not so accomplished as it should and could have been, judged by the writings of his contemporaries. Certain places of naivety and awkwardness in expression are traceable in his handling of the pen. It was probably because he was mainly engaged in the work of translating a foreign language into his own that influenced his formulations of thought and statements. As his language has now become somewhat antiquated, this obtuseness in style has helped to make his thoughts appear more profound and obscure than they actually were that baffled the understanding of so many readers. Next, so far all his authentic works are based on Scriptures such as the Taoist and Buddhist texts — sūtras and shāstras — as the quotations show. This is Āryāvada held as authority in the measurement of knowledge. But these do not show any sign of the realisation of the writer as a spiritual Master, as the German scholar W. Liebenthal alleged. It would be far-fetched to conclude that Seng-zhao had owing to his personal realisation stood for Mysticism or the Divine Ecstasy or the like, as these things were depreciated by the Samgha, and any show of supernatural powers of personal accomplishment by any master, Indian or Chinese, was forbidden on pains of expulsion from the Samgha, a punishment comparable to the excommunication of the Roman Catholic Church. Moreover, there is nothing original in his thoughts so far we can gather.

* * *

It is well known that not all the extant writings of Seng-zhao are authentic. The thesis "On the Namelessness of Nirvāṇa" preceded by a "Letter of Dedication" might be forged by someone else when the originals were lost. The epistle in answer to the Upāsaka Liu Chen (alias Liu Yi-ming) may not be spurious but not of much importance. Several other miscellaneous pieces are left to us with only their titles, or, if existing, of a dubious nature. Thus from among the famous "Four Theses of Seng-zhao," only three are here presented in their English translation. The original Chinese text is one with "Collected Annotations" made by Tsin Yuan in the Sung Dynasty with a postscript dated 1058 C.E. It is a lithography edition made in recent years after a Sung print with slight damages on the edges of several wooden blocks.

Prior to the present translation there were two in circulation, one in English and another one in modern Chinese. The English one, not very popular and known only to a few scholars in China, was done by W. Liebenthal, a German professor in Peking in the nineteen-forties, entitled "The Book of Chao" (included in Monumenta Serica as Monograph XIII, published by the Catholic University of Peking, 1948) . The modern Chinese one was done by Ren Ji-yu, Director of the Institute for Research on World Religions in the Chinese Academy of Social Sciences. It had under separate captions also only three theses, two of which were included in his *Collected Writings* that appeared in its third edition in 1974, Beijing, and the third one in the Journal of Researches of the same Institute in 1979, also Beijing. A word must be said about these two works.

Anyone in the field of literature who has had some experience in writing especially poetry can well understand the lines written in certain moments of inspiration or high creativity can scarcely be altered or written by the same author in another form on another occasion. The task of changing the olden phraseology into a modern one even in the same language is similar to that. It is not easier than to render it into another language. Equally "the taste is lost," as Kumārajīva once remarked about the work of translation in general. Nevertheless, it is of great help to beginners.

With regard to Liebenthal's translation, it should be separately treated apart from his studies found in the same book. The comprehensive collection of lexicographical material, the extensive retranslation of the technical terms into the original Sanskrit, and the broad references made to ancient Chinese literature merit our high esteem. These studies are likely to be omitted by a Chinese scholar, yet they show how great the effort has been made in helping the Western reader to a better understanding of Chinese Buddhism in the so-called Pre-ch'an Period. He must have been partly if not totally guided in his researches by the late Prof. Tang Yung-t'ung (1893–1964) who was then teaching in Peking University where he worked. Prof. Tang Yung-t'ung was an eminent scholar in Buddhology whose *History of Chinese Buddhism* was worldly known. At any rate, whether with or without his guidance, Liebenthal worked intensively on this subject and the results he submitted are highly recommendable to English readers.

But his translation itself is less so. As he himself said: "It is fairly literal but sometimes it seemed impossible to render the meaning without changing the phrasing. In one or two cases the translation is so free that is almost amounts to a mere outline of the content."—Now, we do find the structure of the original entirely changed and rebuilt, and nearly every form is put into a European "pattern" (Denkform). The ancient formula of reasoning characterised by the "turning of the sentences," in fact, a wheeling round and round of the same and often tautological expressions, which should nevertheless be preserved in a faithful translation has been discarded and substituted by his own set of forms, and nearly at every step the terminologies employed are subject to discussion. Hence, numerous interpolations in the text, usually the less the better, as well as so many footnotes are needed to bring out the sense to an approximation.

Thus, on the whole it gives the impression that the translator is being enmeshed in a great thorn-bush hardly able to extricate himself. The trouble with him lies not in his method which is a sound one but in his point of view. Fundamentally he regarded and treated it as any system of European philosophy which he could have avoided. It is there where he stumbled. As he has learned of the great Master Ou-yang Ching-wu the distinction between T'i and Yung (which is simply Being and Becoming in a universal sense) , why not at the same time learned of him that "Buddhism is neither philosophy nor religion"?

The present translation is done in a straightforward way with nothing added or reduced, and made just readable without any embellishment. It is meant to help the readers to a clear understanding of how Buddhism at its first stage of introduction to China was in its theoretical aspect accepted by Taoism, as interpreted by a Chinese monk, Seng-zhao. It is meant for the general reading public instead for only a few scholars.

Usually a new translation should be better than its preceding ones. But in this case it is probably not so, since every translator has his own way. And, as a final remark on the contents of this booklet, it may be said that verbal sophistications and duels and arguments of this kind had a long history which began in Europe since Socrates, in India since Buddha's time, and in China since shortly after Confucius.

Hsu Fancheng Beijing Feb. 15, 1981

ON THINGS UNCHANGING

物不迁论

Life and death interchange, winter and summer alternate in succession. Things move along in a flux, and such is the phenomenon as seen by the common people. But I say it is not so.

夫生死交谢，寒暑迭迁，有物流动，人之常情。余则谓之不然。

How?

It is said in the Sūtra[1]:

"No Dharma ever comes or goes, moves or turns."

If we examine what is meant by non-moving here, we may ask: Is it to abandon motion in order to find stillness? It is to find stillness in all motion. While stillness is seen in all motion, motion in full swing is always found still. Without abandoning motion in order to find stillness, stillness is found not separated from motion. Hence both motion and stillness are rudimentarily not different from each other; yet the deluded people regarded them as otherwise. Because of this, the real Truth has become adumbrated through conflicting views and verbal duels; and the traditional right and straight way turned into meanderings through inquisitive entanglements. Hence it has become difficult to philosophise about the extremities of motion and stillness.

何者?《放光》云:“法无去来,无动转者。”寻夫不动之作,岂释动以求静,必求静于诸动。必求静于诸动,故虽动而常静。不释动以求静,故虽静而不离动。然则动静未始异,而惑者不同。缘使真言滞于竞辩,宗途屈于好异。所以静躁之极,未易言也。

Why?

If the Truth is to be tackled with, then conventional views must be contradicted. If conventional views are to be complied with, then the Truth will be contravened. In contravention of the Truth, people tend to become perplexed about the nature of things, and there will be no return of theirs to the right path. And words in contradiction to the conventional views are held to be insipid and tasteless. Hence, on hearing such talks about the Truth, people of medium intellectual capacity regard them as may or may not be correct, and people of inferior calibre will clap their hands, laugh, and go away.

何者?夫谈真则逆俗,顺俗则违真。违真则迷性而莫返,逆俗则言淡而无味。缘使中人未分于存亡,下士抚掌而弗顾。

With regard to a problem so near to us and yet so inexplicable, is it not that of the nature of things in the universe? Nevertheless, I cannot refrain myself from analysing such a problem and try to extemporaneously concentrate my mind on the problem of the relation between motion and stillness. Can it be said that I am definitely right?

近而不可知者,其唯物性乎?然不能自已,聊复寄心于动静之际,岂曰必然?

1. Fang Kwang, fasc. 5 Pañcaviṁśatisāhasrikā Prājñāpāramitā Sūtra Transl. Mokṣala.

I try to reason it out in this way:

It is said in the Sūtra[2]:

"Fundamentally all Dharma comes not from anywhere, and, if going, reaches also nowhere."

It is also said in the Madhyamaka Kārikāh:

"Looking towards their destinations as things go, it is known that they go, but they do not reach their destinations."

These passages point to the finding of stillness in the motion itself. Obviously the unchangeability of all things can thus be understood.

试论之曰:《道行》云:"诸法本无所从来，去亦无所至。"《中观》云:"观方知彼去，去者不至方。"斯皆即动而求静，以知物不迁，明矣。

What people say of motion is that because a thing in the past does not come to the present in its former condition, so the thing is in motion and not still. What I say of stillness is for the same reason. Because a thing in the past does not come to the present in its former condition, so it is still without motion. It is moving and not still because its former state does not come to the present. It is still and not moving because its present state does not return to the past. The phenomenon is the same, but seen in different perspectives it appeared different. Leeward is the way blocked, windward is the sail smooth. If the right course is taken, where can be any hindrance?

夫人之所谓动者，以昔物不至今，故曰动而非静；我之所谓静者，亦以昔物不至今，故曰静而非动。动而非静，以其不来；静而非动，以其不去。然则所造未尝异，所见未尝同。逆之所谓塞，顺之所谓通。苟得其道，复何滞哉?

It is a pity that people have been deluded since long. They see the truth face to face and are not aware of it. They know already things in the past do not come to the present, yet they hold that things at present can be going. If things in the past do not come to the present, where would things in the present go?

伤夫人情之惑久矣，目对真而莫觉！既知往物而不来，而谓今物而可往！往物既不来，今物何所往？

Why?

If a past thing was looked for in the past, the past thing existed: if it is looked for in the present, it no longer exists. As the thing no longer exists in the present, it can be inferred that it does not come. Yet as the thing existed in the past, it can be known that it did not go away. In the same way, if we examine things in the present, we find they do not go to the past. This is to say that the past thing certainly was in the past, it has not gone from the present to the past; the present thing certainly is in the present, it has not come from the past to the present.

何则？求向物于向，于向未尝无；责向物于今，于今未尝有。于今未尝有，以明物不来；于向未尝无，故知物不去。复而求今，今亦不往。是谓昔物自在昔，不从今以至昔；今物自在今，不从昔以至今。

Thus, said Confucius: "Yen Whei sees everything new; — in the twinkling of an eye it is not the same thing." So said, it is plain that things do not come nor go. If there is not any slight sign of coming and going, what is there that can be moving? Thus a great

2. Tao Hsing, fasc. 9 Daśasāhasrikā Prajñāpāramitā Sūtra Transl. Lokarakṣa.

hurricane may destroy a mountain peak, yet it is always still; currents and rivers may sweep along, yet they are not flowing. Dust and gossamer may float in the air, yet they are not moving; the sun and the moon may pass along the sky, yet they are not circulating. What is there to be wondered at?

故仲尼曰："回也见新，交臂非故。"如此，则物不相往来，明矣。既无往返之微朕，有何物而可动乎？然则旋岚偃岳而常静，江河竞注而不流，野马飘鼓而不动，日月历天而不周。复何怪哉？

"E-e-e!" — so said the Sage: "Life is transient, it flows swifter than the stream!" Thus the śrāvakas attained enlightenment through the realisation of impermanence, and Pratyekabuddhas reached the Truth through the departure from the relative causes. Nay: if all activities in the universe are not in progression, how can any progress made serve as a step forward towards realisation?

噫！圣人有言曰："人命逝速，速于川流。"是以声闻悟非常以成道；缘觉觉缘离以即真。苟万动而非化，岂寻化以阶道？

If we examine the words of the Sage again and again, we find the idea therein very subtle and hidden and difficult to fathom. Things are as if moving yet still; as if going yet staying. This can be grasped by Gnosis, can hardly be proved by facts. Thus to say things are going yet not actually going, that is to encompass the thought of permanence of the ordinary man; and to say things are staying yet not actually staying, that is to explain his thought of the so-called progression. Can it ever be said that by impermanence things can be sent off, and by permanence things can be made to stay?

复寻圣言，微隐难测。若动而静，似去而留。可以神会，难以事求。是以言去不必去，闲人之常想；称住不必住，释人之所谓住（据元康疏，“住”应作“往”）耳。岂曰去而可遣，住而可留邪？

Therefore it is said in the Sūtra[3]:

“The Bodhisattva dwelling among the people who believe in the permanence of things expounds the doctrine of impermanence.”

It is also said in the *Mahāyāna Śāstra*[4]:

“All Dharma being immovable, comes nowhence, goes no whither, and stays nowhere.”

故《成具》云：“菩萨处计常之中，而演非常之教。”《摩诃衍论》云：“诸法不动，无去来处。”

This is to reveal one truth by a paradox in order to guide people of all directions. Can it be said that the idea contradicts itself because of the difference in its wording? Therefore the conception of permanence is talked about, but it means a continuity in progression. The phenomenon of transience is also mentioned, but it is a progression without change. Being without change a thing is passing away yet always still, and without staying it is still though always passing away. Though still yet always passing away, so it goes without change; though passing away yet always still, it is still but does not stay. This is why “the hidden boat can be stolen” as mentioned by Djuang Tze, and why Confucius sighed on coming to the banks of a river. Both sages felt what is passing is difficult to come to a stop

3. Ch'eng Chu, fasc. 1 śiddhiprabhāsasamādhi śūtra Transl. Chih Yao.

4. Ta Chi Du Lun, fasc. 51 Mahāprajñāpāramitā-upadeśa Śāstra Transl. Kumārajīva.

and stay. How can that be understood as saying that what is in the present can be pushed to the past? Thus the idea of the sages, if rightly understood, is different from what is seen and comprehended by the common people.

斯皆导达群方，两言一会，岂曰文殊而乖其致哉？是以言常而不住，称去而不迁。不迁，故虽往而常静；不住，故虽静而常往。虽静而常往，故往而弗迁；虽往而常静，故静而弗留矣。然则庄生之所以藏山，仲尼之所以临川，斯皆感往者之难留，岂曰排今而可往？是以观圣人心者，不同人之所见得也。

Why?

People say a man is of the same body from his childhood to youth, and in a hundred years of life he is the same physical being. He only knows his years have gone by, but he is not aware of the fact that his body was trailing along. — Thus the man who entered the Saṃgha when young and returned home when old was asked by his former neighbors: "Is the former man still living?"

"I am still the former man yet not the former man. "— said he.

All his neighbors were astonished and thought his answer was nonsense.

何者？人则谓少壮同体，百龄一质，徒知年往，不觉形随。是以梵志出家，白首而归。邻人见之曰："昔人尚存乎？"梵志曰："吾犹昔人，非昔人也。"邻人皆愕然，非其言也。

It is said in *Djuang Tze*: "A boat hidden in a creek or a fishingnet concealed in the marshes may be considered as secure, But in the middle of the night a strong man carried it away. The owner who was asleep was unaware of it."— Is it not an illustration of this?

所谓有力者负之而趋，昧者不觉，其斯之谓欤？

（庄子“藏山于泽”，“山”借为“汕”，故此译为“鱼网”。）

Therefore, the Tathāgata, in view of the perplexed thoughts of human beings, cleared off their doubts in many a unique discourse. Basing upon the one undualistic Truth he expounded his doctrines in diverse, even paradoxical forms. Contradictable yet invariable are alone the words of the Sage, perhaps.

是以如来因群情之所滞，则方言以辩惑，乘莫二之真心，吐不一之殊教，乖而不可异者，其唯圣言乎！

Therefore, in talking about the Truth, he promulgated the theory of the unchangeability of things. But for guiding ordinary people, he preached the doctrine of constant flux. Though there might be a thousand different ways of expression, their ultimate end could only be one and the same.

故谈真有不迁之称，导俗有流动之说。虽复千途异唱，会归同致矣。

Yet those people adhering to mere verbal expressions, as they hear the theory of unchangeability, say things in the past never come to their present state, and on hearing about the constant flux, say also things in the present can go back to their past state. Since the past and the present states of things are affirmed, why should they be altered?

而征文者，闻不迁，则谓昔物不至今；聆流动者，而谓今物可至昔。既曰古今，而欲迁之者，何也？

Therefore, to say a “past” would not necessarily mean a time that has passed, since both ancient and modern times perpetually existed and both do not move. Or, to say“going” would not necessarily mean going, that is to say the present does not go back to the ancient times just as the ancient times do not come to the present. As there is neither coming nor going, so there can be no gallop between the ancient and modern times. As nothing is moving, so each thing stays at that very moment as it is.

是以言往不必往，古今常存，以其不动；称去不必去，谓不从今至古，以其不来。不来，故不驰骋于古今，不动，故各性住于一世。

Hence, all Scriptures may in this or that manner differ in their phraseologies and hundreds of schools may vary in their theories, but if one has had realisation, could he ever be deluded by their verbal differences?

然则群籍殊文，百家异说，苟得其会，岂殊文之能惑哉？

Therefore, what people say as "staying", I would say it is "passing". What people say as "passing", I would say it is "staying". Though the terms are different, yet they are the same in truth. — So says the Sūtra[5]: "A positive thesis appears to be its antithesis, who cares to believe it?" This saying then is not groundless.

是以人之所谓住，我则言其去；人之所谓去，我则言其住。然则去住虽殊，其致一也。故经云："正言似反，谁当信者？"斯言有由矣。

Why?

People look for the past in the present and say things never stay, but I look for the present in the past and find things have not gone. If the present went to the past, then the past would have contained the present; if the past came down to the present, then the present would have contained the past. But the present does not contain the past, it can be inferred that things do not come to the present. If the past does not contain the present, it can also be inferred that things do not go. If the past does not come to the present and the present does not go to the past so that everything is left at that very moment as it is, what then is there capable of coming and going?

何者？人则求古于今，谓其不住；吾则求今于古，知其不去。今若至古，古应有今；古若至今，今应有古。今而无古，以知不来；古而无今，以知不去。若古不至今，今亦不至古，事各性住于一世，有何物而可去来？

May then the four seasons turn as swiftly as the wind, and the stars of the Great Bear circulate like lightning, yet if one has grasped this idea in its subtlety, one can understand that these phenomena are ultimately motionless although appearing in swift motion.

然则四象风驰，璇玑电卷，得意毫微，虽速而不转。

Therefore, the merit of the Tathāgata extends over to thousands of generations and remains everlasting. His Truth prevails over hundreds of aeons and stands ever firm. In piling up a mountain, the completion of the the work is initiated through the first basket of earth, and the arrival at the destination after a long distance travelling is anticipated by the first step. That is to say the meritorious actions are indestructible. As they were indestructible, they were never modified though ancient. As there was no modification, there could not be any change.

Now, the reason for the unchangeability of things is transparently clear.

是以如来功流万世而常存，道通百劫而弥固。成山假就于始篑，修途托至于

5. Pu Yao, fasc. 22 Lalitavistara Sūtra Transl. Dharmarakṣa.

初步，果以功业不可朽故也。功业不可朽，故虽在昔而不化，不化故不迁（经下有“不迁故”三字）。则湛然明矣。

So it is said in the Sūtra[6]: “Though the Three Great Calamities may destroy the universe, yet one’s good actions (karma) and their merits are not thereby eliminated.”

This saying is certainly true.

故经云：“三灾弥纶，而行业湛然。”信其言也。

Why?

The cause does not accompany its effect, the effect is produced from the cause. As the cause produces its effect, the cause was not being eliminated in the past. As the effect does not accompany its cause, the cause does not advent to the present. Without elimination and advent the unchangeability of things can readily be understood. What then it there for doubt on the coming and going and what is there for puzzle between activity and inactivity?

何者？果不俱因，因因而果。因因而果，因不昔灭。果不俱因，因不来今。不灭不来，则不迁之致明矣。复何惑于去留，踟蹰于动静之间哉？

Therefore even if heaven and earth turned upside down, it cannot be said that they were not still; and, even if a deluge rose up to the sky, it cannot be said that it was moving. If one can engage his mind with everything at that very moment as it is, then he cannot be far from the truth.

然则乾坤倒复，无谓不静；洪流滔天，无谓其动。苟能契神于即物，斯不远而可知矣。

6. Chan O-han, fasc. 21 Dīrghāgama Sūtra Transl. Buddhayaśa.

ON THE UNREAL-VOID

不真空论

That which is utterly void without coming into and going out of existence, — that is the subtle idea grasped by the metaphysical cognition and the supreme principle of Being. If one is not sagacious, enlightened and of superior comprehension, how can he conciliate the truths of Being and Non-being? So the Superman extends his divine consciousness into the Infinite and nowhere does he meet any barrier to his penetration. His visual and auditory faculties may develop themselves to the utmost, yet they are not affected by the objects of seeing and hearing. Is it not due to the fact that in seeing all objects as they are by themselves void so these cannot burden his spirit?

夫至虚无生者，盖是般若玄鉴之妙趣，有物之宗极者也。自非圣明特达，何能契神于有无之间哉？是以至人通神心于无穷，穷所不能滞，极耳目于视听，声色所不能制者，岂不以其即万物之自虚，故物不能累其神明者也？

Thus riding on his true consciousness and following the right course of things in the universe, the Sage penetrates into everything without any obstacle. Seeing Nature as one movement, he meets everywhere submissive reception. Since there is nothing that he cannot penetrate, he comes to the core of truth through the maze of phenomenal appearances. And, as he meets everywhere submissive reception, he regards each and all as One. All the objects in the universe may be regarded as different from each other, yet they cannot be different in themselves. Since they cannot be different in themselves; it can be known that they are unreal. Since they are unreal, they are phenomenal yet not real phenomena.

是以圣人乘真心而理顺，则无滞而不通；审一气以观化，故所遇而顺适。无滞而不通，故能混杂致淳；所遇而顺适，故则触物而一。如此，则万象虽殊，而不能自异。不能自异，故知象非真象；象作真象，故则虽象而非象。

Hence all beings and I are of the same root, and the right and wrong of one stem. These subtle and obscure and submerged and hidden truths cannot be exhaustively exploited by ordinary men.

然则物我同根，是非一气，潜微幽隐，殆非群情之所尽。

In the recent talks on the principle of Voidness (Shūnyatāvāda) , opinions of diverse schools vary. Now, to approach identity through the way of differentiae, what can be identified? Diverse schools of thought appear in conflict with each other, and they, by their very nature, cannot come to any conclusion.

故顷尔谈论，至于虚宗，每有不同。夫以不同而适同，有何物而可同哉？故众论竞作而性莫同焉。

Why?

A) The theory of Mental Non-existence:

This theory holds that if the mind is not on matter, matter ceases to exist. Thus things in the universe are not non-existent.

The merit of this theory is tranquillisation of the mind, its demerit lies in its ignorance of the voidness of matter.

何则？“心无”者，无心于万物，万物未尝无。此得在于神静，失在于物虚。

B) The theory of Matter in Itself[7]:

This theory holds that because matter does not possess of itself as matter, so it is matter yet non-matter.

Now, if matter is mentioned it should point directly to matter itself. Is it necessary to wait till it has possessed of itself before it is called matter?

This theory simply maintains that matter does not possess itself as matter, it does not realise that matter is radically non-matter.

“即色”者，明色不自色，故虽色而非色也。夫言色者，但当色即色，岂待色色而后为色哉？此直语色不自色，未领色之非色也。

C) Theory of the Original Non-existence:

This theory greatly emphasizes non-existence. Whenever anything is talked about, its non-existence is brought into consideration. So it holds: of what the Sūtras say as non-existent the existence is indeed nil, and by what as not non-existent, there must be also that non-existence.

“本无”者，情尚于无多，触言以宾无。故非有，有即无；非无，无即无。

If we examine the essential idea of what the Sūtras say, we find that it is always held simply that what was non-existent was not really existent, and what was not non-existent was not really non-existent. Why should it be said that here by non-existence this existence must be negated, and there by not non-existence that non-existence does not exist?

These are merely gossips in favor of negations. How can it be said that they are theories supported by actual facts corresponding to the nature of things?

寻夫立文之本旨者，直以非有非真有，非无非真无耳。何必非有无此有，非无无彼无？此直好无之谈，岂谓顺通事实，即物之情哉？

As the name Matter is applied to matter, that which is thus nominated can be called matter; as the name Matter is applied to Non-matter, it is still non-matter though called matter. A thing does not come to actuality by following its name and a name docs not step into reality by following the thing. Therefore the real Truth alone remains silent beyond nominations and descriptions, how can It be defined by words?

夫以物物于物，则所物而可物；以物物非物，故虽物而非物。是以物不即名而就实，名不即物而履真。然则真谛独静于名教之外，岂曰文言之能辨哉？

Yet I cannot be silent, I shall try to bring into some facsimile of the Truth in words. I reason it out thus:

It is said in the *Mahāyāna Śāstra*[8]:

7. Matter=Rūpa in Śkt.
Liebenthal's translation: "Rūpa is not independently existing."
Chin Tao-lin's explanation: "With regard to the nature of Rūpa, it is not possessed of itself; therefore it is Rūpa, but void."
In the Collected Annotations it is explained in terms of cause and effect. Rūpa as we see it is the result or effect and therefore held as void. The author holds that Rūpa as the cause should also be void.

8. Yuan Kang's Commentary Mahāyāna Śāstra, fasc. 6.

"All Dharma is neither existent nor non-existent in phenomenal appearance." — And it is also said in the *Madhyamaka*[9]: "All Dharma is neither existent nor non-existent."

This is the first Real Truth.

然不能杜默，聊复厝言以拟之。试论之曰：《摩诃衍论》云："诸法亦非有相，亦非无相。"《中论》云："诸法不有不无"者，第一真谛也。

If we examine what is meant by "neither existent nor nonexistent," does it mean that everything in the universe should he cleared off and all our senses of seeing and hearing be blocked so that what remains is only silence and quietude and void and emptiness, and then the Real Truth is thus attained?

Verily, it is to approach everything in the right way, so that the thing approached does not offer any resistance to our right cognition, and it is to take it as at once false and real, and so its nature does not change. As its nature does not change, it is existent though non-existent. As nothing offers any resistance, it is non-existent though existent. Being existent yet non-existent, it is the so-called Non-being. Being non-existent yet exist ent, it is the so-called Not-non-being. Thus, it is not that there is no being at all in the universe, it is that every being is unreal. If everything is not a real thing, where should the name of matter be placed upon? So it is said in the Sūtra: "The nature of matter is void, it is not that being destroyed matter is then void."[10]

寻夫不有不无者，岂谓涤除万物，杜塞视听，寂寥虚豁，然后为真谛者乎？诚以即物顺通，故物莫之逆；即伪即真，故性莫之易。性莫之易，故虽无而有；物莫之逆，故虽有而无。虽有而无，所谓非有；虽无而有，所谓非无。如此，则非无物也，物非真物。物非真物，故于何而可物？故经云："色之性空，非色败空。"

This shows that the Sage in regarding the universe treats everything as void, because of its self-nature being void; does it mean that he has to cut his way through by demolishing Being into nothingness?

Therefore, Vimalakīrti talked about his disease as being unreal when he was sick, and in the *Āditya-Samādhi Sūtra*[11] it is also stated that the Four Elements are void. The ways of expression in the Tripiṭ aka may vary, yet the underlying principle is only one.

Again it is said in the Sūtra[12]:

"In the light of the first Real Truth, there is neither accomplishment nor attainment; hut according to conventional conceptions there is accomplishment as well as attainment."

以明夫圣人之于物也，即万物之自虚，岂待宰割以求通哉？是以寝疾有不真之谈，《超日》有即虚之称。然则三藏殊文，统之者一也。故《放光》云："第一真谛，无成无得；世俗谛故，便有成有得。"

Generally speaking, attainment is the false name of non-attain-ment, and non-attainment the real name of attainment.

By the real name, it is real yet non-existent.

By the false name, it is not non-existent, though false.

If it is said to be real, it never existed; if it is said to be false, it was not non existent. This duality in language was never one, yet the principle underlying both was never a duet.

9. id. Madhyamaka Kārikāḥ.

10. Vimalakīrti-nirdeśa Sūtra, fasc. 2 Transl. Kumārajiva.

11. Atisūryasamādhi Sūtra, fasc. 1 Transl. Nie Ch'en-yūan.

12. Pañcavimśatisahāsrikā Prajñāpāramitā Sūtra, fasc. 5 Transl. Mokṣala.

So it is said in the Sūtra[13]:

"'Bhagavān! Are the Real Truth and the conventional truths different?'

'No, not different.' — was the answer."

This Sūtra points out directly the Real Truth in order to reveal the Non-existence, and the conventional truths in order to reveal the Not-non-existence. How can two perspectives of the same thing bring forth two different things?

夫有得即是无得之伪号，无得即是有得之真名。真名，故虽真而非有；伪号，故虽伪而非无。是以言真未尝有，言伪未尝无。二言未始一，二理未始殊。故经云："真谛俗谛，谓有异耶？答曰，无异也。"此经直辩真谛以明非有，俗谛以明非无。岂以谛二而二于物哉？

Consequently all things in the universe have that by which they are non-existent, and that by which they are not non-existent. Having had that by which they are non-existent, they are existent yet non-existent, and, having had that by which they are not non-existent, they are non-existent yet not non-existent. Being non-existent yet not non-existent, this non-existence is not an absolute void; being existent yet non-existent, this existence is not the real Being. If Being is not approaching reality and Non-being not demolishing the phenomenal world, then both are merely different modes of nomination while their underlying principle is one and the same.

然则万物果有其所以不有，有其所以不无。有其所以不有，故虽有而非有；有其所以不无，故虽无而非无。虽无而非无，无者不绝虚；虽有而非有，有者非真有。若有不即真，无不夷迹，然则有无称异，其致一也。

Therefore on hearing the discourses about Dharma, the youth sighed[14]: "All Dharma are neither existent nor non-existent. Because of causes and relative causes, all Dharma arise."

故童子叹曰："说法不有亦不无，以因缘故诸法生。"

In the Sūtra[15] it is also said:

"With regard to the turning of the Wheel-of-Dharma, there is neither turning nor un-turning."

This is said to be turning which is yet un-turning. This is the subtle idea of many a Sūtra.

《璎珞经》云："转法轮者，亦非有转，亦非无转，是谓转无所转。"此乃众经之微言也。

Why?

If to see things in the universe as non-existent is true, then the heretical view is not deceptive. If to see things as existent is true, then the ordinary view is correct. Because things are not non-existent, so the heretical view is deceptive. Because things are non-existent, so the ordinary view is incorrect. Hence to say things are at once non-existent and not non-existent is actually the talk based upon the Real Truth.

何者？谓物无耶，则邪见非惑；谓物有耶，则常见为得。以物非无，故邪见为惑；以物非有，故常见不得。然则非有非无者，信真谛之谈也。

13. Mahāpra jñāpāramitā Sūtra, fasc. 22 Transl. Kumārajīva.

14. i. q. 4, fasc. 1.

15. Bodhisattva-keyura Sūtra, fasc. 13 Transl. Chu Fu-nien.

So it is said in the Sūtra[16]:

"Not there is Mind, not there is no Mind."

In the Madhyamaka Kārikāḥ[17] it is also said:

"Things arise from causes and relative causes, so they are non-existent, but because they do arise therefrom, so they are not non-existent."

If we follow this line of reasoning, we find it is true.

故《道行》云："心亦不有亦不无。"《中观》云："物从因缘故不有，缘起故不无。"寻理，即其然矣。

The reason is: if Being really is, it must constantly be; does it depend upon causes and relative causes (hetupratyaya) to become Being? And, conformably, if Non-being really is, it must also constantly be; does it wait for causes and relative causes for it to become so? If Being cannot by itself be, and must depend upon causes and relative causes for coming into existence, then it can be known that it is no real Being. As it is no real Being, it cannot be called Being though existent.

所以然者，夫有若真有，有自常有，岂待缘而后有哉？譬彼真无，无自常无，岂待缘而后无也？若有不能自有，待缘而后有者，故知有非真有。有非真有，虽有，不可谓之有矣。

With regard to Not-non-being: if all is non-existence in which no activity arises in a perfect stillness, then it may be called Non-being. Then there should be nothing that arises. If things arise, then things are Not-non-existent. It is clear that causes and relative causes give rise to everything in the universe, so the universe is not non-existent.

Therefore it is said in the *Mahāyāna Śātra*[18]:

"All Dharma, all due to causes and relative causes should be existent. All Dharma, all due to causes and relative causes should be non-existent.

"All Dharma of Non-being, all due to causes and relative causes should become existent.

"All Dharma of Being, all due to causes and relative causes should become non-existent."

If we trace these lines of reasoning on Being and Non-being, do we regard them as merely contradictory phrases?

不无者，夫无则湛然不动，可谓之无，万物若无，则不应起，起则非无，以明缘起，故不无也。故《摩诃衍论》云："一切诸法，一切因缘，故应有；一切诸法，一切因缘，故不应有；一切无法，一切因缘，故应有；一切有法，一切因缘，故不应有。"寻此有无之言，岂直反论而已哉？

If it should be means also it is, then it cannot be said as non-existent. If it should not be means also it is not, then it cannot be said as existent. Now, to say Being, it is to reveal the Not-non-existence through Being, and to distinguish Non-existence through Non-being. This is one thing split into two in nomination and there appears only a difference in wording. If their implied sameness is realised, then no differentia can be found in any couple of contradictory terms.

16. Daśasahāsrikā Prajñāpāramitā Sūtra, fasc. 1 Transl, Lokarakṣa.

17. i. q. 3, fasc. 4.

18. i. q. 3, fasc. 80.

若应有即是有，不应言无；若应无即是无，不应言有。言有是为假有以明非无，借无以辨非有。此事一称二，其文有似不同。苟领其所同，则无异而不同。

Therefore, all Dharma cannot be regarded as existent, because ultimately there is the reason for their being non-existent; and cannot be regarded as non-existent as well, because there is equally the reason for their not being non-existent.

然则万法果有其所以不有，不可得而有；有其所以不无，不可得而无。

Why?

If we say all is existent, this existence is not produced from reality. If we say all is non-existent, we see all phenomena are obviously there. The phenomenal appearances are not non-existent, yet they are unreal. As they are unreal, they are then not really existent.

Up to this point, the meaning of the Unreal-Void becomes quite clear.

何则？欲言其有，有非真生；欲言其无，事象既形。象形不即无，非真非实有。然而不真空义显于兹矣。

Therefore it is said in the Sūtra[19]:

"All Dharma are under a false name, unreal. They are comparable to a human figure created by magic (Māyā)." It is not that there is no human figure, but the human figure is not a real man.

故《放光》云："诸法假号不真。譬如幻化人。"非无幻化人，幻化人非真人也。

Now, if an object is sought for by its name, there is no substance of the object corresponding to that name. If the name is sought for through the object , the name has no merit of acquiring the object.[20] Now, if an object has no substance corresponding to its name, it is not an object. If the name has no merit of acquiring the object, it is not a name. Thus the name does not correspond to the substance, and the substance does not correspond to the name. If names and substances do not coincide, where are the objects in the universe?

夫以名求物，物无当名之实。以物求名，名无得物之功。物无当名之实，非物也；名无得物之功，非名也。是以名不当实，实不当名。名实无当，万物安在？

So it is said in the *Madhyamaka*[21]:

"A thing by itself has no thisness or otherness."

Only the man takes a thing as this or that. Another man takes this as that and that as this. "This" and "that" cannot settle to one thing in nomination, but the unenlightened people think in terms of their certainty. Originally there is no thisness nor otherness. If the non-existence of thisness and otherness is realised, what can there be in existence?

故《中观》云："物无彼此。"而人以此为此，以彼为彼。彼亦以此为彼，以彼为此。此彼莫定乎一名，而惑者怀必然之志。然则彼此初非有，惑者初非无。既悟彼此之非有，有何物而可有哉？

19. i. q. 6, fasc. 18.

20. The illustration to this given by the Lakṣaṇa school is: "a man's mouth is not burned by saying 'fire'."

21. i. q. 3, ślokā 7, 9.

Hence it can be known that everything in the universe is unreal. It is merely a name long ever since.

Therefore the arbitrariness of nomination is stated in the Sūtra.[22] And there is the parable of the finger and the horse in *Djuang Tze*.[23] Why words so profound and far and wide in their meaning are not consulted?

Therefore the Sage rides on a thousand transformations and remains unchanged. He steps on ten thousands of doubts and remains always unperplexed. He sees the selfsame voidness of all things in the universe, and does not superimpose a voidness on the universe in order to make all things appear void.

故知万物非真，假号久矣。是以《成具》立强名之文，园林托指马之况。如此，则深远之言，于何而不在？是以圣人乘千化而不变，履万惑而常通者，以其即万物之自虚，不假虚而虚物也。

Thus says the Sūtra[24]:

"O wonderful! Bhagavān! The immovable point of contact of Reality serves as the standing pedestal of all Dharma."

It is not to establish another standing pedestal apart from Reality, the pedestal itself is the Reality. If so, can the Path be far away? In contact with everything it is real. Can the Sagehood be far away? Divinity is felt at once in realisation.

故经云："甚奇，世尊！不动真际为诸法立处。"非离真而立处，立处即真也。然则道远乎哉？触事而真。圣远乎哉？体之即神。

22. i. q. 5.

23. *Djuang Tze*, Ch. 2. Another interpretation of the word "finger" is "the thing pointed at," and the "horse" is "the counting-sticks used in gambling."

24. i. q. 7, fasc. 25.

ON THE WISDOM UNKNOWING

般若无知论

The theory of Prajñā, so void in its spiritual transparency and so obscure in its subtlety as it is, is the supreme terminus of the Three Vehicles. It is the one Truth without a second, and various misinterpretations existed, made profusely by different schools long ago.

夫般若虚玄者，盖是三乘之宗极也。诚真一之无差，然异端之论，纷然久矣。

There was the Indian Śramana whose name was Kumārajīva (344–413 C.E.). He trod on the Great Path when he was young, and he penetrated deeply into Buddhist philosophy. He alone shot above the realm of names and forms, and had his real isations in the most subtle regions above hearing and seeing. Diverse schools in the Western countries were converted and brought to a unity, and by him a healthy atmosphere was brought to the East. He had the intention of enlightening people in different lands, yet he had to conceal his light in the Liang Kingdom (for eighteen years). It is because the Truth cannot be spread at random, and there must be the right occasion for its reception.

有天竺沙门鸠摩罗什者，少践大方，研机斯趣，独拔于言象之表，妙契于希夷之境。齐异学于迦夷，扬淳风于东扇。将爰烛殊方而匿耀凉土者，所以道不虚应，应必有由矣。

In the third year of Hong-shih (401 C.E.) as the Year Star resided in its second position[25] the (Yao) Ching Kingdom took the opportunity of the invasion of the Liangs' and sent an army to encounter it. The army had brought home this master. May the prophecy that Buddhism would spread from the north to the east thus come true, I thought.

弘始三年，岁次星纪，秦乘入国之谋，举师以来之。意也，北天之运，数其然矣。

The Heavenly King of the Great (Yao) Ching state, — he whose virtue goes in accord with the sage-kings of hundreds of generations in the past, and whose grace would extend to the people of thousands of years to come, — manages dexterously his multitudinous quotidian affairs of the state, and yet spreads and furthers Dharma all the day. He is the paradisal refuge of the people of this present decadent generation, and indeed, he is the pillar upholding the Dharma left by Śakyamuni.

大秦天王者，道契百王之端，德洽千载之下，游刃万机，弘道终日。信季俗苍生之所天，释迦遗法之所仗也。

Then an assembly of more than five hundred learned Śramaṇas was convened in the Hsio-yao (Aśoka) Palace. His Majesty Himself took up the work of translation of the Mahāyāna Scriptures in Chinese together with Kumārajīva. What was developed was

25. The 2nd year of the "earth-branch" in a sixty-year cycle.

not only beneficial to the present generation, but would also serve as ford and bridge for crossing over the ocean of births and deaths by people in aeons in future.

时乃集义学沙门五百余人于逍遥观，躬执秦文，与什公参定方等。其所开拓者，岂唯当时之益，乃累劫之津梁矣。

I, in spite of my humble knowledge and shortcomings, had the honor of participating that august assembly. Excellent lectures on special and important topics I heard there and then.[26]

余以短乏，曾厕嘉会。以为上闻异要，始于时也。

And, the Divine Wisdom is subtle and obscure, recondite and inscrutable. It has neither form nor name, and cannot be grasped by words or symbols. Nevertheless, I shall try to put it into an inadequate language according to my vague imagination. Can it be said that the Wisdom of Buddha is ever fathomable?

然则圣智幽微，深隐难测。无相无名，乃非言象之所得。为试罔象其怀，寄之狂言耳，岂曰圣心而可辨哉！

I try to reason it out thus:

It is said in the Sūtra[27]:

"Prajñā is devoid of all forms of being, it has no appearance of coming into being or going out of being." Again it is said in the Sūtra[28]:

"Prajñā sees nothing, knows nothing."

As these passages refer to the action of reflection of the Wisdom, why is it said that it is devoid of form and unknowing? Obviously there must be knowledge without form and reflection without knowledge.

Why?

If there is what is known, then there must be what is not known. Because there is no knowledge in the mind of the Sage, so He knows everything. Knowing without knowledge is called omniscience. So the Sūtra[29] says:

"Buddha knows everything in knowing nothing." It is true.

试论之曰:《放光》云:"般若无所有相,无生灭相。"《道行》云:"般若无所知,无所见。"此辨智照之用,而曰无相无知者何耶?果有无相之知,不知之照,明矣。

何者?夫有所知,则有所不知。以圣心无知,故无所不知。不知之知,乃曰一切知。故经云:"圣心无所知,无所不知。"信矣。

Therefore the Sage vacates his mind and substantiates his reflection. He knows all the time (lit. "day") and yet he does not proceed in the act of knowing. Hence he could conceal his light and veil his brilliancy, and, with an emptied mind he developed his mystic intuition. And by abandoning intelligence and forsaking sense-perceptions, he attained alone his enlightenment in the vast obscurity.

是以圣人虚其心而实其照,终日知而未尝知也。故能默耀韬光,虚心玄鉴,闭智塞聪,而独觉冥冥者矣。

26. Original meaning ambiguous. The sentence may also be translated as "(My) special and important interpretations were offered (to Kumārajīva) above for hearing ever since then."

27. Fang Kwang, fasc. 14 Pañcavimśatisāhasrikā Prajñāpāramitā Sūtra Transl. Mokṣala.

28. Tao Hsing, fasc. 1 DaŚasāhasrikā Prajñāpāramitā Sūtra Transl. Lokarakṣa.

29. Ssu Yi, fasc. 1 Viśeṣacintā Brahmaparipṛcchā Sūtra Transl. Kumārajīva.

Thus the Wisdom has the direct perception penetrating through all profundities, yet it has no knowledge. The Spirit acts and reacts on all occasions without thinking. As it is without thinking, so it can stand sovereignty above the world. As the Wisdom is not knowing, so it can deeply reflect from beyond all actions.

Though the Wisdom stays aloof from all actions, yet it is not without action.

Though the Spirit stands above the world, yet it is all the time in the world.

Therefore the Sage, being infinite in his responses and contacts, admits the ups and downs in the universe. He perceives all that is obscure, yet he makes no effort in reflection. This then is the knowledge of the unknowing Prajñā and the spiritual realisation of the Divine.

然则智有穷幽之鉴，而无知焉；神有应会之用，而无虑焉。神无虑，故能独王于世表；智无知，故能玄照于事外。智虽事外，未始无事；神虽世表，终日域中。所以俯仰顺化，应接无穷，无幽不察，而无照功。斯则无知之所知，圣神之所会也。

But, as it is, it is real yet non-existent; it is void yet not without existence. Is then Divine Wisdom not that which is kept by the sages without discussion?

然其为物也，实而不有，虚而不无，存而不可论者，其唯圣智乎！

Why?

If it is said to be existent, it has neither form nor name.

If it is said to be non-existent, the Sage uses it for reflection.

Because it is used for reflection by being void of itself, it does not lose its power of reflection.

Because it is formless and nameless, it reflects without losing its voidness.

As it reflects without losing its voidness, it mixes itself with the world without any change of itself.

As it is void yet not losing its power of reflection, it acts in contact with the gross material circumstances of the world.

何者？欲言其有，无状无名；欲言其无，圣以之灵。圣以之灵，故虚不失照；无状无名，故照不失虚。照不失虚，故混而不渝；虚不失照，故动以接粗。

Therefore, the Divine Wisdom never ceases for a moment in its action. And in pursuit of it in regard to forms appearances, it can never be temporarily attained.

So it is said[30]:

"He acts presently without mental activity." And, it is also said[31]:

"All the Dharma are being established by Buddha, unmoved in Sambodhi."

Hence, multitudinous as the divine works are, they all can be referred to the one ultimate principle.

是以圣智之用，未始暂废；求之形相，未暂可得。故《宝积》曰："以无心意而现行。"《放光》云："不动等觉而建立诸法。"所以圣迹万端，其致一而已矣。

Therefore, Prajñā can be void yet reflective, the real Truth (para-mārtha) can be formless yet known, all activities can be realised that they are still, and the divine response can be without activity yet acting. This is the spontaneous knowing without knowledge, and the spontaneous action without activity.

30. Pao Tsi, fasc. 1 Vimalakīrti-nirdeśa Sūtra Transl. Chi Chien.

31. i. q. 3, fasc. 20.

What for knowledge and what for activity does it have!

是以般若可虚而照，真谛可亡而知，万动可即而静，圣应可无而为。斯则不知而自知，不为而自为矣。复何知哉！复何为哉！

Question:

By the Sage it is his true Wisdom that illuminates, that alone shines upon everything in the universe. Indefinite in its response to and contact with everyone, it comes always into harmony with the fact at hand.

As it shines upon everything, nothing is left out in his omniscience.

As it comes always into harmony with the fact at hand, no opportunity is being missed by it.

As no opportunity is being missed by it, it must have contact with that which should be contacted.

As nothing is left out in his omniscience, he must have knowledge of that which is knowable.

Possessed of knowledge of that which is knowable, the Sage does not know in vain.

Having contact with that which should be contacted, the Sage does not contact in vain.

Since there is already knowledge and contact, what is the reason for saying that the Sage has no knowledge and no contact?

If you mean that knowledge has been forgotten and contact neglected, this shows that the Sage is not self-affected in his knowledge and contact in order to achieve his selfhood. It may be said that he does not regard himself as having possessed of any knowledge, how can it be said that he has no knowledge?

难曰：夫圣人真心独朗，物物斯照，应接无方，动与事会。物物斯照，故知无所遗；动与事会，故会不失机。会不失机，故必有会于可会；知无所遗，故必有知于可知。必有知于可知，故圣不虚知；必有会于可会，故圣不虚会。既知既会，而曰无知无会者，何耶？若夫忘知遗会者，则是圣人无私于知会，以成其私耳。斯可谓不自有其知，安得无知哉？

Answer:

The merit of the Sage is as vast as heaven and earth, yet he is not benevolent[32]. His brilliancy surpasses that of the sun and moon, yet he is all the more obscure. Can it be said that his mentality is as "tamasic" as wood or stone in its ignorance? Really it is his spirituality that distinguishes him from the ordinary man, and he cannot be understood through his outward acts and appearances. You mean to say that the Sage regards himself as not having possessed of any knowledge, yet he is never without knowledge. Is it then not contradictory to the Sage's idea and a misunderstanding of the meaning of the Scriptures?

答曰：夫圣人功高二仪而不仁，明逾日月而弥昏。岂曰木石瞽其怀，其于无知而已哉？诚以异于人者神明，故不可以事相求之耳。子意欲令圣人不自有其知，而圣人未尝不有知。无乃乖于圣心，失于文旨者乎？

Why?

The Sūtra says[33] :

"Prajñā, being real, is as pure as ether. It has neither apprehension nor perception,

32. "not benevolent" cit. from *Lao Tze*.

33. i. q. 3, fasc. 6.

neither action nor relation."

This means that Prajñā is by itself unknowing. Is reflection needed for it to be unknowing?

If it has knowledge void in its nature and therefore it is called pure, then it cannot be distinguished from ordinary illusory knowledge. Then the Three Poisons and the Four Perversions[34] in all must be pure as well. How is it that the purity of Prajñā alone comes to be respected?

何者？经云："真般若者，清净如虚空，无知无见，无作无缘。"斯则知自无知矣；岂待返照然后无知哉？若有知性空而称净者，则不辨于惑智。三毒四倒亦皆清净，有何独尊净于般若？

If Prajñā is praised as pure because of the purity of its knowledge, Prajñā is not the known. If the known is always pure and the knower Prajñā never pure, then there is also no reason to offer the praise of purity to Prajñā.

Yet it is said in the Sūtra in general that Prajñā is pure. Is it not because Prajñā being by itself and by its self-nature perfectly pure, is fundamentally devoid of illusory knowledge? And, as it is devoid of illusory knowledge, can it be called knowledge at all? Being not only free from the name of knowledge but also free from the act of knowing, it is naturally unknowing.

若以所知美般若，所知非般若。所知自常净，故般若未尝净，亦无缘致净叹于般若。然经云"般若清净"者，将无以般若体性真净，本无惑取之知。本无惑取之知，不可以知名哉？岂唯无知名，无知知，自无知矣！

Therefore the Sage, by means of the unknowing Prajñā reflects upon the Real Truth (paramārtha) which is without appearance. The Real Truth does not exclude the "hare and the horse,"[35] and Prajñā is infinite in its reflection. Hence it contacts without error. And, being correct, it needs no justification. As it is silent, void, and unknowing, there is to it nothing unknown.

是以圣人以无知之般若，照彼无相之真谛。真谛无兔马之遗；般若无不穷之鉴。所以会而不差，当而无是，寂怕无知，而无不知者矣。

Question:

As things cannot express themselves to us by themselves, so names are used to express them. Though the thing is not the name, yet there must be the namable thing corresponding to that name. Consequently a thing cannot be mistaken (lit. "hide") if it is sought after by its name.

难曰：夫物无以自通，故立名以通物。物虽非名，果有可名之物，当于此名矣。是以即名求物，物不能隐。

Now, you say: "The mind of the Sage is unknowing." And again: "The mind of the Sage knows everything." —My idea is: if it is unknowing it does not know; if it knows, it is not unknowing. This is the general rule in the philosophical field and the correct mode

34. Three Poisons: rāga Greed; dveṣa Anger; moha Śtupor. Four Perversions: knowledge contrary to the four noble truths of anitya/impermanence, duḥkha/suffering, anātma/without selves, Śūny/avoidness.

35. Upāsakaśila Sūtra, fasc. 1 Transl. Mokṣala. The story runs： A hare, a horse and an elephant cross the Ganges. The hare swims across, the elephant walks over, the horse walks also sometimes on the bottom. The water of the Ganges is compared to the flow of 12 nidānas, Buddha or Tathāgata the elephant, hare the śrāvaka, and the horse the pratyekabuddha.

of establishing a theory. But to the one mind of the Sage two contradictory statements are applied. In viewing the substance expressed by these words, it does not seem to be relevant.

而论云“圣心无知”。又云“无所不知”。意谓无知未尝知，知未尝无知。斯则名教之所通，立言之本意也。然论者欲一于圣心，异于文旨。寻文求实，未见其当。

Why?

If the statement “Prajñā is knowing” is in accord with the mind of the Sage, then to say it is unknowing is irrelevant, and vice versa. If both statements are not valid, what is then there left for discussion?

何者？若知得于圣心，无知无所辨；若无知得于圣心，知亦无所辨。若二都无得，无所复论哉？

Answer:

It is said in the Sūtra[36]:

“The meaning of the term ‘Prajñā’ is: it is nameless and beyond reasoning. It is neither existent nor non-existent; neither substantial nor void.

“Being void, it does not lose its reflection; and, while reflecting, it does not lose its voidness.”

This is then a nameless Dharma, fundamentally inexpressible by words. And yet, though it is inexpressible by words, it cannot be made known without words. Therefore, whereas the Sage speaks all the day, he actually never speaks[37]. Now, I try to explain this to you in an unorthodox way[38].

答曰：经云“般若义者，无名无说，非有非无，非实非虚。虚不失照，照不失虚。”斯则无名之法，故非言所能言也。言虽不能言，然非言无以传。是以圣人终日言，而未尝言也。今试为子狂言辨之。

（此纯出老庄哲学。）

As regards the mind of the Sage, it is subtle and abstruse, and without form or appearance. So it cannot be said of as existent. Yet, being endless in its actions[39], it cannot be said of as non-existent.

Not being non-existent, there the Divine Wisdom is. Yet, as it cannot be said of as existent, all formulations and principles cease thereby.

Therefore by saying that it is knowing and yet without knowledge, it is meant to illustrate its comprehensive cognition. And, by saying that it is unknowing yet not without knowledge, it is meant to distinguish its phenomenal appearance. In the aspect of its phenomenal appearance, it is not non-existent. In the aspect of its comprehensive cognition, it is not existent. Being not existent, so it is knowing yet without knowledge. Being not non-existent, so it is without knowledge yet knowing.

Therefore, to know is not to know, and non-knowledge is knowledge. One should not split the one mind of the Sage into two by means of the contradiction in statements.

夫圣心者，微妙无相，不可为有；用之弥勤，不可为无。不可为无，故圣智存焉；不可为有，故名教绝焉。是以言知不为知，欲以通其鉴；不知非不知，欲以辨其相。辨相不为无，通鉴不为有。非有，故知而无知；非无，故无知而知。

36. Prajñāpāramitā sūtra in general.

37. cit. *Djuang Tze*.

38. *ditto*.

39. cit. *Lao Tze*.

是以知即无知，无知即知。无以言异而异于圣心也！

Question:

As the Real Truth (paramārtha) is profound and metaphysical in nature, in cannot but be fathomed by Wisdom. Just at this point the capacity of the Divine Wisdom is manifest so it is said in the Sūtra[40]:

"Without having obtained Prajñā, one cannot discern the Real Truth."

So the Real Truth is the object (lit. relative cause) of Prajñā. Through the relative cause we find the subject (Prajñā), then the subject must be knowing.

难曰：夫真谛深玄，非智不测。圣智之能，在兹而显。故经云："不得般若，不见真谛。"真谛则般若之缘也。以缘求智，智则知矣。

Answer:

The Wisdom found through the relative cause is not knowing.

Why?

It is said in the Sūtra[41]:

"Perception not produced in relation to forms of external objects (rūpa) is called non-perception (of rūpa)."

And again[42]:

"Since the Five aggregates are pure, so Prajñā is pure."

Prajñā is the knower. Five aggregates are the known. The known is the relative cause.

So, the knower and the known co-exist in interdependence. They are either correlatively existent or correlatively non-existent.

As they are correlatively non-existent, so all objects do not exist. As they are correlatively existent, so all objects are not non-existent. Where all objects are not non-existent, therefrom all relations (for illusory knowledge) arise. Where all objects do not exist, therefrom no relation (for true knowledge) can arise. Where no relation can arise, there can be no knowledge even if objects were reflected. Whence the relations arise, there the knower and the known arise in interrelationship.

Therefore whether knowledge or non-knowledge, it arises from that which is known.

答曰：以缘求智，智非知也。何者？《放光》云："不缘色生识，是名不见色。"又云："五阴清净，故般若清净。"般若即能知也。五阴即所知也，所知即缘也。夫知与所知，相与而有，相与而无。相与而无，故物莫之有；相与而有，故物莫之无。物莫之无故，为缘之所起；物莫之有故，则缘所不能生。缘所不能生，故照缘而非知。为缘之所起，故知缘相因而生。是以知与无知，生于所知矣。

Why?

As wisdom takes its form (lakṣaṇa) in that which is known, it is then called knowledge. But the Real Truth has no form, how can the real Wisdom know?

This is so because the object is not by itself that which is known; it is born of knowledge. As the known gives birth to knowledge, so also knowledge gives birth to the known. Both come into being through interdependence, and this interdependence is the Dharma of relationship. The Dharma of relationship is primarily unreal, therefore it is not the Real Truth. So the Madhyamaka[43] says:

40. Mahāprajñāpāramitā-upadeśa Śāstra, fasc. 18 Transl. Kumārajīva.

41. i. q. 3, fasc. 11.

42. *ditto.*

43. MK, fasc. 4.

"Because things come into being through causes and relative causes, they are unreal. That which comes into being not through causes and relative causes is real."

Now the Real Truth is real. It is not of any relationship. There is here then nothing produced from relationship. So it is said[44]:

"No Dharma is seen produced without relationship."

Hence to see the Real Truth through the real Wisdom, no object is to be grasped. If the Wisdom does not grasp the object, how can it be knowing?

何者？夫智以知所知取相，故名知。真谛自无相，真智何由知？所以然者，夫所知非所知，所知生于知。所知既生知，知亦生所知。所知既相生，相生即缘法。缘法故非真，非真，故非真谛也。故《中观》云："物从因缘有，故不真；不从因缘有，故即真。"今真谛曰真，真则非缘。真非缘，故无物从缘而生也。故经云："不见有法无缘而生。"是以真智观真谛，未尝取所知；智不取所知，此智何由知？

Yet wisdom is not unknowing. But as the Real Truth is not the object known, so also the real Wisdom is not knowledge. You wish to assert the Wisdom through the relationship and think that the subject in the relative causes must be knowing, But as the object is not one of forms, how can the subject be knowing?

然智非无知，但真谛非所知，故真智亦非知。而子欲以缘求智，故以智为知。缘自非缘，于何而求知？

Question:

By "not grasping the object," do you mean the Wisdom does not grasp the object because of its unconsciousness, or because of its consciousness? If it is due to his unconsciousness that the object is not grasped, then would the Sage not be like someone wandering at night unable to distinguish black from white? If the Wisdom is consciously not grasping the object, then the case is different from non-grasping.

难曰：论云不取者，为无知故不取，为知然后不取耶？若无知故不取，圣人则冥若夜游，不辨缁素之异耶？若知然后不取，知则异于不取矣。

Answer:

It is not being conscious or unconscious and therefore it docs or does not grasp the object. Knowing here is non-grasping, so it can know without grasping.

答曰：非无知故不取，又非知然后不取。知即不取，故能不取而知。

Question:

As regards the non-grasping, it is because the mind of the Sage is not swayed by material objects, so it has no illusory grasping. But without grasping there can be no affirmation (of anything). Without affirmation there can be no relevancy (to any object). What can he then relevant to the mind of the Sage, and how can it be said that the mind of the Sage is omniscient?

难曰：论云不取者，诚以圣心不物于物，故无惑取也。无取则无是，无是则无当。谁当圣心，而云圣心无所不知耶？

Answer:

With regard to no affirmation and no relevancy, it is this:—Because there is no

44. Sūnyavāda-sūtra in general.

relevancy, there is nothing irrelevant. Because there is no affirmation, there is nothing unaffirmed. And because everything is affirmed, so every being is and is not: and because everything is in relevancy, so every object is relevant yet irrelevant. Therefore, it is said[45]:

"All Dharma is seen yet nothing is seen."

答曰：然无是无当者，夫无当则物无不当，无是则物无不是。物无不是，故是而无是。物无不当，故当而无当。故经云：尽见诸法而无所见。

Question:

The mind of the Sage is not incapable of affirmation, but actually there is nothing to be affirmed. Where there is nothing to be affirmed, this non-affirmation should also be affirmed. It is said in the Sūtra that because the Real Truth has no phenomenal appearance, so Prajñā is devoid of knowledge. This is because Prajñā has no knowledge of the phenomena. If non-phenomenal appearance is taken as its object, what harm is done to the Real Truth?

难曰：圣心非不能是，诚以无是可是。虽无是可是，故当是于无是矣。是以经云：真谛无相，故般若无知者。诚以般若无有有相之知，若以无相为无相，有何累于真谛耶？

Answer:

The Sage is not attached to non-phenomena either. Why? If it is held as such, it is again phenomena. Giving up what is in order to go to what is not, that is like descending into the gully by escaping the peak, and in both cases one can equally feel fatigued.

Therefore the Superior Man, even while taking his stand on "existence" (Sat), he does not dwell in it, and on "non-existence" (Asat), he does not dwell in it too. Though he commits himself to neither, he does not abandon either. Therefore he comes into harmony with his environment[46] and shares the sufferings of humanity. He wanders amidst all beings of the Five Planes (dhātu), and silently and placidly he comes and goes. Indifferently he takes no action, yet he takes every action[47].

答曰：圣人无无相也。何者？若以无相为无相，无相即为相。舍有而之无，譬犹逃峰而赴壑，俱不免于患矣。是以至人处有而不有，居无而不无。虽不取于有无，然亦不舍于有无。所以和光尘劳，周旋五趣，寂然而往，怕尔而来，恬淡无为而无不为。

Question:

Though the mind of the Sage is unknowing, it makes no mistakes in its response on all occasions. It is then that responses are given to those which should be responded, and withheld from those which would not be responded. Therefore the mind of the Sage sometimes comes to life and sometimes passes away, Can it be so?

难曰：圣心虽无知，然其应会之道不差。是以可应者应之，不可应者存之。然则圣心有时而生，有时而灭，可得然乎？

Answer:

As to the coming to life and passing away, that happens in the mind. As the Sage has no mind, where does that take place? Yet the Sage is not without mind, only he does not

45. i.q.3, fasc. 2.

46. i.q. 15.

47. *ditto*.

take his mind as mind. He is also not irresponsive, he is merely responding in no response. So the Sage's way of response on all occasions is infallible as the four seasons. Simply because he has the Void as his being; this cannot be made to come to life or to pass away.

答曰：生灭者，生灭心也。圣人无心，生灭焉起？然非无心，但是无心心耳。又非不应，但是不应应耳。是以圣人应会之道，则信若四时之质，真以虚无为体，斯不可得而生，不可得而灭也。

Question:

What is then the difference between the Non-being of the Divine Wisdom and the Non-being of the illusory wisdom, since both have no birth and death?

难曰：圣智之无，惑智之无，俱无生灭，何以异之？

Answer:

The Non-being of the Divine Wisdom is that it is unknowing, while the Non-being of the illusory wisdom is that it knows the Non-being. The Non-being is the same, but the ways to it are different.

答曰：圣智之无者无知，惑智之无者知无。其无虽同，所以无者异也。

Why?

The mind of the Sage is void and silent, and there is no knowledge in it to be annulled. So it can he said of as unknowing, but it cannot be said of as knowing the Non-being. The illusory wisdom has its knowings, so there is knowledge in it to be annulled. It can he said of as knowing the Non-being, but not as unknowing. Unknowingness is the Non-being of Prajñā. Knowing the Non-being refers to the Non-being of the Real Truth.

何者？夫圣心虚静，无知可无，可曰无知，非谓知无。惑智有知，故有知可无，可谓知无，非曰无知也。无知即般若之无也。知无即真谛之无也。

Hence the relation between the Divine Wisdom (Prajñā) and the Real Truth (Paramārtha) is this: Considering their action, they are the same yet different, considering their silence (Being) they are different yet the same. In the sameness there is no regard to thisness or otherness, and in the difference there is no loss of the reflecting power. Therefore those discerning their sameness see the sameness in their difference, and those discerning their difference see the difference in the sameness. Hence they cannot be considered as different nor as the same.

是以般若之与真谛，言用即同而异，言寂即异而同。同，故无心于彼此；异，故不失于照功。是以辨同者同于异，辨异者异于同。斯则不可得而异，不可得而同也。

Why?

Internally there is the light of individual cognition, and externally there is the reality of all existence (Dharma). Though all Dharma is real, it cannot exist without reflection. Both the external and internal combine to form the reflection. Here is then the point where the Sage must differ from the ordinary man in his action. Internally there is the reflection yet it is unknowing, externally there is the reality which is without phenomenon. Both the internal and external fall into silence and both become correlatively non-existent. This is the point where the Sage cannot differ from the ordinary man in his silence.

何者？内有独鉴之明，外有万法之实。万法虽实，然非照不得，内外相与以成其照功。此则圣所不能同用也。内虽照而无知，外虽实而无相，内外寂然，相与俱无。此则圣所不能异寂也。

So it is said in the Sūtra[48] that diverse Dharma do not differ from each other. — Does it mean that the legs of the duck should be lengthened and the legs of the crane shortened[49] or that the peak should be levelled with the ground and the valley filled up with earth so that there will be no more difference? Because difference is not taken up as such, so non-difference can be attained through difference.

是以经云，诸法不异者，岂曰续凫截鹤，夷岳盈壑，然后无异哉？诚以不异于异，故虽异而不异也。

So it is said in the Sūtra[50]:

"O Wonderful, Bhagavān! In the Dharma of non-difference, all Dharma are taught as being different."

And again[51]:

"Prajñā and all Dharma are neither of one, nor of different phenomena."

This is indeed true.

故经云："甚奇世尊！于无异法中而说诸法异。"又云："般若与诸法，亦不一相，亦不异相。"信矣。

Question:

You have said: Considering their action, they are different; considering the silence, they are the same. It is not known whether within Prajñā there is any difference between activity and silence.

难曰：论云：言用则异，言寂则同。未详般若之内，则有用寂之异乎？

Answer:

Activity is the silence, and silence is the activity. They are one in being, so to say "of the same origin but with different names." [52] There is no separate silence without action yet directing the action. Hence, the more obscure the wisdom is, the more clear its reflection; and the more calm the spirit, the more active its response will be. Is it to say that there is difference between obscurity and clarity, activity and silence?

The Sūtra says[53]:

"In non-activity (one is) acting too much." Again, in Ratnakūta[54]:

"Without mind and without perception, all is comprehensively known."

This is the talk on the Supreme spirit and the Divine Wisdom beyond all phenomenal appearances. By referring to the plain words of these Scriptures, the mind of the Sage can be understood.

答曰：用即寂，寂即用。用寂体一，同出而异名。更无无用之寂，而主于用也。是以智弥昧，照逾明；神弥静，应逾动。岂曰明、昧、动、静之异哉？故《成具》云："不为而过为。"《宝积》曰："无心无识，无不觉知。"斯则穷神尽智，极象外之谈也。即之明文，圣心可知矣。

48. i. q. 3, fasc. 22.
49. i. q. 13.
50. i. q. 3, fasc. 23.
51. *ditto*, fasc. 22.
52. i. q. 15.
53. Ch'eng Chu, fasc. 1 Siddhiprabhāsasamādhi Sūtra Transl. Chih Yao.
54. i.q.6.

文
景

Horizon

社科新知 文艺新潮

唯识菁华

徐梵澄 著
梁 珏 译 孙 波 校

出品人 姚映然
策划编辑 李 頔
责任编辑 李 頔
营销编辑 胡珍珍
装帧设计 Timonium lake
设计协力 魏荣辰

出品 北京世纪文景文化传播有限责任公司
（北京朝阳区东土城路 8 号林达大厦 A 座 4A 100013）
出版发行 上海人民出版社
印刷 山东临沂新华印刷物流集团有限责任公司
制版 北京楠竹文化发展有限公司

开本 890mm×1240mm 1/32
印张 14.5 字数：276,000
2024 年 5 月第 1 版 2024 年 5 月第 1 次印刷
定价 98.00 元
ISBN 978-7-208-17493-1/B · 1593

图书在版编目（CIP）数据

唯识菁华 / 徐梵澄著；梁珏译；孙波校 .-- 上海：上海人民出版社，2022
（徐梵澄全集）
ISBN 978-7-208-17493-1

I. ①唯… II. ①徐… ②梁… ③孙… III. ①唯识论—中国—文集 IV. ① B946.3-53

中国版本图书馆 CIP 数据核字 (2021) 第 252469 号